BERNARD K. GORDON, the author, has been
Visiting Professor at the University of Singapore
and a Rockefeller Foundation Fellow in Southeast Asia.
His articles have appeared in *World Politics, Asian Survey,* and
Pacific Affairs, and he is also the author of *New Zealand
Becomes a Pacific Power*. At present Dr. Gordon is
Research Professor of Political Science at
The George Washington University.

The Dimensions of Conflict
In Southeast Asia

The Dimensions of Conflict
In Southeast Asia

BERNARD K. GORDON

Prentice-Hall, Inc., *Englewood Cliffs, New Jersey*

The author wishes to thank Michael Leifer and the Australian National University for permission to reproduce the map, "Cambodia and Its Neighbors," which appears on page 50 of this volume and originally appeared, in slightly different form, in *Cambodia and Neutrality* by Michael Leifer.

For Anita
Ini Buku Dan Tandjung Sari

Acknowledgments

If this book meets some of the goals outlined in the preface, I owe much to many men in Asia and America—though of course I alone am responsible for what is said here. My special debt is to Roger Hilsman, now Professor at Columbia and formerly Assistant Secretary of State for Far Eastern Affairs, for his help over the years. Mr. Hilsman enabled me to begin this study, and Dr. Kenneth W. Thompson of the Rockefeller Foundation ensured its completion, for a Rockefeller Fellowship allowed me to live and work once again in Southeast Asia.

Thanks too to Mr. James W. King of the Institute for Defense Analyses for early support, to Professor R. S. Milne (now of the University of British Columbia) who provided me with a "home" in the University of Singapore's Department of Political Science, and to Mr. Vincent Rock of The George Washington University, for his patience. In the Philippines my deepest debts are to members of the Department of Foreign Affairs, especially Emmanuel Pelaez, formerly Foreign Secretary and Vice-President of the Republic, and also to Julia Palarca and Professors Abueva and Ramos. In Bangkok I must single out Foreign Minister Thanat Khoman, Arand Panyarachun, and Ambassador Konthi, and in Phnom Penh Mr. Charles Meyer. In Kuala Lumpur I was given every kindness by Dato Ghazalie bin Schafie, Tunku Ngah, and Jack de Silva. My welcomes in Indonesia were similarly gracious, and for this I thank Roselan Abdulgani, Ganis Harsono, Suwito, and of course, Dr. Subandrio for his great patience and help.

Less formally, I thank those many friends in Asia—whether scholars, newsmen, diplomats, or Foundation men—for whom the understanding of politics is one of life's joys, and with whom so many ideas have been tested: Tom McHale, Dave Wurfel, Takashi Oka, Mike Leifer, Thomas Critchley, Ivor Kraal, Wang Gungwu, Jerry Schecter, Hiroshi Kitamura, Don Keesing, Tom Hirschfeld, Somsakdi Xuto, Frank Tatu, and Art Rosen. And for their help in seeing the book through all of its stages, my final thanks to Jim Murray and Bill Green at Prentice-Hall, and to Anita and Pamela at home.

B.K.G

Preface

This book hopes to do two things. In the first place, it seems to me that we need to know more about a "differentiated" Southeast Asia, one that is not merely an area that we know is of great interest to Communist China, or otherwise part of the high stakes in the global struggle. It *is* that, of course, but it is also a region of separate and quite distinct nations, a region characterized by political conflicts in addition to the world-wide conflict between the communist and anticommunist nations.

Within the region itself, those conflicts which have little or nothing to do with communism often seem to be by far the most important considerations to the states involved. We need to understand those conflicts, and in doing so we may allow ourselves to see more clearly the separateness and distinctiveness of the nations in Southeast Asia. Most important, probably, is that we free our minds from the perception of "Southeast Asia" as an undifferentiated mass. We must see the states there as separate units; the first part of this book, which analyzes certain major intra-regional conflicts, seeks to do just that. Because those pages deal with the more usual forms of tension and conflict among nations, they should be of interest to anyone concerned with contemporary Southeast Asia and international politics generally.

The second part of the book deals with "cooperation" in the area. Admittedly, there is not much of that, but there are some initial, tentative efforts among leaders in Southeast Asia to establish relatively formal—even institutionalized—patterns of collaboration among their states. That phenomenon is interesting for at least three reasons: first, Southeast Asian efforts at collaboration are not being made in isolation; they are very much a part of world-wide efforts along similar lines—in Africa, in Latin America, and of course, in Europe. Thus, they draw attention as a regional reflection of what appears to be something of a global tendency.

Second, we must understand these local efforts at collaboration for the same reason that we need to understand the conflicts within the area: they are part of the present international politics of Southeast Asia.

And finally, those whose interest is primarily in a science of politics will be drawn to the study of these collaborative efforts in Southeast Asia because they provide an opportunity for more rigorous comparative analysis of state behavior than is usually possible. In other words by examining the processes of collaboration in Southeast Asia we should be able to learn more about patterns and regularities in the behavior of states in this one field of national activity. For we do, as students of politics, already have in our discipline some first generalizations about such behavior, drawn largely from the European experiences in cooperation, collaboration, and integration.

We even have a number of hypotheses about the conditions under which nations collaborate.* By applying to these hypotheses the data that is now available from Southeast Asian efforts, we should be able to determine whether the hypotheses have any likelihood of wider, even universal, application, and thus some merit as predictive tools; or whether they are simply wise conclusions derived from a unique experience in Europe. In either event, this book seeks to clarify our understanding about international relations in Southeast Asia, and in doing so to add to our knowledge about politics among nations more generally.

* Largely as a result of the work of Ernst Haas and Harold Guetzkow.

Contents

*Part Two: Cooperation in
          Southeast Asia*

List of Illustrations

MAPS:

TABLES:

*The Dimensions of Conflict
In Southeast Asia*

INTRODUCTION: A POLITICAL REGION
OF SOUTHEAST ASIA

This book deals with the international politics of Southeast Asia. More precisely, it deals with the conflicts, and the scope of potential cooperation, among the nations of this region. But is that suggesting too much?—*Is* there a political "region" of Southeast Asia? In this context, one specialist on Asian affairs recently wrote that, unlike Europe or the Middle East, Southeast Asia cannot be regarded as a regional unit, but "must be considered as an aggregate of territories." [1] Another expert, a decade earlier, also denied that there is a "region" of Southeast Asia; it is instead, he argued, "merely a place on the globe where certain groups of people, holding little in common, live contiguous to one another." [2]

These views, while perhaps accurate in the past, do not now describe reality. Today, at least three factors force us to consider Southeast Asia as a region. The first is the awareness by Southeast Asia's leaders of the many similar problems they share in common, largely in the area of economic development. Their awareness comes from—for example—regular participation in meetings of the United Nations Economic Commission for Asia and the Far East (ECAFE), and from involvement in many special groups, like the United Nations Conference on Trade and Development in 1964. In addition to sharpening leaders' awareness of their common problems, these meetings add greatly to intra-regional communications, which in turn contribute to consciousness of the "region." No longer do leaders in Bangkok and Manila depend, as they once did, on London and Washington for their knowledge of each other.

The second factor which makes Southeast Asia a "region" is the widespread incidence of conflict, along with some attempts at cooperation, in the area. Both conflict and cooperation are forms of communication; both have led to an unprecedented involvement, by Southeast Asia's leaders, in the affairs of neighbors. Some of this in-

---

[1] P. M. A. Linebarger, "The Psychological Instruments of Policy in Southeast Asia," in William Henderson (ed.), *Southeast Asia: Problems of United States Policy* (Cambridge, Mass.: M.I.T. Press, 1963), pp. 227-228.
[2] Nathaniel Pfeffer, "Regional Security in Southeast Asia," *International Organization* (August 1954), 311-315.

volvement is disruptive, such as Indonesia's campaign against Malaysia; other aspects, such as the plan to establish an Asian Development Bank, are potentially constructive. But in any event Southeast Asia's leaders—and it is the leadership with which we must be concerned if we are to judge whether the area qualifies as a "region"—have been thrown together as never before. Thus, when one critic, seeking to deny that the area is a region, charges that "knowledge of the region as a unit is not yet diffused to the populations which inhabit it," [3] we must ask: how important is that charge within the context of Southeast Asia? Narrow elites, both relatively and absolutely smaller than in the West, dominate the political and economic affairs of all developing nations. Southeast Asia, essentially a village society in which 80 to 90 per cent of its population is rural-agricultural, is no exception. Even in Europe, where consciousness of "region" is high and institutions like the European Economic Community exist to bring about economic and perhaps even political integration, there is a gap between elite attitudes and popular understanding on this subject. In Southeast Asia, with its high illiteracy and underdeveloped communications, the gap between popular understanding and elite attitudes is necessarily much wider. The region's leaders, however, have been thrust into intimate contact with their neighbors, often through conflict; the communications developed as a result are one factor which perhaps more than anything else compels us to accept the fact that a sense of "region" does now exist in Southeast Asia.

The third incentive to accepting the concept of "region" is that a major political force—Communism—has been precisely such an incentive for forty years. The careers of Ho Chi Minh and Tan Malaka, the Indonesian revolutionary, are symbolic. Ho, as Comintern and Soviet agent specially responsible for Indochina and nearby areas in the 1920s and '30s, moved constantly throughout the region.[4] Tan Malaka, "Comintern agent for Southeast Asia and Australia," was similarly well traveled.[5] Marxism stressed that there were common elements in the plight of the Asian peoples and that their independence depended on a Communist victory in all countries. In 1928 the Chinese Communist Party stated that "the triumph of Communism

[3] Linebarger, *op. cit.*

[4] Ellen Hammer, *The Struggle for Indochina* (Stanford, Calif.: Stanford University Press, 1954), p. 82.

[5] Arnold Brackman, *Indonesian Communism* (New York: Frederick A. Praeger, Inc., 1963), p. 23.

in China . . . could not fail to influence neighboring Asia, particularly India, Indochina, Java, and Korea." [6] Today, little has changed, as North Vietnam's Premier recently stressed:

> We must see the situation in the Indochinese peninsula against the background of the general situation in Southeast Asia and . . . with the situation in the southern part of our country. Here we must lay bare the British imperialist scheme in the setting up of Malaysia, aimed at consolidating the British colonialist domination in the countries within that bloc, strengthening the British military base of Singapore, and directly threatening the Republic of Indonesia. [7]

In sum, the incentives for examining the "region" of Southeast Asia derive from the perspective of communications—based on both conflict and cooperation—as well as from Communism. Evidence from each perspective suggests that the nations in Southeast Asia are much more than an unrelated aggregate of states. It indicates that we can learn things of importance by examining the *region*—not only for what we learn about each of the nations separately, but also about the politics among these nations generally and the concept of "regionalism" in particular. In the process we can also come to understand the region's instability, for instability is the one feature of Southeast Asia that gives the region much of its contemporary importance.

Political Conflict in Southeast Asia

Many of the conflicts that divide the nations of Southeast Asia are not really new. The aggravations of existing sores sometimes may give the appearance of "new" tensions, but many of today's problems derive in large part from actions taken long ago. Thus, except for the war in Vietnam, the global conflict between the Communist and non-Communist world has not played a major part in the tension among Southeast Asian nations. Indeed, that war has effectively removed the two Vietnams from much of the region's international politics, [8] and our study therefore deals with the foreign policies of the other states:

[6] *Ibid.*

[7] From the Premier's report at the first session of the National Assembly of North Vietnam, June 27, 1964 (Hanoi: vna International Service in English).

[8] An exception is in the efforts of Cambodia to improve relations with the Hanoi regime: Prince Sihanouk of Cambodia has repeatedly said that he does not expect South Vietnam to retain its independence for long, and he wants to be on good terms with the eventual winner in the Vietnamese struggle.

Thailand, Burma, Cambodia, Indonesia, the Philippines, and Malaysia (along with Singapore).[9]

What kinds of issues contribute to tensions among these nations? Do they differ from those that have led other states in other times to distrust one another? The answer to both questions is very closely tied to the nature of politics in Southeast Asia. These are states that are both old and new. Some writers have called them *the developing countries;* others have used the phrase *nations in transition;* and Professor Fred Riggs has made a strong case for using the term *prismatic societies.* He suggests that, instead of applying the label *traditional society* to an undeveloped nation, we think in terms of a *fused society.* In a traditional, or "fused" society, as he points out, a single structure—whether it be tribe, clergy, or monarchy—performs the basic political functions for the society. Modern, advanced states, on the other hand, have established separate and almost innumerable structures for performing necessarily more complicated functions. Riggs calls these *refracted societies*—"in which for every function, a corresponding structure exists."[10] Prismatic society, he stresses, lies between the extremes of fused and refracted societies and is so called "because of the prism through which fused light passes to become refracted."[11]

The states in Southeast Asia each appear to fit the description of a prismatic society: they exhibit many practices of traditional society, while aspiring to the norms and methods of refracted societies or modern states. Both levels may exist side by side in a single nation, and this can lead to a multitude of internal tensions.[12] This duality

[9] The foreign policies of these nations in comparison with Vietnam's have not been so extensively analyzed. On the "two Vietnams," see Bernard B. Fall, *The Two Vietnams* (New York: Frederick A. Praeger, 1963).

[10] Fred W. Riggs, "International Relations as a Prismatic System," *World Politics,* XIV:1 (October 1961), 149.

[11] *Ibid.*

[12] For example, in reviewing a study of political development in Iran by Leonard Binder, Riggs noted that some leading Iranians, according to Binder, condemn "traditional practices such as nepotism. . . ." But, as Riggs points out: "Nepotism . . . cannot be identified as a traditional system. Hereditary office and ascriptive recruitment are prescribed by the traditional system. It is only the superimposition of norms which substitute achievement-oriented rules, making the appointment of relatives illegal, that creates nepotism. It is this illegality, the contradiction between formal prescription and effective practice, a glaring discontinuity between the ideal and the actual, which is the hallmark of the prismatic condition. Thus what appear as contradictions in Binder's frame of reference are not contradictory in terms of the prismatic model. They are what we expect to

has a clear impact on foreign affairs, both in the sorts of disputes that become important and in the methods used to deal with them. Border disputes, for example, are among the most familiar causes of international conflict, and in Chapter II we will be dealing with one of these: the Philippines' claim to North Borneo. The nations involved seem closer to being refracted societies than any others in Southeast Asia. In fact, the Philippines and Malaysia have tended to deal with their problem in ways that might be expected among refracted states. They have sought, for example, to avoid resorting to the threat or use of force—a virtue popular among the politically advanced nations although not universally practiced by them. A markedly different style of foreign-policy choices, and quite distinct methods of implementing policy, will emerge when the foreign policies of Cambodia and Indonesia are discussed. There, the notion of the prismatic state probably will become more apparent, for the practices of these two nations are relatively less familiar to us than are the methods used by the Philippines and Malaysia.

Territoriality: Western Legalisms and Ancient Empires

Border disputes, ostensibly a "familiar" aspect of international politics, have different roots in Southeast Asia, and traditional Western concepts do not quite seem to fit. For example, the Khmer kingdom associated with Angkor did not wield the kind of political authority, or sovereignty, in all parts of its territory that Westerners associate today with the word *empire* or *kingdom*. Generally speaking, states and empires in Southeast Asian history seldom embodied the territorial implications of sovereignty that developed in the West. The sultans who ruled over different parts of what are now Malaya and Indonesia were not sovereign in the usual Western sense, for they themselves were—to varying degrees and from time to time—subject to the imperial rule of China. When they were at odds with one another or, later, when some of them were engaged in wars against the European powers, they frequently sought the aid of China. The Chinese often regarded these territories as part of China, though not as integral parts. Some, like present-day Vietnam (Annam), were more closely integrated

find." (Fred Riggs, "The Theory of Developing Politics," *World Politics*, XVI [October 1963], 163.)

with Chinese fortunes, and the imprint of Chinese cultural, political, and administrative tradition is very clear there.

Thus the concept of "dual sovereignty," one not too meaningful in Western thinking since the time of Jean Bodin, was not uncommon in Asian history. Its imprecision was paralleled by vagueness on the extent of territory too. Consider, for example, the ancient empire of Majapahit. Modern Indonesians sometimes think of their state as the ultimate successor to Majapahit. Many writings drawn from the thirteenth-century inscriptions known as the *Nagarakertagama*, however, suggest that the "boundaries" of Majapahit included what is now Indonesia, and more. Nevertheless, modern historians increasingly question whether familiar notions of a far-flung domain apply to Majapahit,[13] for that empire does not appear to have exercised the kind of centrally-directed and organized control that Rome wielded in Gaul or the British Isles; and certainly it did not approach the authority of the eighteenth- and nineteenth-century British Empire. Instead, the "empire" of Majapahit may more accurately be interpreted as a series of rulers who considered themselves the supreme authority of a wide realm of islands and mainland territories in Southeast Asia. Majapahit was a sea-based empire with outposts in a variety of places. In those outposts it probably was sovereign; but only a few miles inland imperial rule ended.

Today's leaders, however, are not often familiar with findings of modern historiography; even if they were, there seems little likelihood that they would disregard the old myths. Contemporary Asian leaders tend to accept the ancient legends insofar as they relate to the extent of some ancient empires, and we can probably only applaud their interest in preserving rich histories and traditions. The political significance of their interest, however, is that modern Southeast Asian leaders are products of much *Western* thinking about the nation and state. To their mind, just as to ours, the state necessarily implies territory. It is the essential ingredient of the state and of the nation.

[13] D. G. E. Hall concludes: "So far as the ascertainable facts go, the state of Majapahit was limited to East Java, Madura, and Bali." *A History of Southeast Asia, 2nd ed.* (London: Macmillan & Co., Ltd., 1964), p. 83. In Professor Cady's new book a similar conclusion is reached: While Gaja Mada, the actual ruler of Majapahit (1330-64) boasted of his conquests, Cady points out, they were still extensive. "He claimed control over Bali, Macassar, parts of Borneo, . . . all of lower Sumatra, and the Sunda area in Western Java, *but much of this control probably amounted to little more than receipt of vassal tribute.*" John F. Cady, *Southeast Asia: Its Historical Development* (New York: McGraw-Hill Book Company, Inc., 1964), p. 141. Emphasis added.

Not surprisingly, therefore, these leaders may get just as incensed about seemingly worthless pieces of territory as have their counterparts in European and American history. The precise charting of a boundary, probably never very important to some of the ancient kingdoms and empires,[14] can now—because of this superimposition on Asian traditions of Western legalisms about sovereignty and the state—lead to some quite intense disputes among the independent states of Southeast Asia.

One source of the problem is that many of today's independent nations are successor states to what were merely *parts* of the same kingdom or "empire" in the dimly recorded past. The European colonial powers, for their own reasons, often divided territories that had previously been part of a larger unit. Thus some of the lines the French drew around Laos, Annam, Cochin-China, and Cambodia were meaningful and some were not. Yet those demarcations have become today's "fixed" boundaries. In other cases old territorial divisions that were the result of pre-European intra-Asian conflicts were sometimes hardened by the Europeans, in moves related largely to intra-European diplomacy, as they administered and "protected" the separate territories as part of their empires or spheres of influence.

Even the Japanese, the last outsiders, contributed to these patterns. During World War II Japan "returned" to Thailand certain parts of French Indochina. Later, under pressure from the victorious Allies, the Thais relinquished those territories, but many Cambodians today fear that Thailand still covets their land. Similarly, as World War II drew to a close, the Japanese military decided that the former Dutch East Indies were readier for independence than was British Malaya. Thus when Indonesia—under Japanese sponsorship—proclaimed its independence, it included only the former Dutch territories. If Japan had decided differently, what is now Malaysia and Singapore might have been part of Indonesia. Many Malaysian leaders fear that Indonesia will try to "correct" that accident of history.

Of course not all the scores of invasions and conquests which have shaped Southeast Asian history find parallels in present territorial conflicts among the now-independent states. Yet even the briefest

---

[14] International conflict in Southeast Asia in the pre-European period was more commonly concerned with the control of a given commodity trade, trading routes, and the cities and entrepôts which were centers of trade—and thus of income. For the rich history that sentence so brutally passes over, see Cady, *op. cit.*, Chaps. 2-4, 7-8, and Hall, *op. cit.*, pp. 12-204.

glance at the ethnographic map of Southeast Asia reveals the effects of the region's checkered history. Indeed, the very concept of Southeast Asia as an historical and geographic entity is likely to bring to mind an image of loosely extended and overlapping empires. That history has left us with an area especially fertile in disputes over who owns what, and dozens of population islands surrounded by ethnically different peoples. Often these communities do not live in harmony with one another, and some look across national borders for support.

Thus the Shan peoples of Burma, many of whom desire more autonomy or even independence, look to the adjacent and ethnically similar Thai for support. Until recently they were not always disappointed. Similarly with regard to the Muslim, or Moro, population of the southern Philippines. These people have hardly been integrated into Philippines society and culture; instead they have much closer commercial, cultural, and religious ties with Indonesians in nearby islands.

These illustrations, at least, concern dissidence within a framework of relatively well-defined borders. But in a number of cases—as between Cambodia and South Vietnam—the borders are not so generally agreed on. And in other instances, where borders are clearly defined, there are some openly competing claims to the same tract of land. One illustration is the dispute between South Vietnam and Cambodia over the ownership of some tiny islands; another is the Philippines' claim to North Borneo. Yet at least one dispute over territorial "ownership" appears to have been resolved when the World Court awarded the Prah Viharn Temple to Cambodia in 1962. (The temple dispute threatened to enflame even further the relations between those two states.[15]) Finally, there are also some "latent" disputes which can be anticipated but which have not yet erupted into open conflicts among states. These will be touched on, but it is probably best to focus attention on those territorial disputes which have already aggravated international politics in Southeast Asia. Of these, probably none has received more attention recently than the Philippines' claim to North Borneo.

[15] For details on that affair, see L. P. Singh, "The Thai-Cambodian Dispute," *Asian Survey*, XI:8 (October 1962), 23-26.

Part One: Conflicts in Southeast Asian International Politics

CHAPTER I: PHILIPPINES FOREIGN POLICY AND THE NORTH BORNEO CLAIM

The government of the Philippines claims that it, not the new Federation of Malaysia, is the rightful sovereign in Sabah (North Borneo). This dispute has become one of the central issues in the international politics of Southeast Asia. When the claim was first lodged in 1962, there were many informed people who found it difficult to take the matter seriously, but within a year the dispute had assumed major proportions.

The conflict is a remarkably complicated affair from the point of view of history, international law, or linguistics. It quickly gave rise to a large number of essays, and international lawyers in particular are likely to have a field day debating some of its aspects. Moreover, the controversy is heavily laced with factors bound to attract interest —including heirs who cannot agree on which of them is the real sultan of Sulu; frantic searches through the old archives of Madrid for legal documents; and rumors of a $30 million payoff and several kinds of double-dealing by presidents and prime ministers. All the same, a serious historical and legal dispute is unquestionably involved.

Before the claim was lodged, the Malayan and Philippine governments had been on the friendliest of terms, but the claim led ultimately to a diplomatic break. Naturally, the deterioration of relations which followed the dispute also meant that almost all work was suspended within the Association of Southeast Asia (ASA), the cooperative effort which these two governments, along with Thailand, had launched in 1961. Thus it is evident that some portion of the mutual trust which had been developed between Kuala Lumpur and Manila has been eroded; it will not be restored readily. Malayan officials were annoyed by the Philippines' decision to lodge the claim, and Filipino leaders, in turn, were upset by the Malayan and Malaysian reaction to their claim.

Thailand and Indonesia were also involved. It is clear that the Philippines' efforts since 1962 to establish warmer relations with the Indonesian government were facilitated by its claim against the proposed Malaysia. Indonesia had already intimated what its attitude toward Malaysia would be, and Manila's claim came almost simultaneously with this developing tension. Thus, Djakarta could only welcome its new anti-Malaysia ally. It may even be that the Philippines entered into its new relationship with Indonesia for the express purpose of pressing its dispute with Malaysia, for Malaysians soon found themselves with two unfriendly neighbors where there had been only one. By the same token, as Manila tried to pull back somewhat from its anti-Malaysia posture two years later, Indonesian officials wondered about the good faith and steadfastness of their new friends in Manila.

And Thailand—largely in the person of its foreign minister, Thanat Khoman—has been unhappily involved in an effort (in 1963 and 1964) to act as mediator between the parties. Thanat himself, who seems to have questioned from the beginning the wisdom of Manila's decision to press its claim, was understandably disappointed when his efforts met with no success whatever, for the dispute has meant that cooperative efforts in the ASA framework have had to come to a stop once more, and it is clear that the Thai leader regarded ASA as one of his own personal achievements. Even more important, Thai leaders are particularly sensitive to any threat to the region's relative stability, and so open a conflict between the only two other Western-aligned states in Southeast Asia could not be viewed with equanimity in Bangkok.

It must be stressed, therefore, that the dispute had fairly wide effects. An understanding of these effects will lead to an understanding of the main points of the foreign policies of each of the nations involved. In particular, an examination of this dispute will also shed light on the substance and the process of foreign policy in the Philippines. For example, why was this territorial claim first lodged in 1962, when the Philippine government has been in control of its own foreign affairs since 1946? Allegations have been made that the most elementary forms of corruption were involved in the resuscitation of a claim which had lain dormant for at least a generation. The clarification of these propositions requires a more detailed examination of the claim.

Basis of the Claim

Although the dispute is terribly complex, there are at least a few events which are not contested, and a chronology of these follows:

December 29, 1877: Baron de Overbeck, operating as agent for the British firm of Dent Brothers, received a cession of territory in North Borneo, extending from Jesselton on the west coast to the Sibuco River on the east.

January 22, 1878: Baron de Overbeck, having learned that some of the northern and eastern portions of this territory had been ceded earlier (1704) to the sultan of Sulu by the sultan of Brunei, entered into an agreement with the sultan of Sulu for the purpose of acquiring clear title to some of the lands mentioned in the 1877 agreement. The crux of the dispute: the government of the Philippines maintains that this 1878 agreement provided merely for the lease, rather than the cession, of these territories.

November 1, 1881: The British North Borneo Company, successor to Dent, was granted a royal charter.

1888: By agreement between the British North Borneo Company and Great Britain, North Borneo became a protectorate of the British Crown.

1946: The British North Borneo Company gave up all rights in North Borneo, and the territory became a colony.

June 21, 1962: President Macapagal of the Philippines, who had not fully accepted the validity of British sovereignty over North Borneo for at least fifteen years, announced that his government, as the successor to the sultan of Sulu, intended to claim North Borneo as part of the Philippines.[1]

September 16, 1963: Malaysia was established, and North Borneo—which had been a British colony—became part of Malaysia. The Philippines withheld recognition of Malaysia by recalling its ambassador and reducing its diplomatic representation in Kuala Lumpur to consular level on the grounds that "Malaysia" was a new state. Malaysia replied by recalling its ambassador in Manila, thus breaking off diplomatic relations.

Almost all other related events, especially those which occurred between 1878 and 1946, are in dispute. At the heart of the dispute is the Philippines' contention that the agreement of January 22, 1878, was

---

[1] *Malaya/Philippines Relations* (Kuala Lumpur: 1963), p. 22. Here, in Appendix IV, is an extract of President Macapagal's "State of the Nation" Address of January 28, 1963, in which he tells of his interest in a Philippine claim to North Borneo, dating back to 1946-47. See also Frances L. Starner, "Malaysia and the North Borneo Territories," *Asian Survey,* III:11 (November 1963), 526.

not a cession of territory, but merely a lease (an annual payment for which was stipulated in the agreement) and that—whatever the nature of the original agreement—no transfer of sovereignty was (or could) ever have been involved. The basis for this argument is that only sovereigns and their representatives can transfer, accept, and hold sovereignty. Because Baron de Overbeck represented no sovereign entity, the Philippines contends that the agreement affected only property rights, not sovereignty. If accepted, this argument would render invalid all the later transactions which purported to alter the status of the North Borneo territory.

There are dozens of other complications, some arising out of the terms and wording of the original agreement, and others resulting from the actions taken and commentaries made by the affected governments. Consider first the method of payment. The 1878 document stipulated that Baron de Overbeck and his successors would pay to the sultan of Sulu an amount equivalent to $5000 annually. Some observers claim that the "very manner in which payment . . . is made, which is annually in perpetuity, and the smallness of the amount offered . . . underline the nature of the transaction as one of lease." [2] But others hold that the method of compensation does not affect the permanence of the transfer:

> That payment was to be made annually in no wise alters the matter. Such payment was given, not as rent, but as a pension to compensate for the loss of (in theory) income-producing lands. There is nothing strange about this; it was standard practice, and surely it was a good bargain for a sultan to receive a regular and secure income simply for signing away a hunk of useless jungle.[3]

Professor K. G. Tregonning, a recognized authority on the history of British Borneo, is convinced that the government of the Philippines

[2] Pacifico A. Ortiz, "Legal Aspects of the North Borneo Question," *Philippines Studies,* II:1 (January 1963), 44. Ortiz argues that "It is characteristic of sale that the consideration should at least equal the value of the object, and should be paid outright or within a terminable and definite time; as it is characteristic of lease that the consideration be paid from time to time as long as the tenancy exists."

[3] R. H. Leary, "Sulu and Sabah," *Far Eastern Economic Review,* IV (July 1963), 20. It must also be said that in the author's conversations with attorneys on this subject, the comment is regularly made that the method of payment is quite similar to what is known today as an annuity. They argue that it is perfectly acceptable practice for the seller of a property to demand and obtain payment annually or at any other interval, and for any period, finite or not.

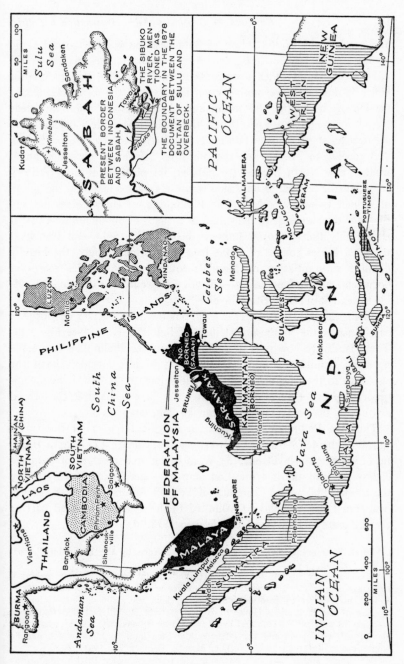

I:1

and/or the heirs of the sultan of Sulu have no valid historical claim to any portion of North Borneo. After consulting the original of the 1878 treaty (and other documents as well) in the Public Records Office in London, Tregonning reported that, in the English-language version of the treaty, the sultan and his successors "grant and cede . . . forever and in perpetuity all the rights and powers belonging to me over all the territories and lands being tributary to us. . . ." [4]

According to Tregonning, the sultan of Sulu never possessed all of what is now North Borneo (or Sabah), for portions of that territory came into British hands only as a result of cessions made by the sultan of Brunei (who still rules). The Philippines, of course, does not say that it is the successor to the sultan of Brunei; Manila maintains that it claims only the territories formerly belonging to Sulu. But just what those territories consist of is far from clear. Interestingly, the heavily detailed substantiation of Manila's formal claim includes scores of documents and commentaries—but not a single map or drawing indicating the extent of the territory involved.

Furthermore, the 1878 treaty mentions the Sibuco River on Borneo's east coast as the southernmost limit of Sulu's domains (see Fig. I-1). Those lands are now part of Indonesia, but the Philippines has made no claim against that state. Inasmuch as Manila considers itself the successor to the sovereign rights of the sultanate of Sulu, it might appropriately make an effort to recover all those lands, but the official attitude is that only one thing can be done at a time. [5]

Thus the Philippines' claim raises at least three major questions: (1) Was the 1878 transfer of territory permanent? (2) Was a transfer of sovereignty involved? (3) What is the precise extent of Manila's claim? At least the last question may have been partly answered by the former Philippines Secretary of Foreign Affairs, Mr. S. P. Lopez, who stated that the claim "is limited to the area that formed part of the sultanate of Sulu as of the deed in 1878." [6]

---

[4] K. G. Tregonning, "The Claim for North Borneo by the Philippines," *Australian Outlook*, XVI:3 (December 1962), 285.

[5] Observers may suggest that there are fundamental reasons for not making a claim against Indonesia as well, the size of her armed forces being among these. Indeed, in response to questions on why no claim was made against Indonesia, Speaker of the Philippines House of Representatives H. Villareal said that if he were armed only with a .45, and had two possible adversaries, one of whom was also armed with a .45 and the other with a Sten gun, he knew which one he would tackle. Interview with author, Manila, October 23, 1964.

[6] Mr. Lopez added that "accretions to the territory under British administration, if any, cannot properly be claimed by us, unless the British themselves volun-

It may be that a group of judges, perhaps at the World Court, will someday have to render a decision on the first question. If so, they will have to conduct an examination on the meaning, in 1878, of the Malay word *padjak*. Like the rest of the text, that word is written in Arabic script and in the Malay language in what was probably the original copy of the treaty. Tregonning has consulted the official British translation which carries the words,

> "we . . . Sultan of Sulu . . . *grant and cede* of our own free and sovereign will . . . forever and in perpetuity all the rights and powers belonging to me over all the territories and lands being tributary to us on the mainland of the island of Borneo. . . ." [7]

The Philippines government, on the other hand, presents an English-language translation prepared by a language specialist, Professor Harold Conklin of Yale University. That text reads:

> We . . . Sultan of Sulu . . . do hereby desire *to lease* of our own free will . . . and assigns forever and until the end of time, all rights and powers which we possess over all territories and lands tributary to us on the mainland of the island of Borneo. . . . [8]

The issue, therefore, seems to revolve about the critical word *padjak*, although even Malaysian officials do not deny that its usual meaning today is *lease* rather than *cede*. On the other hand, there is some doubt as to its meaning in 1878, for language does change. More significant, however, the words *in perpetuity* or *forever and until the end of time* appear in all versions, and these certainly suggest permanent transfer. [9]

There remains the question: Was a transfer of sovereignty involved? This question presents perhaps the most intricate legal tangle of all. Manila maintains that no transfer of sovereignty could have taken place in 1878, because Dent Brothers and Co. (which Baron de Overbeck represented) was not a sovereign entity. Thus, Manila contends, all later changes in the territory's status—from protectorate to colony to incorporation in Malaysia—are invalid. According to this argument,

---

tarily include these areas with the rest of North Borneo in the settlement." Interview with a correspondent of the *Free Press* (Manila), reprinted in *Larawan*, VIII:1 (Washington, D. C.: Embassy of the Philippines, October 26, 1962).

[7] Tregonning, *op. cit.*, p. 285. Italics added.

[8] Reprinted as an appendix in *Philippine Claim to North Borneo*, I (Manila: Bureau of Printing, 1964), p. 61. Italics added.

[9] Some British officials have hinted that the original treaty was in English. If so, London has not yet been willing to prove this.

Overbeck and Dent were "relinquishing" a sovereignty they did not possess and consequently had no right to turn over.

Manila's present position is bolstered by a number of statements made earlier by British officials. Undoubtedly, the most significant of these statements is found in a letter written by Lord Granville (then Britain's Foreign Secretary), to his minister in Madrid in 1882, only four years after the original treaty was signed:

> The British Charter [establishing the British North Borneo Company] . . . differs essentially from the previous Charters granted by the Crown . . . in the fact that the Crown in the present case assumes no dominion or sovereignty over the territories occupied by the Company, nor does it purport to grant to the Company any powers of government; it merely confers upon the persons associated the status and incidents of a body corporate, and recognizes the grants of territory and the powers of government made and *delegated by the sultans in whom the sovereignty remains vested*.[10]

Nevertheless, only six years later, in 1888, Great Britain established a protectorate over North Borneo, and proclaimed that "all rights of sovereignty over the said territories are vested in the British North Borneo Company." The point at issue, then is clear: How does Britain justify the Company's attainment of "sovereignty" by 1888, when only a few years earlier the British Foreign Secretary himself had specifically denied that sovereignty resided anywhere but in the person of the sultan? The Philippines, of course, holds that nothing whatever had changed: "We do not see how this protectorate agreement . . . can possibly divest the sultanate of Sulu of the latter's sovereignty. . . ."[11] There has been no formal statement either by Britain or Malaysia in response to this question. British officials may be relying upon the protocol signed in 1885 by Spain, Britain, and Germany, in which Britain agreed to recognize Spain's sovereignty over the Sulu Archipelago—i.e., the islands between Mindanao and Borneo. In return, the Spanish government renounced "all claims of sovereignty over the territories of the mainland of Borneo which belonged or may have belonged to the sultan of Sulu."[12] Thus Britain and Malaysia

---

[10] Reprinted in *Philippine Claim to North Borneo, op. cit.*, p. 117. Italics added.
[11] *Ibid.*, p. 122 fr. 21.
[12] Ortiz, *op. cit.*, p. 35. The text of the protocol is also found in *Philippine Claim to North Borneo, op. cit.*, p. 119, where there are slight textual differences from the Ortiz version.

may now maintain that the 1885 protocol cleared the way for the establishment of the protectorate in 1888, for according to accepted international law at that time, Spain had sovereignty not only over Sulu's domains but also throughout the Philippines. Thus the British view (and again within the perspective of nineteenth-century international law) is likely to be that Spain was empowered to renounce the sultan of Sulu's claims on the Borneo mainland.[13]

Great Britain may also contend that international practice has for at least seventy years accepted its sovereignty over North Borneo. Professor Tregonning has made this point well:

> These protectorate agreements, which recognized the boundaries of Sarawak, Brunei, and North Borneo, were never challenged by any other party. They were the basis of affairs until 1946, when . . . the territory became a colony. . . .[14]

And of course it is true that, despite occasional demurrals by the sultan's heirs and sporadic commentaries by American officials who were responsible for the foreign affairs of the Philippines until 1946, there was no formal objection to the status of North Borneo until 1962. Indeed, several international agreements signed after the 1885 protocol seem to reinforce the view that no nation doubted Britain's sovereignty over North Borneo.

Motives for the Claim

It was not until January 1962 that a Manila columnist, Napoleon Rama, wrote a series of articles entitled "North Borneo is Ours!" in the Philippines *Free Press*. From that time on, events moved very quickly, and six months later, President Macapagal informed Britain that the Philippines was laying claim to North Borneo. Why, after all those years, did Manila decide to lodge this claim?

It is too easy, and also misleading, to answer simply that Diosdado

---

[13] None of this, of course, has anything to do with "self-determination," regarded by many observers as part of modern international law, but certainly not accepted in the 1880s. If the dispute should come before an international tribunal, both the Philippines and Malaysia are likely to invoke self-determination. Malaysian officials already stress that with elections already having been held in Sabah, and with additional elections acceptable to them, no change in sovereignty is justified. This is also implied by the results of the United Nations' Survey of September 1963, in which Secretary-General U Thant found that a majority of the people of Sabah (and Sarawak) wish "to join in the Federation of Malaysia."

[14] Tregonning, *op. cit.*, p. 287.

Macapagal's election as President in late 1961 allowed him finally to fulfill a burning ambition to recover North Borneo, although he is one of the few prominent Filipinos with a long-standing familiarity with the claim.[15] But wider factors in the domestic politics of the Philippines, revolving especially around the renewed nationalistic emphasis, seem to have led to the President's decision.

Rama, the reporter whose series of newspaper stories ostensibly brought the claim to public attention, concedes that the articles were generated by someone else.[16] By most accounts, the articles aroused some interest in informed Manila circles, and undoubtedly in foreign embassies, but apparently very little concern or enthusiasm among the Philippine public. Though articles on the subject—generally written in flamboyant terms—ran for several months in a number of newspapers, they certainly did not call forth public demonstrations, student marches, or any of the other modern manifestations of nationalistic sentiment. Indeed, during the early months of 1962, the North Borneo "issue" was commonly regarded as the product of a Manila newspaper circulation war.[17] This view apparently was shared by the British government, which was described by the newspapers as an unscrupulous landgrabber, for Britain tended to ignore the clamor.

It is often contended now that London's attitude was a major error, and that if Britain had expressed a willingness to discuss the claim— first with the representative of the sultan's heirs, and later with Philippine officials—the dispute might have been avoided. But the British attitude is understandable. For example, the attorney who represented the sultan's heirs (Nicasio Osmeña) reportedly was asking for a cash settlement of the claim of between $20 and $40 million. That may have seemed sufficiently bizarre to British officials for them to decide not to give the matter serious consideration. Moreover, the sultan and his heirs had complained about the North Borneo arrangement

[15] As he has explained, he first became interested in the territory when he was a junior member of the foreign service in 1946, and in 1948 he sought the help of an American law professor, whose views confirmed Macapagal's suspicions that a valid claim existed. Later, as a member of congress in 1950, he authored a resolution urging the government to press the claim, and although this passed the house of representatives, the senate did not concur. Macapagal appears to have said nothing else about the matter publicly for twelve more years, until 1962.

[16] Interview with the author, Manila, October 1964. It is possible that Rama obliged, in return for some favor, but at any rate he decided to "give it a try," and several well-written articles appeared.

[17] This was the view of, among many others, a leading official in the U.S. Department of State. Interview with the author, Washington, D. C., June 1962.

before (beginning six months after the treaty was first signed),[18] and British officials may have concluded that this was just another attempt to obtain more money.

There was little evidence that most Filipinos cared about the North Borneo affair at all. The editors of Manila's newspapers, for example, soon decided that circulation could be increased more rapidly by the case of Harry Stonehill, an extremely wealthy American whose activities in the Philippines since 1946 were linked to widespread official corruption. The dramatic proceedings which led to Stonehill's eventual deportation from Manila in August 1962 easily diverted press attention from the North Borneo claim. Thus, it seemed likely that the "North Borneo affair" would soon go the way of earlier, short-lived crusades by Manila's rather frantic press. Even Vice-President Pelaez, who was then also Foreign Secretary of the Philippines, spoke warmly during this period (in an interview with the author) of his impending plans for intensive cooperation with Malaya in ASA. In the course of this interview, Pelaez referred only once—and then flippantly—to the need "to settle this North Borneo thing." [19]

The mistake made by all these informed people seems to have been an underestimation of President Macapagal's pique and of those political elements which would aggravate it. The best explanation of why the dispute has gone so far is that President Macapagal, in an effort to establish a mild irritant, unleashed forces greater than he had foreseen.

NORTH BORNEO AND A PHILIPPINE "IDENTITY"

It is clear that Macapagal was annoyed by his relations with the United States early in 1962. To begin with, there had been a recurrence of the many commercial irritants inherent in the "special" Philippines-American relationship when U.S. officials impounded a shipment of Philippines tobacco.[20] The Stonehill affair was another re-

---

[18] See "The Philippine Claim to North Borneo," in *Larawan,* IX:9 (Washington, D. C.: Embassy of the Philippines, December 24, 1963), for a chronology of these events. Also see the story by Aleko Lilius, "How England 'Stole' North Borneo!" in the *Chicago Sunday Tribune* October 14, 1945), recently reprinted by the Philippine government.

[19] Interview with the author, Manila July, 31, 1962.

[20] There was another of these upsets in August 1963, when the United States announced restrictive quotas on imports of Philippine dresses and embroidery. As David Wurfel writes: "Dressmaking is an industry that employs more than 300,000 persons . . . and an immediate uproar followed, with threats of demon-

minder of an unsavory aspect of the relations between Filipinos and Americans, and Macapagal's handling of this problem—particularly the fact that he seemed willing to let Stonehill "get away"—had brought him some stiff criticism.[21] But perhaps the major factor in Manila's decision to press the claim was anger over the failure of the U.S. Congress to appropriate funds for the $73 million War Damages Claims Bill. (Congress did not refuse to pass the appropriation, which had already been authorized; it simply adjourned without getting to it.) This inaction, after a series of promises begun by President Roosevelt, was considered by Manila to be an inexcusable breach of faith and a shocking insult.

This led to some remarkable events, all of which were intended to express Manila's extreme displeasure with the United States. In rapid succession, President Macapagal announced that he was cancelling his scheduled trip to Washington (where he was to speak with President Kennedy), changed the Philippines Independence day from the 4th of July to a June date symbolizing the revolt against Spain, and changed the name of Manila's famous avenue, Dewey Boulevard (in commemoration of the U.S. Admiral) to Roxas Boulevard. Then, under the transparent cover of actions designed to "play a greater role in Asia," the Philippines set out to strain its relations with Great Britain, another major Western power, and particularly to cast a shadow on the proposed new state of Malaysia which Britain was actively furthering and which the United States had tacitly endorsed.[22]

The Philippines' claim to North Borneo must be seen in the light of these events. If it was part of President Macapagal's intention to remind the United States and the West that his country could no longer be taken for granted, undoubtedly he succeeded. For the first time in years the West—and the United States in particular—was forced to think about Philippines' nationalism. Many events, large and small,

---

strations at the U. S. Embassy." "A Changing Philippines," *Asian Survey* (February 1964), 703.

[21] Macapagal had smarted under criticism during the 1961 election campaign, in which President Garcia had characterized him as a man with a "colonial mentality." In the Philippine context, this can mean only that one is too subservient to the American, and part of President Macapagal's concern, once he won the election, may have been to demonstrate that he could be as independent of American influence as anyone else.

[22] In a statement that could not have pleased President Macapagal, President Kennedy later declared that Malaysia is "the best hope of security for that very vital part of the world." See transcript of Presidential Press Conference, *Washington Post* (February 15, 1963).

seemed to take on new meaning.[23] An old strain of Pan-Malay senti-ment, which had long attracted some Filipinos but which generally had been discounted, seemed to acquire new significance as Manila exerted considerable effort to improve relations with Indonesia—a de-velopment directly related to the Philippines' claim to North Borneo.[24] Malaysian leaders in particular regarded Manila's sudden friendship with Djakarta, their major enemy, as a cynical attempt to pressure them and saw in it another manifestation of the relative shallowness of Philippine policy. Insofar as it seeks to explain a particular tactic, that thesis appears essentially correct, but it needs refinement and elaboration. The North Borneo claim was a catalyst in Manila's turn toward Djakarta: not only did it provide a reason for closer associa-tion with Indonesia, but it also helped to revive certain latent political currents in the Philippines. In the broadest sense, these currents repre-sent the widespread desire among articulate and informed Filipinos to be accepted in Asia as Asians rather than as an "Asian branch" of the United States. More specifically, they represent the desire to be accepted by Indonesia, a nation which evokes decidedly ambivalent feelings—both of attraction and fear—among many Filipinos.

The urge to demonstrate a specific identity is not new to the Phil-ippines; it has been commented on regularly by most knowledgeable observers of local politics and foreign policy there. In part, it is re-lated to a sentimental attraction for the Pan-Malay idea, which ap-peals to many Filipino intellectuals: "It gains prominence in the Phil-ippines now partly because of a strongly felt need to identify more closely with Asia." [25] The Borneo claim provided both a tactic and an opportunity to fulfill some of this need.

[23] By "small" events we mean, for example, isolated personal "slights" which Americans had come to regard as a common manifestation of Philippine nation-alism. Perhaps wrongly, resident Americans felt that they detected a pattern in so often being placed at the end of a line; or waiting for a particularly long time at a store counter; or having a cup of coffee "accidentally" spilled on their laps. By 1962, this sort of incident came to be regarded as part of a larger trend.

[24] As an initial comment, Guy Pauker's observations may be cited: "President Macapagal became . . . increasingly involved in a Philippine claim to an unde-fined part of Sabah, which brought about a Philippine-Malaysian conflict not directly related to Indonesia's pursuits. Added to a growing Philippine quest to find for herself an 'Asian identity,' this led in 1963 to an increasing *rapproche-ment* between the governments in Manila and Djakarta." "Indonesia in 1963: The Year of Wasted Opportunities," *Asian Survey* (February 1964), 689.

[25] David Wurfel, "A Changing Philippines," *op. cit.,* p. 704. Wurfel, long a close student of Philippine politics, wrote the chapters on the Philippines in *Government and Politics in Southeast Asia,* George McT. Kahin (ed.) (Ithaca, N. Y.: Cornell University Press, 1964).

As a tactic (and it seems clear that Malaysian suspicions on this point are correct), President Macapagal launched his "Greater Malay Confederation" proposal as a means to forestall Sabah's inclusion in Malaysia. Closing ranks with Indonesia would confront the Malaysia proposal with two opponents. As an opportunity, the claim to Sabah gave added legitimacy to those who already were urging closer relations with Indonesia. For certain prominent Filipinos the Pan-Malay concept was a vehicle in which, along with Indonesia and Malaya, the Philippines finally would find its true identity in Asia.

The thesis that the new relationship with Indonesia was a tactic aimed at improving Manila's chances for recovering North Borneo is illustrated by a very important and confidential study prepared by the University of the Philippines—a study commissioned by President Macapagal himself. The following excerpt from one of the authors' introductory remarks describes why the study was undertaken:

> President Macapagal was hopeful that, with the confederation proposal, he had effectively met the criticism in the foreign—specifically, British —press that the Philippines' claim to North Borneo at this time was disrupting the formation of a Federation of Malaysia which would be a stable and "powerful bulwark against Communism in this part of the world."

> At the behest of Undersecretary Salvador P. Lopez, President Carlos P. Romulo [of the University of the Philippines] asked Dean Cesar A. Majul to form a faculty committee to cooperate in the "preparatory studies which President Macapagal has instructed the Department of Foreign Affairs to undertake concerning the establishment of a Malayan Confederation." [26]

The study itself contains a large section called "The Confederation Proposal and the North Borneo Question," which explains first that by 1961 Britain had planned to relinquish control over North Borneo by incorporating it into a proposed Malaysia Federation, and then adds:

> The Philippines, quick to realize the implications of such a federation, gave official notice of its claim to sovereignty over North Borneo. . . . What are the implications of the proposed Federation of Malaysia? As far as the Philippines is concerned, its formation would mean the transfer of sovereignty over North Borneo from the United Kingdom to the new

---

[26] Alejandro M. Fernandez, "The Greater Malayan Confederation Proposal: Cultural, Economic, and Political Considerations," in *Proposed Outlines of a Greater Malayan Confederation,* p. 47. Unpublished.

federation. . . . This would complicate our North Borneo claim by the coming in of a new party or, at the worst, would mean the forfeiture of that claim.

This clearly leaves two courses of action, which are not mutually exclusive, that the Philippines can pursue. *One course of action is already being pursued: i.e., President Macapagal's confederation proposal. This course of action would be fruitful provided* it succeeds in superseding, or preventing the formation of, the Federation of Malaysia, *as the President apparently intended.* The idea is twofold; (1) to prevent the British from unilaterally transferring sovereignty over North Borneo to a federation which excludes the Philippines; and (2) to keep open the avenue to a negotiated settlement of the status of North Borneo.[27]

These comments show clearly that Macapagal's famous "confederation proposal" was seen, even by his own advisors, as a mere tactic designed to help press the North Borneo claim. They were written late in the summer of 1962, when the proposed "confederation" was to include only the Philippines and Malaya/Malaysia. But in December 1962, when a revolt broke out in Brunei and it became evident that Indonesia openly supported this and other anti-Malaysia demonstrations, real incentive for Philippines-Indonesian cooperation was established. Accordingly, Macapagal soon after began to speak of the "Greater *Malay* Confederation" including Indonesia (this became "Maphilindo"). He made a second request to the University of the Philippines for an amended study, taking into account the enlarged concept of a confederation. This is the point at which those Filipinos, in government and out, who already were disposed to a friendlier relationship with Indonesia were no doubt most encouraged. To them the dispute over North Borneo came as a marvelous opportunity, for it led directly to Maphilindo. In Macapagal's own words:

. . . through the long eclipse of their civilization, the Malay peoples have waited for this moment. If they fail to seize it, another opportunity may not come again during the lifetime of this generation, but if they seize the moment mightily with both hands, it can mark the beginning of a new golden age for the peoples of Malay stock.[28]

---

[27] *Ibid.*, p. 94. Italics added.
[28] Conclusion to Macapagal's speech before the Manila Overseas Press Club, August 21, 1963. His final words were: "In Maphilindo and through Maphilindo, nourished constantly by their vision and enterprise, the Malay peoples shall be borne upon the true, the vast, the irresistible wave of the future."

Similarly, in one of his most famous statements, Macapagal has likened Indonesia, Malaya, and the Philippines to "triplets who, after birth, were placed under the care of three different foster-parents. . . . Now that they have come of age and achieved independence, they should try to rediscover their common origin and common destiny."

But perhaps one of the clearest indications that some sophisticated Filipinos are caught up in a search for national identity is found in the "Suggested Course of Action on North Borneo," included in the University study commissioned by Macapagal:

> I am suggesting that our government seriously consider *unofficially supporting a national movement,* led by Filipino Muslim leaders, *aimed at the recovery of North Borneo* from the British before the proposed Federation of Malaysia is born. Our government must not restrain any spontaneous [sic] movement directed toward this end.

Having made this suggestion, the author then concluded that one of the main benefits of such a policy would be that "a direct confrontation with the British . . . *would boost our prestige in the eyes of fellow Asians, who up to now tend to regard us as Asian puppets.*[29]

THE "OPPORTUNITY" AND MACAPAGAL'S ADVISORS

Even more important than the circulation of such ideas in Manila is the fact that they have had a number of exceptionally well-placed supporters and spokesmen—particularly in the Department of Foreign Affairs. The most prominent of these was Salvador P. Lopez, and it is also likely that Juan M. Arreglado, then Counselor of the Department of Foreign Affairs, found a more attentive audience for his markedly pro-Indonesian convictions than ever before. Lopez, who had been attracted to the Pan-Malay idea in his student days, was Undersecretary in 1962-63, and became Foreign Secretary in mid-1963. Among British and Malaysian officials, he is now commonly regarded as the chief architect of the Manila-Djakarta *rapprochement* which, they feel, is aimed at weakening Malaysia. And when, after less than a year in office, Lopez was transferred by President Macapagal (April 29, 1964), Filipino observers commented openly that Macapagal must have concluded that Lopez's pro-Indonesia attitudes were too pro-

[29] Fernadez, *op. cit.,* Appendix III, p. 96. Italics added.

nounced. As one reporter put it, the dismissal of Lopez would ease "an apparent overdose of sympathy in the administration toward Indonesia." [30]

Lopez had come to office in July 1963, when Vice-President Pelaez (concurrently Foreign Secretary) resigned in the wake of corruption charges instigated by Macapagal. (Pelaez subsequently sought and lost the presidential nomination of the opposition party.) It is unlikely that foreign-policy attitudes were a major consideration in President Macapagal's desire to get rid of Pelaez, but there are a number of indications that, even before the break, Palaez had differed with Macapagal's developing approach toward Indonesia.[31]

During his tenure, Pelaez had never been noticeably partial to Indonesia. When he spoke in 1963 about Maphilindo—the symbol of the new Philippines-Indonesian relationship—he was at pains to stress that nothing very real was involved in that concept, though he felt that the agreement to consult regularly was of some importance. In contrast, he felt great pride in his role in furthering ASA, in which Indonesia was not included. In late June 1963, only days before his resignation, he showed every interest in continuing to maintain and develop ASA.

Lopez, on the other hand, had indicated as early as mid-1962 that ASA evoked no enthusiasm in him. Interviewed in June 1963, on the same day that Pelaez discounted the importance of Maphilindo, Lopez was remarkably optimistic about the new concept—even to the point of dismissing, ignoring, or eventually doing away with ASA. This idea was rejected by Pelaez: using almost the same words that Malayan officials chose, he said that there was no cause for Thailand to feel "left out" of Maphilindo, because "it cannot be regarded as a serious development."

These preferences clearly were known to President Macapagal. A prominent Philippines senator, and a former confidant of President Macapagal, has assured this author that he was present early in 1963 when Macapagal said to Pelaez: "Manny, you've got to go slow on this

[30] Oscar Villadolid, diplomatic reporter for the *Manila Bulletin,* April 30, 1964. Villadolid added that during Lopez's tenure "a noticeable preference for Indonesia, in some instances at the exclusion of Malaysia, has caused considerable concern in and out of government."

[31] For this comparison of Pelaez and Macapagal, I draw on interviews in Manila with Emmanuel Pelaez (July 1962, June 1963, October 1964), and S. P. Lopez (July 1962, June 1963), as well as the statements of informed observers both in and out of the Philippine government.

ASA thing; our foreign-policy effort has to focus on North Borneo, and everything else must take a back seat." [32]

Thus, when Lopez replaced Pelaez, there seemed every reason to believe that whatever pro-Indonesian tendencies were building up in the Philippines' foreign policy would very likely be enhanced. At an interview during which Lopez expressed his considerable enthusiasm for the Maphilindo concept, even an accompanying Filipino official was startled, later confiding surprise that "S.P. is so incautious about Indonesia." But this enthusiasm was precisely what President Macapagal needed in his effort to press the North Borneo claim and to enlist Indonesian support for the anti-Malaysia posture it implied. One of Lopez's first speeches as Foreign Secretary gave the measure of his conviction that the Philippines, in its search for its "true" identity, must accelerate its "clear orientation toward Asia":

> . . . in the end, the powerful affinities of race, culture, and geography and the imperatives of regional security and common destiny will inevitably push us toward our racial kin and next-door neighbors in Southeast Asia.[33]

This was the view of Juan Arreglado, the other senior Philippines diplomat whose opinions appear to have been important in shaping the cordial Djakarta-Manila relationship. Arreglado, like Lopez, must have considered the North Borneo claim an opportunity not to be missed. A former ambassador to Indonesia, Arreglado had by 1962 acquired a reputation in diplomatic circles for vehement anti-American statements. These were mixed with expressions of warm regard for Indonesia, and private urgings for a closer relationship with Djakarta. For example, in an article published in May 1963, Arreglado argued that "throughout all of Asia there can be no truer and better friend of the Philippines than Indonesia.[34] In an unmistakable reference to the foreign policies

---

[32] Senator Raul Manglapus, interview with the author, Manila, October 1964.

[33] Salvador P. Lopez, "Foreign Policy: Transformations and Reconsiderations," Address before the Manila Rotary Club, August 29, 1963. Also see Lopez's comments in "The Crisis of Malaysia and the Future of Maphilindo," Address at a Convocation of the University of the Philippines, October 4, 1963, and his address to the eighteenth Regular Session of the United Nations General Assembly, October 8, 1963, in which he said that "Maphilindo was a glorious improvisation," and that the Manila summit which led to it was received in Manila "amidst euphoria." All of these speeches reprinted by the Philippines Embassy in Washington, D. C., in *Larawan*, Series IX, Nos. 8, 12, and 13, respectively.

[34] Juan M. Arreglado, "Our Relationship with Indonesia," *Progressive Review*, I:1 (Manila: May-June 1963).

of former Foreign Minister Serrano, which had included tacit assistance to the 1958-59 Indonesian rebellion, Arreglado stressed that it was in Manila's interest to have a strong, united, and stable Indonesia "rather than a weak Indonesia which might become the victim of subversion and disintegrative tendencies." [35]

Arreglado's article also contained an unmistakable reference to a very well-known article by the former Chief of Military Intelligence, Captain Carlos Albert, which described the size of Indonesia's armed forces and "the massive Indonesian arms build-up" as "an entirely new and disturbing factor, . . . the most ominous development in the Southeast Asia region, if not in the entire Far East. . . ." [36] Arreglado, however, took a very different view, and his words are also instructive for the light they shed regarding his opinion of the Philippines-American defense ties in SEATO:

> How big that [Indonesian] army and navy should be, no other nation could pretend to know the answer better than the Indonesians themselves. For, after all, the primary responsibility for the defense of their country and the preservation of their territorial integrity, rests with them. *No self-respecting nation would ever entrust duty to any foreign power or any combination of foreign powers, however friendly or powerful they might be.*[37]

Arreglado's influence on the Philippines' policy toward Indonesia is also evident in the previously secret documents which President Macapagal used in preparing for the June 1963 conference with President Sukarno and Tunku Abdul Rahman, Malaysia's Prime Minister. That was the meeting at which the foundations were laid for Maphilindo, the loose consultive organization formed by the three governments. Arreglado, in his article, conceded that

[35] Arreglado was, of course, intimately familiar with Manila's assistance and acquiescence in efforts to aid these "disintegrative tendencies." Indeed, Subandrio said to this writer that Serrano, whose anti-Indonesian attitudes were well-known in Djakarta, had commented openly to him that Indonesia really was probably too big a country to administer effectively, and that—according to Subandrio— Serrano had even used the words *break up* in this context. Interview with the author, Djakarta, July 1963.

Similarly, Fernadez commented that: "surface manifestations to the contrary notwithstanding, Indonesia is still nursing a grudge against the Philippines for its role in harboring Indonesian rebels and unofficially aiding them during the 1958-61 civil war between Djakarta and the outer Islands. *Op. cit.,* p. 48.

[36] Captain Carlos J. Albert (PN) Ret., "Warning to All: Indonesia's Arms Buildup," *The Sunday Times* (Manila: January 20, 1963).

[37] Arreglado, *op. cit.* Italics added.

Indonesia and the Philippines may be different from each other in their national perspectives and institutional trappings, but when it comes to the fundamentals of political morality and international policies, they have certainly many things in common, particularly in their determination to uphold *individual liberty, human dignity, self-determination for dependent people, elimination of all forms of colonialism,* and respect for the territorial integrity and national independence of all nations—big or small.[38]

Compare that statement with the hitherto classified "Philippines Proposal for the Establishment of a Malay Confederation" (the document prepared for President Macapagal's use at the conference) which, after stressing the "common underlying culture" of the Malay peoples, states:

In spite of varied political experience, there exists among the Indonesians, Malayans, and Filipinos a common recognition of the *dignity of the individual, respect for human rights and fundamental freedom,* and desire for economic and social progress. A definable core of compatible values is clearly discernible.[39]

The year following these statements, characterized by the formation of Maphilindo, saw near-ridiculous efforts by President Macapagal to demonstrate a Filipino "identity" with Indonesia. When he visited Indonesia in February 1964, he gushed about the ties of "race, culture, and geography" which allegedly bind together Indonesia and the Philippines. He asserted that Rizal, the national hero of the Philippines, "is an important intellectual link" between the two countries, and that Rizal's writings "are widely read and quoted in Indonesia and have, in fact, inspired the Indonesians in their struggle for independence." [40] The truth is that Indonesians would treat very lightly indeed the suggestion that they owe anything to Rizal—about whom most of them have not heard until very, very recently.[41]

[38] *Ibid.* Italics added.
[39] From the document given to this writer by officials in the Philippine government. Italics added.
[40] From Macapagal's speech, "The Challenge to the Malay Peoples," at the University of Gadjah Mada, Jogjakarta, February 25, 1964.
[41] The author has asked a number of Indonesian officials in Djakarta about Rizal, and other pretensions by Filipinos that Philippine nationalism "inspired" Indonesians. The Indonesian leaders have *heard* about Rizal, to be sure, but largely as a poet, and then only recently. This conclusion, that Rizal has been of no importance in the Indonesian nationalist movement, is concurred in by specialists on Indonesian affairs.

The 1963-64 period was also one of vain efforts by Macapagal to act as a bridge between Indonesia and Malaysia, ostensibly in his role as an Asian statesman. The spate of meetings among the leaders of the three countries came to a fruitless end in Tokyo in June 1964, precisely one year after Maphilindo was formed. During that year the foreign policy of the Philippines described a wide circle: it began with pleasant but not close relations with Indonesia, swung to an extreme of maudlin cordiality, and finally returned to the point at which it had started.

The career of Lopez himself during that period is illustrative of this wide swing in foreign policy. His advent to office was accompanied by efforts at Philippines-Indonesian *rapprochement,* and to many observers, Lopez is symbolic of the excesses of Philippines policy during that period. In his own country, Lopez came under increasing criticism for the marked pro-Indonesian posture he and Macapagal had adopted. By January 1964, a leading member of Macapagal's own party had made several demands for immediate recognition of Malaysia.[42] In March, Lopez felt called upon to defend his policies against severe press criticism, and denied once again that he was merely "toeing the Indonesian line." [43] In April, both Ferdinand Marcos, President of the Senate, and Lorenzo Sumulong, Chairman of the Senate Foreign Affairs Committee, subjected Lopez and Macapagal to scathing criticism. Marcos, for example, accused Macapagal of "treading on dangerous ground" in his close attachment to Indonesia's Sukarno.[44] Macapagal himself, perhaps admitting more than he intended, defended the policy on the grounds that it had "effectively served our national interest in terms of our claim to Sabah." [45] By May, when Lopez was relieved of his post, most of his comments on Malaysia were indistinguishable from the statements emanating from Djakarta, even including references to "neocolonialism" and "imperialism." He was at one with Dr. Subandrio in challenging United Nations Secretary-General U Thant's statement that the peoples of Borneo did indeed prefer to join with

[42] Statement of Senator Raul Manglapus, January 12, 1964, reported by Radio Malaysia (Kuala Lumpur), January 13, 1964.

[43] Manila *Chronicle* (March 25, 1964).

[44] From Marcos's speech of April 10, 1964, in commemoration of Bataan Day. This is the speech in which Marcos, who later defeated Macapagal for the presidency in the November, 1965 elections, charged that had Macapagal "consulted with Filipinos who love freedom . . . he would surely have been told to oppose moves to glorify the Indonesian . . . dictator."

[45] From Macapagal's statements to the press, in answer to the attacks of Marcos and Sumulong, April 10, 1964.

Malaysia.[46] His insistence that a great number of Filipino and Indonesian "observers" accompany the United Nations investigating team (he demanded more "observers" than there were members of the United Nations team itself) nearly brought about the collapse of the whole operation.

But perhaps the most startling of all Lopez's actions, and one which indicates the disfavor into which he has fallen, came after his dismissal as Foreign Secretary. In October 1964, in his role as chief delegate to the United Nations, Lopez warned that the Philippines' claim to North Borneo would be placed on the agenda of the General Assembly—unless Malaysia agreed to submit the issue to the World Court. Apparently he had acted upon his own initiative, for within hours President Macapagal announced that his government had no intention of bringing the issue to the United Nations at that time. This event, a classic diplomatic bungle for the Philippines, probably also marked the highest point reached in their search, by some Filipinos, for an Asian identity and— more specifically—for acceptance by Djakarta. But Macapagal's refusal to support Lopez was symbolic of the obvious effort in Manila to pull back from the close relationship with Indonesia which he represented [47]—another manifestation of the striking ambivalence in the Philippines' attitude toward its enormous neighbor.

Siren of the Celebes Sea:
Indonesia and the Philippines

Indonesia apparently has something of a siren-like effect on the minds of many Filipinos, particularly of those who feel constrained to prove their Asian identity. Many leading Filipinos are aware of the chaos in Indonesia's economy, the size of its Communist movement, and its failure to establish democratic government. Yet Indonesia, like a giant Lorelei, continues to lure Filipino intellectuals and leaders alike. Indonesia's attractions lie in its flamboyantly Asian nature, its symbolism as an ethnic and cultural homeland of the Malay

[46] This is not to say that U Thant's "ascertainment" was a perfect operation; the point, however, is that both Indonesia and the Philippines agreed *in advance* to "welcome Malaysia" on the basis of U Thant's findings. When it became clear that the findings would not be favorable to them, Manila and Djakarta began to complain about the United Nations' "procedures."

[47] We would cite once again Oscar Villadolid's comment that Lopez's relief would ease "an apparent overdose of sympathy in the administration toward Indonesia." *Manila Bulletin* (April 30, 1964).

peoples, and its pretensions to be the very model of a revolutionary Asian nationalist state.

These attractions have had an effect in Manila, particularly on Filipinos who are unsure of their own heritage and who are searching for an identity more fundamental than that derived from the three foreign influences—the tutelage of Christianity, the veneer of Spanish civilization and culture, and the American political and economic imprint. This relationship is reinforced by Indonesia's recognition and exploitation of its attractions. Having themselves been courted for so long in Moscow, Peking, and Washington, Indonesians are familiar with the techniques of impressing visitors. Thus there has been a major campaign to attract Filipino newspapermen to Indonesia; once there, they find every facility put at their disposal.[48] Philippine government missions, too, have been accorded the red-carpet treatment in Djakarta, and even some of the most hard-headed of Manila's businessmen and trade leaders have been impressed. The members of one such mission, after having signed a multimillion-dollar trade agreement in Djakarta in May 1963, seemed to realize only after returning to Manila that there really was not much present scope for trade between the two nations.

The Filipinos' susceptibility to Indonesian overtures is increased by their relative lack of knowledge of their big neighbor,[49] but it is complicated by three basic elements in their overall attitude: (1) their feelings of superiority, deriving especially from a recognition of their own economic and political advancement; (2) their admiration for the largest Malay state, reflected in the desire to be "accepted" by it; and (3) their very definite apprehension, derived primarily from Indonesia's large size and population.

The Philippines' feelings of superiority toward Indonesia are perceptible both in economic matters and, to a lesser extent, in political affairs. Some Filipino businessmen, for example, apparently hope that Indonesia's more backward economy will make it a market for the

[48] Reporting what has long been an open secret in his profession, a Manila newsman wrote recently that "by cultivating influential Filipinos, the Indonesians have partly succeeded in winning some segments of the free-swinging press. Local Sukarnophile journalists willing to write daily columns on U.S. imperialism . . . prosper." (Oscar S. Villadolid, "Sukarno Makes Trouble in the Philippines," *The Reporter*, XXIII:3, (August 12, 1965), p. 23.

[49] For example, the sections devoted to Indonesia in the officially sponsored study already referred to are not at all well done, and do not reflect a sound understanding of Indonesian affairs. Nevertheless, this study formed the basis for President Macapagal's thinking on confederation of his Maphilindo proposal.

products of the expanding industry of the Philippines. They tend also to assume (and here some Manila officials join them) that Indonesia will willingly accept the Philippines' leadership in technical and economic development.[50] In fact, however, any economic or technological advantage which the Philippines may possess is not acknowledged by Indonesia. Dr. Subandrio has made it clear that his colleagues disdain the economic advancement of the major industrial nations, to say nothing of that of the Philippines:

> A steel mill, a chemical plant, some technical advice, these things we can get anytime; from the Russians, from [the] Americans, from the Germans. But to develop national identity—that takes years, and even in Indonesia we have only begun to accomplish that now.[51]

Surprisingly, even Indonesian economists dismiss the suggestion that the Philippines has much to offer their country. At a meeting of the Planning Council of the National Economic and Social Institute, many of Djakarta's most able economists expressed considerable derision— almost contempt—for the Philippines' "pretensions" to advancement. One speaker commented that it was "pure and utter nonsense" to think that the Philippines was in a position to assist Indonesia; the two countries, he went on, "are approximately at the same level of industrial development." No one present challenged this preposterous claim.

The same pattern prevails in the political sphere, in which some Filipinos think that the Philippines can serve as a model for, or act as a moderating influence on, certain of Indonesia's policies. Some Filipino leaders have broadly hinted that cordiality between Manila and Djakarta should be welcomed, because it could exert a "Westernizing" influence on their Indonesian counterparts. Thus, when President Macapagal announced his plans for the Greater Malaysia Confederation (that eventually became Maphilindo), the officially sponsored study argued, as one of federation's merits, that "The Philippines would serve as a restraining force to the political tendencies of Indonesia which may

---

[50] See statement of Philippine Secretary of Commerce and Industry Cornelio Balmaceda on the potential for trade among the Maphilindo countries (Washington, D. C.: Embassy of the Philippines, October 30, 1963). The relevant documents, each signed jointly by Dr. Suharto, Indonesia's trade minister, and Rufino Hechanova, secretary of the department of commerce and industry, are: the joint communiqué; the trade agreement; the protocol regarding economic cooperation; and the agreement on technical and scientific cooperation, all signed in Djakarta, on May 27, 1963.

[51] Interview with the author, Djakarta, July 4, 1963.

be described as becoming increasingly favorable toward Communist objectives." [52] This is a suggestion to which Indonesian leaders are extremely sensitive, for they take the view that—in the political sphere as in the economic—the Philippines has nothing of value to teach them.[53] Indeed, the attitude in Djakarta traditionally has been that the Philippines is only slightly less politically "backward" than Malaya. This attitude was clearly expressed by Foreign Minister Subandrio of Indonesia in July 1963, even as the two countries were ostensibly embarking on their newly cordial relationship. He expressed with asperity his conviction that the Philippines (like Malaya) must first find, establish, and recognize its own "national consciousness and identity" before it could be taken seriously by Indonesia.[54]

THE NAGGING FEAR OF INDONESIA

The fact that Filipino leaders are at such pains to stress their role as a potential "good" influence on Djakarta is itself of some importance, for it grows out of their nagging fear of Indonesia. President Macapagal was repeatedly warned by some associates that his alliance with Indonesia, designed to further the Sabah claim, might have unforeseen—and undesirable—consequences. These warnings were a manifestation of the duality inherent in the Philippines' perception of Indonesia. It is significant, for example, that the "special relationship" with Djakarta was not Macapagal's first policy choice in mid-1962, when he was casting about for a means to forestall the establishment of Malaysia. Instead, his first expressed choice was a Greater Malayan confederation,

---

[52] Estrella D. Solidum, "Background Paper on Indonesia," in "Proposed Outlines . . ." *op. cit.,* Appendix IV, p. 272.

[53] Late in 1964, Philippine Ambassador to Djakarta Reyes stated that he was well aware that relations between his country and Indonesia were not as cordial as before. Part of the reason, he said, was that *Sukarno and Subandrio resent expressions in Manila that the new relationship with Indonesia was justified by the opportunity it provided to "moderate" Indonesian policies.* "They think we want to bring them into the Western camp," the ambassador concluded. Interview with the author, Djakarta, October 27, 1964.

[54] Interview with the author, Djakarta, July 4, 1963. Much of this talk of the need for the Philippines and Malaya to assert their "national consciousness" is simply another way of saying that Indonesian leaders feel that the Filipinos must leave SEATO, and Malaya the Commonwealth, before Djakarta will give them serious consideration as Asian partners. Thus it seems correct to say, as Guy Pauker has commented, that the Manila agreements of August 1963 "constituted a diplomatic triumph for Indonesia." For in those agreements both Malaya and the Philippines stated officially that their Western bases are "temporary in nature." In Pauker's words, this was "no mean achievement for Indonesia." "Indonesia in 1963: The Year of Wasted Opportunities," *op. cit.,* 689.

which would have included only the proposed Malaysia and the Philippines. It is beyond question that Macapagal saw in confederation a means of incorporating North Borneo with the Philippines, or at least keeping alive its claim to the territory. This was well expressed in the 1962 study he commissioned:

> The establishment of the Federation of Malaysia will render the Philippine claim over North Borneo more difficult to pursue. Therefore, if the Greater Malayan Confederation proposal fails, other alternatives for pursuing the Philippine claim are immediately indicated.

This tends to make a mockery of the emotional overtones that Lopez and Macapagal later imputed to the Philippines' new relationship with Indonesia and to Maphilindo (which caused Lopez to say that Maphilindo is the "fruition of the dreams of many generations of Filipino and other Malay heroes").[55] Obviously, the new policy trend was not at all emotional: it was merely an alternative—another method by which Manila might press its claim to North Borneo and oppose the new state of Malaysia. It is also clear that those goals have priority over cooperation with Djakarta, for Filipinos continue to nurture a measure of fear and anxiety over Indonesia. Indonesia's very size provides cause for apprehension, as do the size and role of its Communist party and related groups, its friendly relations with the Communist bloc, and the size and equipment of its armed forces.

Moreover, as Albert's "warning" article pointed out, the Philippine Muslim South—over which Manila cannot always exercise effective control and which is characterized by a population only loosely integrated with the rest of Filipino society—is perceived to be a potential breeding-ground for Indonesian-led subversive movements. "Outside of the Huk area at the heights of the campaign," Albert noted, "we have had to maintain the largest concentration of armed forces in the tiny province of Sulu." Albert did not go so far as to say that there has yet been any separatist movement among the Moros of that region, but he concluded:

> A well-organized propaganda campaign, emphasizing Indonesian affinities, magnifying differences and justified grievances of our Muslim

[55] S. P. Lopez, "The Crisis Over Malaysia and the Future of Maphilindo," Speech at the University of the Philippines, October 4, 1963. This was also the period of euphoria during which Macapagal, visiting in Indonesia, commented that similarities in the two countries' educational programs derives from "the deep well-springs of our racial subconscious experience." Macapagal's address at the University of Gadjah Mada, February 25, 1964.

Filipinos, stage-managed incidents, coupled with submarine-supplied arms [and] munitions, could create a most serious national security situation for the Philippines. It is time our people and leaders started considering all aspects of this situation.[56]

Clearly, "this situation"—and other possibly undesirable effects of the new relationship with Indonesia—have occurred to a number of prominent Filipinos, as angry comments by Macapagal's former colleagues (usually made as they resigned their party membership) would indicate. Even the amended study commissioned by Macapagal recognized the problem that Indonesia might pose in the future. When the scope of the study was enlarged to take into account Indonesian membership in the proposed confederation, the authors considered the consequences that might arise "should Indonesia be left out":

Philippine and Indonesian relations will be strained in view of the anticipated hostile attitude of Indonesia. It would then become necessary to evaluate whether the defense arrangements of the Confederation would offset or neutralize *Indonesia's attraction to the Muslim population in Mindanao*, which situation could pose a grave threat to Philippine political security.[57]

The study also discusses the possible consequences of a close relationship with an Indonesia included in the confederation. Observing that one of the reasons for which the prime minister of Malaysia, Tunku Abdul Rahman, had proposed the establishment of Malaysia was to provide for Malay dominance over Malaya's large Chinese contingent, the authors warned Macapagal that his proposed Greater Malayan Confederation posed a problem:

. . . it appears that Indonesia, on account of its population and economic potential will overshadow the rest. However, for the protection of their interests, *the natural tendency would be for Malaya and the Philippines to gravitate closer toward each other to maintain a closer balance between member states.*[58]

[56] Albert, *op. cit.* This article, written several years ago, is strikingly evocative of the very techniques that Indonesia has applied recently in its confrontation of Malaysia, including the submarine-supplied arms and munitions.
[57] Estrella D. Solidum, "Background Paper on Indonesia," "Proposed Outlines . . . ," *op. cit.,* Appendix IV, p. 272. Italics added.
[58] *Committee Report*, "The General Nature of a Confederation and Its Applicability to the Malay Peoples," *ibid.*, p. 11.

The tendency, of course, has been decidedly different: Macapagal's flirtation with Indonesia has caused a number of internal difficulties, to say nothing of its effects on the Philippines' relationship with Malaya.

The Impact of North Borneo on Philippines-Malaysia Relations

The most obvious result of President Macapagal's decision to claim North Borneo has been the erosion of the mutual warmth and trust which had developed between Kuala Lumpur and Manila. Malaysian leaders feel that the Philippines' sacrifice of the once-excellent relations between the two countries is based on three dubious factors: a charlatan, "Nick" Osmeña; the spurious political argument that possession of North Borneo is vital to Philippines security; and Sukarno's Indonesia —Malaysia's chief enemy.

Nicasio Osmeña, a colorful and prominent Manila lawyer, was the attorney for a group of the heirs to the sultan of Sulu, who claimed that Sabah (North Borneo) still belonged to them. On their behalf, Osmeña organized a group called the Kiram Corporation, whose major purpose apparently was to sell land, for Osmeña, anticipating a multi-million dollar sale, apparently attempted to have either Britain or Malaysia "buy" North Borneo from the Corporation. Malaysian leaders suspect, moreover, that at least some Filipino officials held shares in the Corporation. The further likelihood that Osmeña sought to interest high Malaysian officials (including the Tunku himself) in some sort of cash "arrangement" reinforces suspicion of Philippine intentions in this entire affair. (Osmeña reportedly claimed that he was acting for President Macapagal, and later that he was attorney for Azahari, the leader of the Brunei revolt of December 1962.) During his visit to Kuala Lumpur in January 1963, Osmeña vainly sought an audience with the Tunku, allegedly maintaining that he could help settle both the North Borneo claim *and* the Brunei revolt, if Malaya tendered a suitable offer of cash, land rights, and other concessions. Indeed, Osmeña asserted in a newspaper interview that the Tunku had secretly offered about £26 million to the sultan's heirs in settlement of the Sabah claim—a statement angrily denied within hours by the Tunku himself.[59] With Osmeña's death later in 1963, the Philippine govern-

---

[59] Information on some of these events is carried in the *Straits Times* (January 18, 1963) and in a broadcast of Radio Malaysia (Kuala Lumpur: January 18, 1963). It was in that broadcast that Rahman announced he had no intention of meeting with Osmeña.

ment succeeded the sultan's heirs. On these grounds, the Philippines began to press its claim as a matter of states sovereignty—a claim which, large because of its dubious origins, has failed to persuade Malaysian officials to a charitable view.

Furthermore, Malaysian officials find it difficult, for a number of reasons, to accept at face value the Philippines' argument that the claim is a matter of "vital national security." First is the fact that the Philippines never before raised any question about the relation of Sabah to national defense. Any early complaints about the status of Sabah derived from the charge that Britain had been guilty of a "land-grab." The Philippines now maintained, however, that the newly formed Malaysia would be a militarily weak state, beset by internal difficulties. Manila pointed especially to the leftist-oriented Chinese population of Singapore and Sarawak, and Singapore's expulsion from Malaysia in August 1965 supports the thesis of Malaysia's weakness. The crux of Manila's argument, therefore, is that Malaysia may disintegrate and/or come under Communist control, and that either or both possibilities would—if North Borneo were part of Malaysia—present a new security problem for the Philippines.

There is no difficulty in demonstrating this aspect of Manila's argument because—unfortunately for their future relations with Malaysia—Philippines spokesmen, in their eagerness to prove their point, have uttered some very unfriendly remarks about their neighbor. Even Vice-President Pelaez, presenting his government's claim at the British-Philippines talks in London, said that "a close examination of the Malaysia idea . . . would reveal that it would be, we regret to say, hardly viable." [60] President Macapagal's 1963 State-of-the-Nation message, however, was more specific:

> It is vital to the security of the Philippines that North Borneo be not placed under the sovereignty and jurisdiction of another state, particularly a state on the Asian mainland like Malaya. In the event, God forbid, that Malaya succumbs to the potent Communist threat on the Asian mainland, with North Borneo under Malaya, there would be created a situa-

[60] Republic of the Philippines, *Philippine Claim to North Borneo*, Vol. I (Manila: Bureau of Printing, 1964), p. 15. In fairness to him, it should be noted that this comment of Pelaez's came almost a year before Malaysia actually was formed. In Pelaez's view the Philippine government should have recognized Malaysia as soon as the Secretary-General's "ascertainment" was completed, and "thereby put an end to the whole problem." Interview with the author, Manila, October 20, 1964.

tion in which a Communist territory would be immediately at the southern frontier of the Philippines, which would pose a grave and intolerable threat to our country.[61]

The map of Southeast Asia which accompanied the Philippines' claim carried a legend with equally dire predictions, and might be cited as a modern example of geopolitics at their crudest. It purportedly showed "how essential North Borneo is to Philippine security. . . . Sabah is the gate to open Philippine Sulu Sea like a cork to the open end of a bottle":

> Should Malaya succumb to the Communist threat . . . there would be created a situation in which a Communist territory would be immediately at the southern frontier of the Philippines. North Borneo is only eighteen miles away from the nearest island of the Philippine archipelago. It is as vital to Philippine security as East Guinea [sic] is to Australia.[62]

Not surprisingly, these unneighborly predictions—coming as they did after several years of remarkably friendly relations—stirred some bitterness in Malaya. But, of course, many of Manila's speculations about the future of Malaysia are highly debatable, and this reinforced Kuala Lumpur's suspicion that they were transparently insincere. For example, it seems inconsistent that the Philippines, proud of its anti-colonial tradition, should object so strenuously to the demise of colonialism—which, after all, the formation of an independent Malaysia represents. This inconsistency seems all the greater because the former colonies of Sarawak and North Borneo joined, in Malaysia, a notably responsible and enlightened group of leaders—leaders, moreover, who had regarded the Philippines as a real friend and ally.

Of course, even before Singapore's secession it had to be acknowledged that Malaysia—like many other new nations—might not survive, but it must also be stressed that Malaysia has a better chance than most. First, Malaysia enjoys the best educational standards, the highest living standards, and the highest per capita income record in all Southeast Asia. Moreover, despite the restrictions on civil liberties (designed to guard against precisely the internal troubles predicted by

---

[61] Extracts from Macapagal's speech reprinted in *ibid.*, pp. 6-7. Palaez had explained the three "vital interests" which the claim involved: "sovereign rights, national security, and the peace . . . of the geographical area. . . ." *Ibid.*, p. 1.

[62] From the map legend appended to *Ibid.*, p. 20.

the Philippines), the country seems to be a stable democracy. The only other country in Southeast Asia to which that term—with its accepted connotations—might be applied is the Philippines itself. Finally, although their concern about the Communist threat to Malaysia may be genuine, Filipino leaders know that the new state has been accorded the most solemn defense guarantees Britain can give, and—as its confrontation with Indonesia illustrates—these include very material demonstrations of military support from Australia and New Zealand as well. Indeed, it might have been supposed that the Philippines, like any nation anxious about its own security, would have had reason to welcome heartily the advent of a friendly and well-defended neighbor.

It is in this context that many observers have questioned the sincerity of Filipino leaders who argue that their security would be *enhanced* by a land border with Malaysia. If Manila's prediction of Malaysian susceptibility to Communist control were to be fulfilled, the Philippines might well find more protection in its present boundaries, with a stretch of sea separating it from the anticipated turmoil. Instead, the Philippines appears to be seeking the privilege of sharing land borders with Asia's two most upsetting elements: Indonesia, the leaders of which proudly declare they must help "all oppressed peoples" (particularly those on their own borders); and Malaysia, presumably about to become part of the Chinese Communist empire.

These inconsistencies, which are as obvious to many Filipinos as to others, have been a major factor in the reconsideration of the manner in which the claim to North Borneo should now be pressed—if at all. There is no more lucid critique of Philippine policy on this point than the scathing indictment of Macapagal by his former colleague, Vice-President Pelaez. After noting that Indonesia had placed troops on Malaysian territory, and that "justice and fairness are on the side of Malaysia," Pelaez charged Macapagal with following a "naïve, shortsighted policy" which had brought dishonor to the nation:

> Under the stewardship of President Macapagal, our Malaysia policy has undergone a transformation that is glaring in its lack of direction and naïve in its attempt to play for the grandstand.[63]

After two years of trying to make the North Borneo claim a cornerstone of his foreign policy, President Macapagal achieved neither

---

[63] Pelaez in a speech in Manila, April 14, 1964.

widespread domestic support for this goal nor the goal itself. His policies, and his flirtation with Indonesia, succeeded only in making the Philippines look foolish. As a result, within two years after the claim was lodged it was apparent that the Philippines was groping for some face-saving means by which to retreat from their earlier position. No longer did officials stress "security" aspects; instead, they preferred to deal with the claim as a "purely legal" dispute[64]—for, at worst, submission of the claim to the World Court would postpone its resolution for several years, by which time (if the Philippines lost its case) everyone would have forgotten the clamor. In the meantime, however, the Philippines had adopted a very negative attitude toward Malaysia and —when that country came formally into existence on September 16, 1963—Manila took steps that finally led to a break in diplomatic relations. After months of strained relations, the Philippines apparently had second thoughts, however, and for a long time seemed about to reverse its decision and re-establish full diplomatic ties. The re-establishment of consular relations, in the spring of 1964, was taken as an indication that President Macapagal was seeking some way to ease the strained relations with Kuala Lumpur. Indeed, he eventually declared that Manila deplored the landings of Indonesian guerrillas on the mainland of Malaya, breaking his previously massive silence on this clear example of aggression.

Considering the developments discussed in this chapter, that decision represented an important shift in Philippine policy. In part, it reflected President Macapagal's recognition of the negative consequences of his overtures to Indonesia. But while Manila was "learning" about Indonesia, its once-excellent relationship with Kuala Lumpur sustained considerable damage. Important leaders in both capitals now feel they have been shabbily dealt with by the other side. President Macapagal maintains that, at one of their meetings, the Tunku said he had no objection to submitting the Sabah claim to the World Court. The Tunku denies it. For his part, the Tunku, and other Malaysian officials as well, bitterly resent Macapagal's apparent willingness to side with

[64] I base this conclusion on extensive sets of interviews in Manila in 1962, 1963, and 1964. In October 1964, among those consulted on North Borneo were Mr. Mauro Mendez, the foreign secretary; Mr. Librado Cayco, the undersecretary; and members of the "Borneo Panel," including its chairman, Representative Jovito Salonga, Senator Raul Manglapus, and Mr. Battista, the Minister in charge of the "North Borneo desk" in the department of foreign affairs.

Djakarta in an effort to exert pressure on Malaysia. For these and other reasons, the mutual trust that had been developed among leaders in the Philippines and Malaya through collaboration in ASA, and that was so deeply eroded in 1962-64, will not be easily or quickly restored.

CHAPTER II: CAMBODIA AND HER
NEIGHBORS

Cambodia's relations with her neighbors amply illustrate three broad concepts often used to describe all of Southeast Asia: a meeting-ground for the great cultures of India and China; a modern example of Balkanization; and the main battlefront in the global confrontation between Communism and the West.

Nowhere, for example, are the Indian and Chinese cultural influences so apparent as in comparisons between Cambodia and Vietnam. In Vietnam, innumerable aspects of culture, society, and administration reveal the imprint of its ten centuries of domination by China. In Cambodia, the impact of India on the culture of the Khmer people is readily apparent in architecture, in religion, in dance forms, and perhaps even in the influence of Nehru's neutralism on Prince Sihanouk.[1]

The two countries also provide an excellent illustration of contemporary Balkanization. French withdrawal from Indochina marked the re-emergence of problems and animosities which had been muted for generations.[2] Some of the problems derive from—or were intensified by—French actions during the colonial period, and these have troubled Cambodian-Vietnamese relations since independence. Those problems

---

[1] As the Cambodian government itself has explained, most of Indochina is inhabited "by a people popularly known as 'Annamite' (now Vietnamese) whose culture derives from China, *while Cambodia with a civilization which is Indian in origin,* is clearly distinguished. . . . See Royal Government of Cambodia, *Memorandum by Cambodia on her Territories in South Vietnam* (Geneva: Imprimerie Gloor, 1954), p. 1. Or see Joseph Buttinger's comment: "the culture of Cambodia . . . is 'Indianized,' in contrast to the Sinicized culture of Vietnam." *The Smaller Dragon: A Political History of Vietnam* (New York: Frederick A. Praeger, Inc., 1958), p. 51.

[2] See Charles A. Fisher, "Southeast Asia: The Balkans of the Orient?" *Geography* (November 1963), 347-67, and Fisher's excellent new book, *Southeast Asia: A Social, Economic and Political Geography* (London: Methuen & Co., Ltd., 1964), Chapter I.

Several of the problems left behind by the French, or generated by their colonial policies, will be discussed below. They relate essentially to the Vietnamese minority that now lives within Cambodia; border decisions made by the French at Cambodia's expense, particularly on Cochin-China, and which in turn has left a large Cambodian population in South Vietnam; a dispute over certain islands; and a nagging controversy about certain funds left over from the banking institution established by France for all of Indochina.

created by tensions over ethnic minorities reveal undertones of irredentism strongly reminiscent of recent Balkan experience.

Finally, like all the countries of Southeast Asia, Cambodia and Vietnam are touched by the global struggle between East and West Cambodia and South Vietnam are more directly and intimately affected, for they have come to be regarded as pawns in the Cold War contest. Partly because economic and political development, and hence nationalism, was more advanced in Vietnam, that country was the major battleground in the long, bloody struggle against French colonialism. In consequence, Vietnam was divided in two: a pro-Western regime based in Saigon; and a Communist regime based in Hanoi. That division, in turn, has caused Vietnam to become a battleground once more —this time in the larger-scale conflict between East and West. To Cambodia, which has proclaimed its neutrality in the Cold War, this turn of events has meant its own daily and direct involvement in the global conflict. This neutrality intensifies and reinforces Cambodia's traditional disagreements with its neighbors: embattled South Vietnam to the east, and pro-Western Thailand (a SEATO member) to the west.

Shrinking Cambodia

One source of disagreement between Cambodia and her neighbors involves territorial conflicts—but these have little in common with the territorial dispute between Malaysia and the Philippines. The controversy over North Borneo created mutual distrust where none existed before, and there at least seemed to be a practical potential for the re-establishment of friendly relations and even cooperation between Manila and Luala Lumpur. Between Cambodia and her neighbors, on the other hand, no such potential exists, and their contemporary relations must be viewed against a long-standing background of mutual distrust and animosity.

To understand the competing territorial claims that concern Cambodia, it must first be noted that modern Cambodia comprises a much smaller area than Khmer governments once ruled. Cambodian leaders are acutely aware of their national history, and the events which have reduced their domains since the twelfth century. Then, the Khmer Empire known as Chen-La apparently ruled almost all Indochina—including Laos and much of South Vietnam. Even in the late seventeenth century Cambodia included the whole of Cochin-China (the Mekong Delta and the Ca Mau peninsula) as well as the area of Modern Cambodia (see Figs. II-1, II-2).

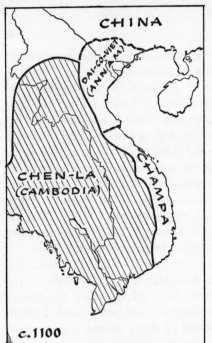

II-1

II-2

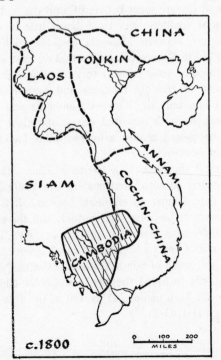

II-3

In 1673, however, Cambodia began to suffer the series of excisions relevant to today's territorial problems. By 1701, the Ca Mau peninsula was lost, and finally the entire Mekong Delta fell to the Vietnamese.[3] Meanwhile, Cambodia's difficulties with Thailand, her western neighbor, had not lessened, but continued: a series of Thai invasions, beginning in the thirteenth century, finally forced the Cambodians to abandon their ancient capital, Angkor, after 1431.[4] Although Cambodia exhibited a few sporadic bursts of energy after that, it was not able to withstand the revival of Thai power, or the pressure exerted by the Vietnamese.[5] Indeed, by the 1750s, Cambodia was caught between its two neighbors' challenges to each other's supremacy. By the early nineteenth century, Cambodia had become a vassal of Thailand and Vietnam and, although the Thais seem generally to have had more influence, Cambodia paid homage to both (see Fig. II-3).[6]

Yet the Thai and Vietnamese seem never to have completely relinquished their hopes of acquiring even more Cambodian territory. Thus, in 1795, five Cambodian provinces were "transferred" to Thai control, and in 1835 the Vietnamese took steps to "incorporate what was left of Cambodia."[7] Finally, in 1845, a "solution" to Cambodia's unenviable position was reached when the three parties agreed that Cambodia should come under joint Thai and Vietnamese "protection."

It was at this point that France (and Britain) intervened. The French argue that their intervention, and the eventual incorporation of Cambodia into French Indochina, "saved" the Khmer kingdom from further Thai and Vietnamese incursions. From the Cambodian (and Thai) view, the power of France merely replaced that of Vietnam. Thus, in 1867, France forced Thailand to renounce all claims to Cambodia as a whole, and although it confirmed Thai control of the two western provinces of Battambang and Siam Reap (where Angkor is), French troops later occupied Thailand's second most important port

---

[3] Since 1673, when they ceased warring with other Vietnamese of the north, the Vietnamese of Cochin-China had begun to settle in large numbers in the Delta: "They devoted their attention to southward expansion at the expense of the Chams and Cambodians. . . . See D. G. E. Hall, *A History of Southeast Asia* (London: Macmillan & Co., Ltd., 1964), p. 394.

[4] Angkor was captured in 1313, 1351, 1420, and 1473, although none of these conquests resulted in permanent occupation.

[5] For example, in 1594 the Cambodian capital of Lovek was taken briefly by the Thais, and in 1654 the city was overrun by the Annamites.

[6] Often the kings of Cambodia were crowned in Bangkok, but repeatedly requested, and were invested with, the simultaneous status of vassals to Vietnam.

[7] Hall, *op. cit.*, p. 438.

of Chantaburi, and then the town of Trat as well.[8] To get them out, Thailand had to relinquish (1907) the two western provinces.

Thai leaders never forgave France, and they seized the opportunity of its fall to Germany in 1940 to exert pressure to recover the "lost" provinces. Accordingly, in the Japanese-imposed Tokyo agreements of May 1941, the Vichy regime instructed its representatives in Indochina to transfer these territories to Thailand. It was a short-lived triumph, for in 1946—under a French threat to veto Thailand's application for membership in the United Nations—Thailand relinquished the territories to France once more. Finally, in 1954 they were for the most part incorporated into independent Cambodia.

The decisions which established Cambodia's border with Vietnam were also taken unilaterally by the French and were devoid of Cambodian influence. In 1949, the French decided that Cochin-China, which Cambodians had continued to regard as theirs, should be incorporated within Vietnam. There were some protests from Cambodia, but when Cambodian and Vietnamese independence was formally established at Geneva in 1954, Cochin-China became part of what is now South Vietnam.

Cambodia and Vietnam: Boundary Disputes

Cambodia's fear of Thailand today centers on Thai irredentism and the "lost" provinces, but its fear of Vietnam has a firmer basis: the possibility of outright absorption by Vietnamese imperialism. Thus, although Cambodian leaders distrust Thailand, their animosity toward the Vietnamese appears to be far deeper and more widespread.[9] For

[8] To provide justification for these occupations, the French seem to have regularly distorted events, showing Siamese aggressive intentions, and so on. See Hall, *op. cit.*, Chapter 37, esp. pp. 657-64. In a remarkable book published in 1941, in the heyday of Thai expansionist sentiment and cooperation with Japan, a famous Thai diplomat and official wrote that "Many of the Thais until this day tatooed the word *Trat* on their arm in order not to forget the French." See Luang Vichitr Vadakarn, *Thailand's Case* (Bangkok: University of Moral and Political Sciences, 1941). The author, regarded as an extreme Thai nationalist until his death in the early 1960s, was at the time minister of state.

[9] Attitudes toward the Thai seem ambivalent, and it was consistent with the practice of earlier Cambodian kings that Prince Sihanouk took up brief residence in Bangkok in 1953, as part of his preindependence campaign to embarrass France. There was also upset in Bangkok, "where the arrival of a monarch whose ancestors had been vassals of the Siamese Crown caused Marshal Phibul's government some embarrassment." Donald Lancaster, *The Emancipation of French Indochina* (London: Oxford University Press, 1961), p. 274. This visit, it should be pointed out, has never been forgotten by Sihanouk nor forgiven, for he feels that he was not

one thing, Cambodians have an intimate knowledge of the energies and
skills of the Vietnamese. In Phnom Penh alone, Vietnamese now account for 28 per cent of the city's population, and there are at least
350,000 in the country as a whole.[10] These Vietnamese, along with the
Chinese inhabitants of Cambodia, dominate the nation's economy, but
there is a difference: it was the Vietnamese whom the French em-
ployed to administer their Cambodian protectorate. French colonialism
in Indochina (Cambodia and Laos in particular) involved relatively
few Frenchmen—in 1937 there were only about 4000 French officials
and 11,000 French military personnel in all of Indochina.[11] The size
of the territories and the almost total absence of trained Cambodians
meant that the administration had to be entrusted to someone else. In
Laos and Cambodia, it was entrusted to the Vietnamese. They ran the
government offices, while the Chinese infiltrated the economic sphere:

> Thus, whereas Vietnamese were employed as clerks in the French-staffed
> civil service and in French business houses, . . . the local Chinese com-
> munity . . . profited from the Cambodian distaste for commerce and
> lack of business acumen to engage in economic activities on an extensive
> scale. . . .[12]

Whenever a Khmer came into contact with government power, it
was usually a Vietnamese face he saw; the thousands of Vietnamese
minor officials were visible evidence of Cambodia's subjection to
foreign rule. This fact, coupled with the Cambodians' knowledge of

---

given proper treatment in Bangkok. One account states that the Thai government,
surprised by his unannounced arrival with a company of thirty-four others, "admitted him as a political refugee and lodged him in Bangkok's most luxurious
hotel. But it refused to let him head a government-in-exile or to use Thailand as
his intermediary for presenting Cambodia's case to the United Nations." Virginia
Thompson and Richard Adloff, *Minority Problems in Southeast Asia* (Stanford,
Calif.: Stanford University Press, 1955), p. 189.

[10] Fisher, *Southeast Asia, op. cit.*, p. 570. Thompson and Adloff, *op. cit.*, p. 174,
state that in 1944 there were about 250,000 Vietnamese in Cambodia. This would
seem to indicate that, even after World War II, and allowing for statistical in-
accuracies, the movement of Vietnamese into Cambodia under French auspices
probably continued. The Khmers, in their own capital city, are a distinct minority;
for, in addition to the Vietnamese population of 28 per cent, the Chinese account
for another 30 per cent of the city's total.

[11] Lancaster, *op. cit.*, p. 63, fn. 11. Professor Bernard Fall, in conversations with
this author, has reported that in 1925 there were (excluding French schoolteachers)
only about 1000 French civil servants in all of French Indochina. These figures
are consistent with the information provided by Thompson and Adloff, *op. cit.*,
p. 172, who report that there were just 506 French officials before World War II.

[12] *Ibid.*, p. 70.

Vietnam's expansionist tendencies in the past (which resulted in its acquisition of Cochin-China), has contributed to their widespread animosity toward Vietnam and the Vietnamese. Thus most observers conclude that Cambodians, although they do not trust the culturally similar Thais, generally harbor a much deeper hatred and fear of the Vietnamese.

Beyond these historic enmities, there have arisen many more problems which have intensified Cambodian-Vietnamese tensions since independence. Of these, the territorial disputes are only the most obvious.

In 1949, even before Cambodia achieved independence, its leaders protested to the unilateral French decision to incorporate Cochin-China within Vietnam.[13] Then, at the 1954 Geneva meetings, Cambodia's foreign minister renewed his country's claim to that territory. He warned that statements assuring Vietnam's territorial integrity did not "imply the abandonment of such legitimate rights and interests as Cambodia might assert with regard to certain regions of South Vietnam. . . ."[14] Once again, it was Cochin-China which figured most prominently in these "rights and interests." Then, in 1956, Cambodia again took France to task for her role in this affair. In a letter to *Le Monde*, the Cambodian prime minister recalled that his country's leaders had protested as early as the nineteenth century, when France drew the boundaries that separated Cochin-China from Cambodia, and he made it clear that Phnom Penh still regarded the frontier with Vietnam as unjust.[15]

PHU QUOC AND SIHANOUKVILLE

These claims have been kept alive, and the further estrangement between Cambodia and South Vietnam—brought about by other problems—has made the border disputes even more bitter. Beginning in 1956, the Cambodian government shifted its foreign-policy emphasis from its claim to Cochin-China (probably recognizing that there was little hope of success on that score) to repeated complaints about Vietnamese occupation of some six or seven islands, the largest of which is Phu Quoc. To understand Cambodia's special interest in this island, it is necessary to note that Thai and Vietnamese expansion left Cambodia with a relatively small shoreline on the Gulf of Siam. Its major

---

[13] Michael Leifer, *Cambodia and Neutrality* (Canberra: Australian National University, 1962), p. 23.

[14] *Ibid.* Also see Buttinger, *op. cit.*, p. 60

[15] Buttinger, *op. cit.*, p. 60, fn. 35.

access to the sea is still the port of Saigon. Consequently, Cambodians have for some years been apprehensive about this critical dependence on Vietnam's willingness to allow continued use of the port for their trade.

As early as 1946, the French promised Cambodia that "thenceforth Saigon would not be Cambodia's sole outlet to the sea," [16] and since then Cambodian leaders have taken measures to reduce this dependence, including the effort to develop a port at Kampong Som (Sihanoukville). Later, when France met with representatives of her Indochina territories at the Pau Conference of 1950 (which established the framework for the Associated States of Indochina) Cambodia was given further guarantees: the Vietnamese promised that the port of Saigon—to be regarded as "autonomous"—would, "together with facilities for access," be kept open to Cambodia and Laos.[17] But it is clear that Cambodia has never fully believed these assurances, and South Vietnam underscores the reasons for this anxiety by occasionally reminding Prince Sihanouk that if he causes too much difficulty the port of Saigon will be closed to Cambodian trade.

These considerations impelled Cambodia to devote considerable effort to developing a major harbor on the Gulf of Siam, and even some thought to relying upon Bangkok, in the absence of Saigon, as an outlet to the sea:

> So eager has Cambodia become to slough off the last vestiges of its dependence on Saigon that in January 1953 it began negotiations with the Thai government for the initiation of direct railroad express service between the capitals of the two countries.[18]

But of course there is little in Prince Sihanouk's present relationship with Thailand to warrant any heavier reliance on the port facilities in Bangkok than on those of Saigon.

These facts reinforce Cambodia's incentive to develop the port of Sihanoukville, perilously close to the large Vietnamese-occupied island

[16] Thompson and Adloff, op. cit., p. 181.

[17] Lancaster, op. cit., pp. 211-12. Lancaster, who has an intimate knowledge of these problems, and serves now as a member of Prince Sihanouk's governmental secretariat, has written that "the impending abolition of French internal control in Indochina had aroused misgivings among the Cambodians and Laotians in regard to Vietnamese intentions, which the brief period of the protectorate had lulled but not removed," and that "the Cambodians . . . had inherited, together with the imperial traditions of the vanished Khmer empire, a fear of the prolific and industrious Vietnamese. . . ." Ibid., p. 210.

[18] Thompson and Adloff, op. cit., p. 182.

CAMBODIA
AND HER NEIGHBORS

0   100   200   300
MILES

II-4

50

of Phu Quoc (see Fig. II-4). (South Vietnam was given the island of Phu Quoc by France, together with Cochin-China, for the island generally had been regarded as a portion of Cochinchinese territory.) Some smaller islands to the northwest of Phu Quoc also concern Sihanouk, who maintains that they all belong to Cambodia. Now, more than ever, he fears that Vietnamese possession of these bits of land will perpetuate South Vietnam's control over Cambodia's policies: with South Vietnam in possession of Phu Quoc, a Cambodian decision to cut all ties with the port of Saigon could soon be nullified. As Sihanouk himself has said:

> . . . the loss of the islands and the territorial waters which surround them would lead to the stifling of the port of Kompong-Som . . . and very soon to the end of our independence.[19]

The problem has recently been aggravated by South Vietnam's decision to convert Phu Quoc into a full-fledged naval base. Although its alleged purpose is to block "Viet Cong infiltration from Cambodia by sea," [20] the same facilities could later be used for the purpose Sihanouk fears: to block Cambodia's new port. It was, no doubt, with these possibilities in mind that Prince Sihanouk has markedly increased his demands for the return of these islands.

But Sihanouk experienced a rude shock (which probably reinforced his anxieties) when South Vietnam responded to his incessant demands by making counterdemands. In March 1960, and again in April 1962, Saigon demanded that a group of islands near Phu Quoc be returned to Vietnamese sovereignty. The islands are all quite small,[21] and seem to offer no economic or population resources. On the other hand, they may represent a potential problem to the Saigon government in its war against the Viet Cong. This was the view expressed to a *New York Times* reporter writing from Phu Quoc in 1962. At that time, South Vietnam laid major stress on its need to retake Koh Ses Ream, and Koh Thmey, two bits of land northwest of Phu Quoc. The reporter was told that these islands were being used as training and rest

---

[19] In *Cambodian News*, I:2 (May 1960) as quoted by Leifer, *op. cit.*, p. 26.

[20] Homer Bigart, in *The New York Times* (April 13, 1962). Phu Quoc was the island on which leaders of the South Vietnamese government came close to death in December 1964, when their aircraft was fired upon by Viet Cong units present on the island.

[21] Some of the islands concerned are Koh Thmey (Isle de Milieu), Koh Ses Ream (Isle Aloh), Koh An Tay (Isle de Picque), Koh Takeau, and Koh Po.

centers for Viet Cong guerrillas who were transported by junk to and from forays on the mainland of South Vietnam.[22]

It is characteristic of the relations between Saigon and Phnom Penh that Cambodia soon responded to this report (it has often been remarked, only half in jest, that Prince Sihanouk is the only Khmer who regularly reads American newspapers). According to Cambodian spokesmen, the *Times* report led the Royal Navy's "general staff" quickly to refute all South Vietnam's allegations. Koh Ses Ream, they maintained, is uninhabited, except for fishermen who occasionally use it as a temporary shelter, and "the only life on the island is the lookout post of the Royal Cambodian Navy." Koh Thmey, slightly larger, has a population of about fifty fishermen, and a few acres of land devoted to the cultivation of coconut palm.[23] This information had probably been available to Saigon all along, for it soon became clear that South Vietnam was not taking its counterclaim at all seriously. In August 1962, the late Ngo Trong Hieu, then Minister for Civic Action, disclosed the reason for Saigon's action. (Ngo, among the most extreme of Vietnam's anti-Cambodian officials, even conceded involvement in the 1959 "Dap Chuuon" affair—an effort to unseat Sihanouk.) President Diem's claim to the two tiny islands, Ngo explained, was "totally artificial . . . and contrived." Saigon decided to dispute ownership of the islands, he added, largely to annoy Prince Sihanouk: "to make such an extreme claim [that] we would not be bothered by having to negotiate with Sihanouk for a long time."[24]

This episode may be amusing, but it did not end there. Phu Quoc, the 230-square-mile island now in South Vietnam's possession, directly faces the long-sought port of Sihanoukville. Thus in 1964 Prince Sihanouk once again began to press his claim for at least that island and revived Cambodia's old claim to Cochin-China. In a note handed to the French embassy for transmittal to Saigon, Cambodia reminded South Vietnam that "its right of sovereignty [to Phu Quoc and Cochin-

[22] See Bigart's report, *op. cit.* Unlike Phu Quoc itself, it could not even be contended that these two small islands were important for the production "of a main item in the Vietnamese diet, fermented fish sauce"!

[23] *Cambodia News* (Washington, D.C.: Royal Embassy of Cambodia, July 13, 1962).

[24] Interview with the author, Saigon, August 8, 1962. The Vietnamese show a fine appreciation for Sihanouk's sensitivities, for it is altogether likely that this claim did in fact "drive him crazy," just as the "Free Cambodia" (Khmer Serai) radio broadcasts are alleged to do, and it is possible even now that Saigon supports the Cambodian dissidents operating from outside of Cambodia.

China] was never proscribed but assumed provisionally by France." [25]

The Significance of Cambodia's Disputes With Her Neighbors

There is a fundamental difficulty in assessing the significance of these claims, and that of other disputes between Cambodia and her neighbors. The difficulty lies in the complex task of distinguishing between those statements issued in Phnom Penh merely for effect, and those that represent Cambodia's operating assumptions. One must never forget that every consideration of Cambodian foreign policy is affected by its historically precarious position—with pro-Western Thailand and South Vietnam on either side and with the massive presence of Communist China felt through fragile Laos and Communist North Vietnam.[26] Thus its border dispute with South Vietnam is only ostensibly a *border* dispute. The Philippine-Malaysian dispute over Sabah, for example, can be viewed as a separate and distinct problem; it does not derive from centuries of animosity, nor is it a consequence of the Cold War. While the Philippines' claim to North Borneo may have been inspired by the desire to demonstrate "identity," it was not lodged solely for its "demonstration effect." Many Filipinos believe they have a valid claim to North Borneo, and therefore hope to deal with the case "on its merits." [27]

Cambodia's problems with her neighbors derive from a very different set of conditions. The basic condition is the fact that the continued existence of the state cannot be taken for granted. Thus, in order to preserve the existence of the state, many of Prince Sihanouk's pro-

[25] Communiqué of the Cambodian ministry of foreign affairs, January 4, 1964. Sihanouk once again showed how great a value he attaches to the port project in the wake of his decisions, in 1963-64, to terminate all U.S. foreign aid to Cambodia. He had the gall, some might say, to ask that while all other aid projects should be terminated, "we can only except the completion of a task under the former aid system—that is, the repairing of the Khmer-U.S. friendship road joining Phnom Penh and Sihanoukville." Phnom Penh Radio, January 21, 1964.

[26] In late June 1964, the Prince explained on a visit to Paris "the main lines of Cambodian policy." Included as the second principle was "an unshakeable determination not to allow expansionist neighbors—who in the course of the past five centuries had reduced Cambodian territory to its most elementary expression—to take possession of the smallest bit of our territory." Reported on July 1, 1964.

[27] Philippine leaders know, moreover, that should their case ever come to the World Court—unlikely as that is—a decision one way or the other would probably be accepted by both parties.

nouncements on foreign affairs are made almost exclusively for their "demonstration effect." It is in the interests of Cambodia to present to its immediate neighbors an image of a foreign policy that has considerable latitude. For years, for example, Sihanouk managed to accept a continuing assistance program—including military aid—from the United States, despite the public complaints of Thailand and South Vietnam and the tacit misgivings of Communist China. Until 1963, he accepted no military assistance from the Communists, but only from France and the United States. Indeed, Sihanouk was asked to justify this policy by no less than Chou En-lai, and maintains that the Chinese leader was satisfied that Cambodia's acceptance of American military assistance neither impinged upon his sovereignty nor represented any threat to Chinese interests.

Similarly, Sihanouk has been careful not to allow his relations with Thailand and South Vietnam to deteriorate too far simultaneously. For almost ten years he succeeded in this delicate task. Until 1963, many of his anti-Western pronouncements were roughly balanced by remarks critical of Communism as well, and he has never made any secret of his distaste of Communism.

But as South Vietnam seemed less and less likely to withstand the pressure from the North, Prince Sihanouk first hinted, and then stated publicly, that Communism represents the wave of the future in Southeast Asia, and that the region inevitably must come under some form of Chinese hegemony. As he explained recently to his people:

> Dear children, we do not want to become Red. But some day we will have to accept it because we will be unable to avoid it; that is, provided we are able to safeguard our territorial integrity. We do not want to become like the [nonexistent] Cham. We want only to maintain forever the Khmer nation and the Khmer flag. Most of the countries which have become Red have maintained their national flags and their names are mentioned with great honor in the list of United Nations members.[28]

Sihanouk has made innumerable statements with the same thesis: he does not want Communism for Cambodia ("frankly speaking, both the two great powers are depraved") but, if necessary, "we will all become Communists together." [29] For example, in the wake of the 1962

[28] From Prince Sihanouk's speech of February 21, 1964.
[29] From Prince Sihanouk's speech, November 3, 1962, at Samathy Ram Pagoda, Kampong Speu province.

Cuban missile crisis, Prince Sihanouk assured his people that China would not desert Cambodia as Russia had deserted Cuba:

> Cambodia is not guaranteed by Russia but by the CPR [Chinese Peoples' Republic]. It seems to me that the CPR will not make any concession as old Mr. Khrushchev had done. Whereas Mr. Khrushchev is soft, China seems to be fractious. Old Khrushchev prefers peaceful coexistence in order not to show that he is fond of war. As for China, it seems that it fears nothing and is more severe than old Khrushchev.[30]

No doubt these remarks were designed to evoke a favorable attitude in Peking. The one consistent tactic in Cambodian foreign policy since 1961-62—in an environment notorious for inconsistency—is the evident warming of relations between Cambodia and Communist China. There have been a remarkable number of high-level visits between Phnom Penh and Peking. This is very important to Sihanouk, because he perceives international relations in Southeast Asia essentially as a pattern of interaction between "bosses" and "puppets"—an attitude perhaps not surprising in the leader of a state which was for centuries a vassal to others.

Thus Prince Sihanouk has long assumed that Washington could dictate to Bangkok and Saigon their policies toward Cambodia.[31] He has complained bitterly that the Free Khmer Radio—which is directed against his regime and which irritates him terribly—is broadcast from Thailand with transmitters supplied by the United States. If the Americans wanted to, he has said repeatedly, they could stop such actions. Similarly, in his calls for a four-nation conference to affirm Cambodia's neutrality and its borders, Sihanouk has underlined his conviction that some nations just naturally have to do what their masters tell them. As he said recently: "If the Americans sign this agreement and under them their children [the Thai and Vietnamese] do not honor it, it will

---

[30] *Ibid.*

[31] In 1961 it was reported that U.S. Ambassador Trimble "had found it impossible to convince Sihanouk that Washington is unable to influence Thailand and South Vietnam toward a more conciliatory tone in their relations with Cambodia." Leifer, *op. cit.,* p. 34, citing *The New York Times* (November 19, 1961). Later, in his speech of November 3, 1962, Prince Sihanouk stated that "the U.S. Ambassador came to tell me that but for U.S. persuasion Thailand and South Vietnam would have pushed things further in dealing with Cambodia. . . . However, the Thai and South Vietnamese have not stopped their aggressive activities."

be bad . . . because the Americans give them rifles and ammunition to enable them to do evil things." [32]

Sihanouk apparently sees the Hanoi-Peking relationship in like terms. A journal close to Sihanouk reported that when he went to Peking in 1956, "he was informed that if he had any trouble with the Viet Minh he had only to appeal to Peking to have it stopped." [33] Sihanouk does not hide his conviction that such assurances from Peking are important—particularly in light of his open distrust of all Vietnamese, north *and* south. For him the central concern is that Cambodia is constantly in danger of being swallowed up altogether, like Champa. Thus the model with which he views the conditions for a continued existence for his small country is simply this: to benefit from the differences between those nations which have control over Cambodia's destiny.

THREE LEVELS IN THE SEARCH FOR SURVIVAL

Cambodia's effort proceeds at three levels: in the relations between North and South Vietnam; in the relations between North Vietnam and Communist China; and in the relations between Communist China and the United States.

Over the short-run, Prince Sihanouk benefits from the conflict between Hanoi and Saigon. Certainly one of the reasons that Cambodia has not been more severely pressed by South Vietnam in recent years is that Saigon has had its hands full with the war against the Viet Cong (sponsored by North Vietnam). To be sure, the two countries often traded press insults with each other (particularly in President Diem's last years), but South Vietnam exhibited remarkable restraint in not undertaking more drastic action against the provocative Sihanouk. Nor was Saigon powerless to do so. First, of course, it might close the port of Saigon to Cambodian trade.[34] In addition, and in re-

---

[32] From Sihanouk's speech of February 21, 1964, reported on Phnom Penh Radio, February 21, 1964. The Prince concluded his remarks by warning that all three states must come together to sign a pact with him: "Therefore, I have asked these three great and bold thieves to come together to sign with us. We will not agree if they come separately. . . . we will not agree if the Americans and Vietnamese come without the Thai, . . . if the Thai and Vietnamese come without the Americans, nor if the Americans and Thai come without the Vietnamese. It is necessary for the three to come together to sign with the Khmer."

[33] Leifer, *op. cit.,* p. 32, citing *Réalités Cambodgiennes* (July 14, 1961).

[34] Late in 1962 Sihanouk again acknowledged the dependence on Saigon: "If we shut our frontier, we would face many difficulties because our lives depend on the Mekong River. . . . Once the frontier is closed, there will remain . . . only

taliation for certain of Cambodia's restrictions on the role of its resident Vietnamese population, South Vietnam could engage in an open contest of repression against its Khmer minority. (In Cochin-China, there are between 450,000 and 600,000 *Khmer Krom*—Vietnamese of Cambodian descent.) Sihanouk has alleged that certain repressive measures have already been undertaken, but these do not seem very harsh. Even Cambodia's complaint to the United Nations, alleging "genocide," charged South Vietnam merely with forcing the assimilation "of 600,000 Cambodians . . . , obliging them to assume Viet-Nam-sounding names, systematically limiting the study of the Cambodian language, and obstructing the practice of the Buddhist religion." [35] This policy of cultural assimilation seems somewhat less repressive than some Cambodian measures designed to inhibit the activities of its resident Vietnamese. As Leifer reports, Cambodia implemented a law in 1956 "which banned eighteen professions to foreigners. This hit numerous Vietnamese." [36]

In the face of these actions—and even with Prince Sihanouk's decision to break political relations with South Vietnam just before the fall of the Diem government—Saigon has not acted very sternly toward Cambodia. One of the most serious grievances between the two countries, of course, is Prince Sihanouk's constant complaint that the South Vietnamese army, searching for Viet Cong units, crosses into Cambodia and on occasion destroys property and kills Cambodians. This is true, but it is notable (in view of the ostensibly hostile state of affairs between the two countries, and the fact that Saigon has at its disposal major facilities for doing even greater harm to Cambodia's interests) that, soon after the fall of the Diem regime, Saigon publicly apologized for one such incident and offered to pay for the property damages and to compensate the bereaved. This restraint certainly seems to stem from Saigon's desire to avoid more troubles than it has already, and no doubt it has been urgently requested by American advisors to South Vietnam.

Cambodian leaders recognize this inhibition of South Vietnam, and they are particularly conscious of the potential threat to Cambodian territorial integrity should Vietnam be unified. Minister of Defense

---

. . . Sihanoukville and this will be a major problem." Sihanouk speech of November 3, 1962.

[35] United Nations General Assembly Seventeenth Session, XX (A/SPC/SR. 332, October 22, 1962), p. 9.

[36] Leifer, *op. cit.*, p. 25. He adds that in 1961 the Cambodian press printed several veiled threats of new repression against the resident Vietnamese population.

General Lon Nol has said that the reunification of Vietnam, under any arrangement, is the event he most fears—for it would give traditional Vietnamese ambitions an opportunity for revival.[37] Thus the first level at which Cambodia seeks to preserve itself is through the continuation of a divided Vietnam. This is also made clear in Prince Sihanouk's 1962-63 requests for an international conference to affirm Cambodia's neutrality and its present borders. He hoped, by the treaties he proposed, to formalize the promises of both North and South Vietnam to respect Cambodia's territory.[38] But Sihanouk recognizes that the security indirectly provided by the present internal Vietnamese conflict may be short-lived, so he also exerts efforts on a second level: for an external guarantee.

The second level focuses on Cambodia's policy toward Communist China and is concerned with the potential relationship between the Asian giant and Vietnam. Sihanouk expects that a unified Vietnam will be a vassal to Communist China, which would then be the only nation able to provide the necessary assurances for Cambodia. He has made no secret of his conviction that something better than assurances from Vietnam—North or South—is needed. Early in 1964, even while he said he was hoping to sign a boundary agreement with South Vietnam (including a recognition "that the islands of Kep and Ream belong to Cambodia"), he explained that he must still have an agreement with Hanoi, "because the North Vietnamese will certainly win the war." [39]

> Since we signed with Mr. Khanh—and I do not know when he will be overthrown—Mr. Khanh will have agreed to respect Khmer territorial integrity. But at that time, Mr. Ho Chi Minh may say: "How can that

[37] Interview with the author, Phnom Penh, August 1962. It will be remembered that the major population movement of the Vietnamese into Cambodian Cochin-China began in 1673, when the rival great families of north and south Vietnam finally ended their long hostilities. When the author asked General Lon Nol whether it might be in Cambodia's interests to do what she could to preserve the present division between Hanoi and Saigon, he smiled and agreed emphatically, with the words: "You should be a military staff officer."

[38] Royal Government of Cambodia, *Draft Declaration of the Neutrality of Cambodia*, and *Draft Protocol to the Declaration on the Neutrality of the Kingdom of Cambodia* (1962). Mimeo. These agreements, which Cambodia hoped would be signed by Burma, Canada, Communist China, France, India, Laos, Poland, Thailand, the Soviet Union, Britain, the United States, and *both* Vietnams, provided that the boundaries with Vietnam and Laos are established "by the frontiers traced on the maps of the Geographical Service of Indochina in use before the Paris Agreement of 1954." Article I of *Draft Protocol . . .*, p. 6.

[39] From Sihanouk's speech of February 21, 1964, reported by Phnom Penh Radio.

man represent Vietnam and sign the agreement? It is I who represent Vietnam." If Mr. Ho Chi Minh says this it will be bad for us.[40]

Sihanouk made it clear that this agreement with South Vietnam would be only a temporary expedient, but "we must first accept this temporary thing because the North Vietnamese are still far from us."

Weeks later, apparently after a series of unsuccessful efforts, Sihanouk made his fears perfectly clear: "Hanoi," he complained, "gives no better response than Saigon" on the question of respecting Cambodia's boundaries.[41] In this statement lies the explanation for Cambodia's increasing warmth toward Communist China. It would be an oversimplification to say that Prince Sihanouk simply wants to be on the winning side, because he does not envisage the "winning side" as a monolithic entity. The history of relations between China and Vietnam suggests that the two will be separate and distinct, particularly if Hanoi gains sovereignty over the whole of Vietnam. Thus Prince Sihanouk recognizes that, when and if Vietnam is unified under Communism, he will have to look to some third agent to contain traditional Vietnamese energies. At present, it seems to Phnom Penh that this "third agent" will be China.

But why should China endeavor to protect Cambodia against a Chinese associate? Part of the answer, as Sihanouk has pointed out on several occasions, is Peking's desire to demonstrate to the world that it does not necessarily want to incorporate the small states along its rim. Prince Sihanouk hopes that Cambodia, like Burma, will be used by Peking to show that it can maintain peaceful relations with nearby small and weak states.[42] The greater part of the answer, however, is Sihanouk's recognition that Cambodian alignment with the West would be seen as a threat to Communist interests in Southeast Asia (just as a Communist-dominated Cambodia would be a devastating blow to the security of Thailand and South Vietnam).

But in recent statements Sihanouk has made it exquisitely clear that his last hope for the continued existence of Cambodian independence depends, in the final analysis, on the relations between Com-

---

[40] *Ibid.* General Nguyen Khanh, who was then Premier of the South Vietnamese government, was later overthrown.

[41] From Sihanouk's speech of April 1, 1964, reported by Cambodian Radio, April 12, 1964.

[42] Prince Sihanouk expressed these hopes at Bandung in 1955. See George McT. Kahin, *The Asian-African Conference* (Ithaca, N.Y.: Cornell University Press, 1956).

munist China and the rest of the world—particularly the United States. This is the third level at which Prince Sihanouk hopes to find security for his country. It is one more illustration of a paradox in international politics: not all nations benefit from conditions of peace and stability. As Sihanouk has said:

> . . . we are able to survive thanks to People's China. I do not know whether People's China loves us. I know that for its own interests at present People's China must protect us. As for the future, I do not know. There may be a change. However, *I must thank the Americans for disputing with People's China. If they are on good terms with People's China we would be dead.*[43]

In another, more recent speech, Sihanouk explained further:

> Dear venerables and children, you must know that no one likes us, including the people who support us. Let us take for example the assistance brought by the Communists. The Communists do this not because they like us; they must do so, otherwise they will lose face and will be defeated by the free world and the Americans. Even though the Communists do not want it, People's China promises us that if the Americans dare walk into Khmer territory the Chinese will, in the Khmer's place, fight the Americans until the Americans are defeated.[44]

And most recently, the Prince addressed American readers in words that illustrate beyond question Cambodia's dependence on continued conflict in Asia:

> I concede again that after the disappearance of the U.S.A. from our region and the victory of the Communist camp, I myself and the People's Socialist Community that I have created would inevitably disappear from the scene.[45]

If Cambodia is viewed as a beneficiary of conflicts—regional, Asian, and global—its foreign policy will be seen to possess considerable in-

---

[43] From Sihanouk's statement at the morning session of the sixteenth national congress on December 31, 1963. Italics added. To put a fine point on it, he added, "I want to thank the Americans. The Americans are really stupid because they do not want to recognize People's China and because they only know how to mistreat the Chinese. I thank you very much, Messieurs the Americans. If you, the Americans, continue to insult the Chinese, the latter will be sure to come and protect the Khmer. I find this a very good situation for us."

[44] From Sihanouk's speech, reported on May 12, 1964.

[45] Letter to *The New York Times*, June 4, 1965.

ternal cohesion and logic. This internal consistency helps to explain Sihanouk's seemingly erratic behavior. Essentially, Cambodian policy consists of three elements: a goal, an operating principle, and a method. The fundamental goal and purpose of Cambodian foreign policy is survival. The operating principle designed to achieve this goal is to establish that survival is a value for those other states which have potential control over Cambodia's destiny. The method by which to implement this principle is constantly to focus on Cambodia the attention of world leaders directly concerned with Southeast Asia. Cambodia, lacking the usual ingredients of power and influence, must exploit the one asset it does possess: the mutual interest of other states in Cambodia's continued independence.

Sihanouk, in order to attach international value to Cambodia's own basic goal of survival, has endeavored constantly to draw attention to his country and himself. He speaks incessantly, almost daily, on foreign policy, for it is essential to his purpose that he occupy the center of attention and never be taken for granted.[46] His speeches have become notorious for their expressions of his vanity; for his threats first to one side and then to the other in the Cold War; and for his disconcerting tendency to reveal in public what an ambassador may have told him in strictest confidence only hours earlier. But his public utterances are always carefully noted, for there is no telling what new bombshell they may explode.

To the Vietnamese, and especially to the Thai, Sihanouk's behavior is maddening. Foreign Minister Thanat of Thailand recently complained of the "vociferous statements by an ex-king who wants to lay his country at the feet of Communist leaders unless Western nations beckon to him to take back a few million dollars of aid which he spurned, and fall on their knees to receive his diktat. . . ."[47] At about the same time, Thailand's Deputy Prime Minister Praphat warned: "We must, however, one day put an end to the most vile acts of

[46] As will be seen in Chapter IV, this is fortunately a role for which Sihanouk's personality is admirably suited. The French detected some of Sihanouk's tendency to speak out, with apparent great frankness, when they chose him to become king of Cambodia. Lancaster reports that when still in his teens, Sihanouk "possessed a capacity for short-lived enthusiasm and an artless candor which appeared to qualify him for the position of a protected monarch." Lancaster, *op. cit.*, p. 97. It would seem that there were other qualities in the young king's character that remained undetected at the time.

[47] Foreign Minister Thanat Khoman, "Which Road for Southeast Asia?" *Foreign Affairs* (July 1964).

Sihanouk . . . [who] considers it all a stage play. . . . The actions of Prince Sihanouk do not differ from those of a toad who sits in a coconut and dreams of immense deeds." [48]

Prince Sihanouk seems to have chosen his operating principles only after 1956. In 1954-55, for example, he came quite close to aligning his country with the West, and observers have agreed that, at the time, "Cambodia was the most anxious of the Indochinese states to be militarily associated with the United States." [49] But shortly thereafter (and, according to Prince Sihanouk, as a result of his meetings with Nehru in 1956), he adopted his special brand of "neutrality." [50] The explanation is not that a Western military pact was no longer needed in 1956; if that were so, Prince Sihanouk might have again indicated some interest in such an arrangement when Viet Minh pressures on South Vietnam were renewed in 1959-60. A more fundamental explanation lies in the fact that a pact with the United States would have reduced Cambodia's freedom of action: it would have prevented the request for aid from Communist China and, worse, would probably have evoked China's enmity as well. That was a consequence to be avoided: first, it is necessary for Cambodia to be in a position to benefit from the different approaches of North Vietnam and Peking; second, if Communist China is ultimately to control Southeast Asia, Cambodia would not wish to be too closely identified with the West.

Sihanouk's overriding purpose, therefore, has been to demonstrate to all observers that Cambodian foreign policy contains a certain unpredictability, and thus to preserve a relative freedom of action. This explains his willingness to accept military assistance from the United States for eight years and his simultaneous disinclination to request or accept (if one had been offered) a closer defense relationship. As Leifer has observed, this arm's-length relationship with the United States enabled Cambodia to "demonstrate to the Chinese that there existed an

[48] Quotations from General Praphat's speech, March 1964 press conference, in a statement of the Cambodian government (in reply), March 20, 1964.

[49] Leifer, *op. cit.*, pp. 9-10, citing with approval the conclusion reached by George Modelski in *SEATO: Six Studies* (Melbourne: Cheshire, 1962). Thompson and Adolff, *op. cit.*, p. 196, state that "since June [1954] the king has been vainly angling for an American commitment guaranteeing Cambodia's territorial sovereignty and, in return, has indicated his country's willingness to join a Western security system for Southeast Asia."

[50] "Since [Nehru] expounded a few principles in international relations . . . , I have been following them." The *Hindustan Times* (April 3, 1956), p. 3, cited by Leifer, *op. cit.*, p. 10.

alternative if ever pushed too hard, particularly by its nearer neighbor, Communist North Vietnam." [51]

Reducing Tensions and the Potential for "Latent" Disputes

Analysis of Cambodia's behavior toward its neighbors leads to the conclusion that Prince Sihanouk does not consider it in his country's present interest to have a condition of stability on its borders. For Cambodia, the gains from stability would be dubious, but the price for achieving them would be high: a great amount of Cambodia's freedom of action, and possibly its continued existence as an independent state. If this analysis is correct, the usual descriptions of Cambodia's foreign affairs require fundamental reassessment. Most observers have concluded that Cambodia's traditional and historical difficulties with Thailand and Vietnam have been "intensified" by the Cold War. This thesis is stated best by Professor Fisher: "Cambodia's relations with Thailand, as also with Southern Vietnam have deteriorated, and . . . [the] *root cause* lies in growing differences over the alignment of foreign policy as a whole." [52] Leifer, too, writes that "Cold War differences have aggravated a relationship which traditionally was never a happy one." [53]

These and similar analyses do not go far enough, for the fundamental point is that the differences between Cambodia and its neighbors, which appear to be a consequence of the Cold War, are actually essential to Cambodia's foreign policy. This does not deny that Cambodia's neutrality has indeed strained relations with its pro-Western neighbors: from the viewpoint of Bangkok especially, a Cambodia too friendly to the Communists, or under Communist control, would be anathema. The late Premier Sarit of Thailand lashed out at Sihanouk for "making . . . [Cambodia] a springboard for launching attacks on neighboring countries by Communist armed forces." [54] With such attitudes common among Thai leaders, it is hard to conceive of friendly relations between Prince Sihanouk and Bangkok officials.

But a major point often overlooked is that the different Cold War

[51] Leifer, *op. cit.*, p. 13.
[52] Fisher, *Southeast Asia, op. cit.*, p. 569. Emphasis added.
[53] Leifer, *op. cit.*, p. 27.
[54] Sarit statement of October 1961, quoted by D. Insor, *Thailand* (London: George Allen & Unwin, 1963), p. 121.

alignments of Cambodia and its neighbors have merely aggravated the traditional enmity between them. This conflict is not the "unavoidable price" Sihanouk must pay for his neutrality in the Cold War; it is a central thesis of Cambodian foreign policy. Sihanouk needs an environment of tension, and it is reasonable to conclude that, if the Cold War differences were somehow resolved, he would concentrate upon other areas of tension between Cambodia and its neighbors—seeking only to avoid a simultaneous confrontation with both Bangkok and Saigon.

There are plenty of potential disputes between Phnom Penh and both Bangkok and Saigon. For example, Prince Sihanouk can always revive the specter of Thai irredentism—a danger he cites regularly even now, when he lists evils that surround beleagured Cambodia. Nor should it be thought that the settlement of any one border dispute with Thailand would insure peace on that front. For instance, in 1958-62, Prince Sihanouk engaged in a seemingly major on-and-off dispute with Thailand over the ownership of an ancient temple known as Kao Prah Viharn (or "Preah Vihear"). Some observers called it the "most serious" dispute ever to arise between the two countries. Indeed, the controversy over a temple barely accessible from either country did inflame tempers in both Bangkok and Phnom Penh. But even when the World Court awarded Cambodia sovereign control over Kao Prah Viharn in June 1962, there was no perceptible improvement in relations between Bangkok and Phnom Penh, and Sihanouk has continued to rail against the "evil" intentions of the Thai. Early in 1964, he said once again that "Some Thai have written that their territory extends to the Mekong River, where the [Cambodian] Royal Palace is. . . . So you can see the Thai want to seize our territory. . . ." [55] Should Prince Sihanouk ever wish to revive a major oratorical campaign against Thai irredentism, he will have laid the groundwork for his charges.

Of course, some of the Cambodians' fears are real. Few Thai leaders were happy about having to relinquish Battambang and Siam Reap under French pressure in 1946, and many would like nothing better than an opportunity to reacquire these provinces. According to officials in the Thai foreign ministry, the World Court's decision on Kao Prah Viharn led some Thai army officers to plead with Premier Sarit for permission to "march right to Phnom Penh." [56] Despite the soldiers' assurances that they could "have lunch in Phnom Penh," Sarit refused to

[55] From Sihanouk's speech of February 21, 1964, reported on Phnom Penh Radio.
[56] Interviews with the author, Bangkok, July 1962 and June 1963.

grant permission, though he himself was tearful over the Court's decision.

Similarly, there are plenty of latent disputes between Cambodia and Vietnam, both North and South. The problems surrounding the minority populations—Khmer in South Vietnam, Vietnamese in Cambodia—are only the most obvious. Even Sihanouk has conceded that this is a problem which can be left—if need be, temporarily—"on the back burner." In March 1964, explaining his proposals for a Four-Power Conference on Cambodian Neutrality, he claimed that they "would be a sacrifice for us. . . . In our drafts we have not even attempted to safeguard the interests of our 600,000 Khmer Krom compatriots [in Vietnam]." [57] Thus, should Sihanouk ever wish to revive the charges of "cultural genocide," there will be enough room for conflict on that score.

Another Cambodian dispute with Vietnam, to which Sihanouk seldom refers now, could be lodged against Saigon—and Hanoi, too, should reunification be accomplished under the latter's auspices: the running controversy over the millions of dollars left from the days of the Associated States of Indochina. This framework had been established at the Pau Conference of 1950. The member states agreed on an "autonomous" port of Saigon; a national bank and a single currency; a customs union; and the apportionment of the total customs revenues.[58] These agreements were abrogated by the 1954 Geneva Conference, which brought independence to the states of Indochina. Even before that, the unilateral French decision in 1953 to devalue the *piastre* (the single established currency until independence) had upset all the Indochinese states.[59] Early in 1954, Cambodian spokesmen began to make clear that they were dissatisfied with their share (according to the Pau agreements, 23 per cent [60]) of the joint customs revenues. Phnom Penh, badly in need of funds to resolve its acute economic difficulties in the country, was even more irritated by Vietnam's contention that it could

---

[57] From Sihanouk's speech of March 9, 1964. The Prince probably exaggerates when he uses the figure of 600,000 Khmer Krom, although there is no positive way of knowing by how much. Hall, *op. cit.*, p. 835, says that there are 400,000 Cambodians in Vietnam (and 300,000 Vietnamese in Cambodia). Fisher, *op. cit.*, p. 559, also says that there were, as of 1955, 300,000 Vietnamese in Cambodia, but gives 480,000 for the Khmer Krom in Vietnam. This agrees well with the figure given by Thompson and Adloff, *op. cit.*, p. 181, of 450,000 Cambodians in Cochin-China.

[58] Lancaster, *op. cit.*, p. 211-13.

[59] *Ibid.*, p. 270.

[60] *Ibid.*, p. 212, gives the "provisional" figure as 22 per cent.

not then pay the almost 800 million piastres which had already accrued to Cambodia's credit. At the time, this sum would have "gone far to help balance Cambodia's budget for 1954." [61]

This problem has never been solved. In May 1954, during a period of acute inflation, Cambodia declared that it would take measures to recover the blocked customs revenues. Then came Dienbienphu, the collapse of French colonialism in Southeast Asia, and (in September 1954) the establishment of the separate states of North Vietnam and South Vietnam. Since then, Cambodia has been unable to gain any satisfaction from Saigon, which soon became involved in its own difficulties with Hanoi. From time to time, Cambodia has claimed that the sum owing to it is much larger than that blocked in 1954. Although Saigon has occasionally offered to make restitution to Phnom Penh, the two governments have not been able to agree on the figure. As a result, large sums of money are now blocked in Paris, available to neither Cambodia nor South Vietnam. The dispute is particularly galling to Cambodia (which does not enjoy the massive foreign assistance lavished on South Vietnam) and has frustrated other countries which have attempted to mediate the conflict. But no solution is in sight, and the problem remains a device which Prince Sihanouk can use whenever he feels disposed to exacerbate the already-embittered relations between Cambodia and South Vietnam.

The Essentiality of Foreign Policy to Cambodia

Many students of foreign policy have alleged that a state may create an international crisis or embark upon a foreign adventure in order to resolve, or divert attention from, some internal difficulty. A variation of this thesis is the theory that a foreign crisis will help to reduce tensions among competing groups within a state by allowing them to rally around an overriding "national interest." Today, that theory is often applied to Indonesia,[62] and in the past it has found application in Fascist Italy, Nazi Germany, and Communist China.

This thesis can be extremely misleading, for some foreign policies otherwise difficult to understand may in fact be based on actual foreign-policy goals. Perhaps some of Hitler's early foreign adventures were designed to help consolidate internal support for the Nazis, but it is

---

[61] Thompson and Adloff, *op. cit.*, p. 194.

[62] See Donald Hindley, "Indonesia's Confrontation with Malaysia: A Search for Motives," *Asian Survey* (1964), 904-13.

not necessary to argue that the domestic confidence he had established by 1937-38 was significantly increased by the adventure on which he embarked in 1939. Instead, Nazi Germany's foreign policy at that point was related directly to real foreign-policy goals.

Cambodia, too, has real foreign-policy goals, and most of Prince Sihanouk's foreign policy can, in fact, be understood as the method he has chosen for achieving those goals, rather than as a means of dealing with any internal problems. His behavior is understandable as a reaction to his external environment, and as a means toward his primary goal: the preservation of Cambodia as an identifiable—and independent —national entity.

The essential characteristic of Cambodia's foreign policy, therefore, is its negative quality, and its fundamental source is Cambodia's uncertainty about its continued existence. Thus the problems in which Cambodia is involved and which Sihanouk chooses to emphasize, whether they concern ethnic irredentism or border disputes, are absolutely different in nature from the seemingly similar problems facing other states in Southeast Asia.

The Philippines' claim to Sabah, for instance, has almost no relation to its national existence. In the foreign policies it adopts—whether disruptive or conciliatory—it can reasonably afford even to make mistakes, for few (if any) of these foreign policies are central or basic to its continued existence.[63]

Cambodia, however, can afford few real mistakes in foreign policy. Although there is no significant internal dissension, the fact that the continued existence of the state itself cannot yet be taken for granted sheds new light on the seemingly erratic and disconnected moves that Cambodian leaders make in foreign affairs. For some years to come, Cambodia cannot be expected to participate in actions that would seem to "stabilize" the environment in Southeast Asia, such as attempts at regional cooperation. As long as the basic condition of Asia's international politics is instability, Cambodia must retain her capacity to benefit from that instability.

---

[63] This is well understood by Philippine leaders. As Vice-President Pelaez (himself engaged at the time in a preconvention contest for the presidential nomination) remarked to the author in October 1964: "No election in this country was ever won or lost on any foreign-policy issue."

CHAPTER III: INDONESIA AND MALAYSIA

Another state in Southeast Asia whose foreign policy goals are presently incompatible with stability in the region is Indonesia. Like Cambodia, Indonesia has objective and definable foreign policy goals, and like Prince Sihanouk, President Sukarno follows an activist approach in foreign policy. Indeed, the generally dynamic quality that characterizes much of Indonesia's politics also applies to its foreign policy, and the cardinal feature of that policy in Southeast Asia, proclaimed since early 1963, has been *Ganjang Malaysia!* This phrase, printed on banners that wave over Indonesian streets and roads, scrawled on the walls of Indonesian buildings, and shouted repeatedly by Indonesian leaders, means *Crush Malaysia!* [1] The campaign launched by Indonesia against Malaysia represents the most activist trend in the international politics of Southeast Asia today and, barring only the bloody struggle in Vietnam, is the most serious conflict in the region. To understand it requires a search not only into its causes but into its effects and consequences.

The major tangible effects of the conflict have been the severance of Indonesian-Malaysian relations[2] and, since mid-1963, the infiltration of Malaysia by Indonesian armed volunteers at such a rate that Malaysia presented a formal complaint to the United Nations Security Council in September 1964. Its most dramatic result was Indonesia's decision, in January 1965, to withdraw from the United Nations—because Malaysia had been given its expected one-year seat on the Security Council. One of its intangible results was the unprecedented pattern of intense communications developed by Indonesia, Malaysia, and the Philippines in 1963. The governments of these states learned

---

[1] Recently Indonesian spokesmen have tried to point out that *ganjang* does not mean literally *crush* but should better be interpreted as *chew*. Presumably, Malayans (whose language is in many ways identical with Bahasa Indonesia) do not need the English translation. President Sukarno once said to an anti-Malaysia audience: "A few moments ago I received your statement to devour Malaysia. Yes, the word *devour* has become well-known everywhere . . . some people used the word *swallow*, but I think Jogjakarta citizens like the word *devour* better." Sukarno speech in Jogjakarta, September 25, 1963.

[2] And as we saw in Chapter I, Philippine-Malaysian relations were also broken when Malaysia was established.

more about one another than ever before,[3] which should help resolve
the issue of whether or not Southeast Asia is a political region.

Immediate Consequences: High-Level Diplomacy

A chronology of the confrontation as it grew, subsided, and intensified once again will, to begin, be useful.

The Indonesian government first formalized its opposition to the
proposed new state of Malaysia in February 1963, when Foreign Minister Subandrio declared that Malaya's premier "has always been
hostile to Indonesia." [4] On the same day, President Sukarno charged
that "we are being encircled. . . . We do not want to have neocolonialism in our vicinity. We consider Malaysia an encirclement of the Indonesian Republic. Malaysia is the product of . . . neocolonialism." [5]
Soon afterward, in response to suggestions by Philippine Vice-President
Pelaez, an informal, second-level conference was held in Manila when
ECAFE met there in March. But, although Pelaez met with Dr. Subandrio and Deputy Prime Minister Tun Razak of Malaya, little seems
to have been accomplished.[6]

Finally, after efforts by Thailand to smooth Philippine-Malayan differences, Tunku Abdul Rahman of Malaysia agreed to go to Manila
for the ASA meeting.[7] There he spoke with President Macapagal, who

[3] Assessing the impact of Malaysia, one observer concluded that "not for centuries has there been the extent of interaction among Southeast Asians themselves
that exists at the present time." Richard Buttwell, "Malaysia and Its Impact on the
International Relations of Southeast Asia," *Asian Survey* IV:7 (July 1964), 946.

[4] *Straits Times* (February 12, 1963). References to the *Straits Times* in this
book are to "straight news" reports as carried by the wire services (usually
Reuters). References are never to editorials. In the case of the Subandrio statement cited here, the *Washington Post* (February 12, 1963) carried the same news
item. The *Straits Times* has been cited only because its pages reflect a good
chronology of events as reported in wire service dispatches.

[5] From President Sukarno's speech, given at the opening of the Joint Conference
of the Central and Regional National Front Committee, Djakarta, February 13,
1963.

[6] In addition, the Sabah claim was then disturbing Malayan-Philippines relations, so that the top-level meeting of ASA had to be postponed twice. They were
first scheduled to be held from December 10-15, 1962, and then from January
12-17, 1963. But Sheikh Azahari, whose Brunei revolt was warmly supported by
Indonesia, fled to Manila, where he was given Philippines government protection.
This decision to harbor a major anti-Malaysia dissident was obviously not
welcomed in Kuala Lumpur.

[7] The Philippines had by now told Azahari to leave, and Indonesia gave him a
travel visa. The British had already withdrawn his passport, and according to
Indonesian press sources of January 31, 1963, Azahari left on this visa "under
oath" by the United Arab Republic and Indonesian embassies.

was intent on arranging a meeting between Sukarno and the Tunku. The most that could be accomplished, however, was an agreement to call for subministerial conferences. These meetings, held in mid-April 1963, marked the first formal three-way conversations designed specifically to deal with problems surrounding Malaysia.[8] It was hoped they would lead to a summit conference, but the verbal attacks launched by the Malayan government in Kuala Lumpur and the Indonesian government in Djakarta had become venemous. Sukarno, for example, charged that the incipient formation of Malaysia symbolized the continuation of colonialism, which Indonesia opposed as a matter of principle: "The Tunku," Sukarno added, "does not understand this principle."[9] To this, the Tunku replied a few days later by declaring that Sukarno "is acting like a Hitler" and labeling him a "Red Chinese stooge."[10]

In late May and early June, however, as Indonesia seemed (for the first time in years) about to undertake steps toward economic stabilization, President Sukarno suddenly appeared to have abandoned his extreme position. From Tokyo, where he was to conduct negotiations with American oil companies, Sukarno invited the Tunku to visit with him for a few days—a remarkable invitation, because the two men had been trading insults for months. After stopping briefly in Manila to inform President Macapagal, the Tunku flew to Tokyo, where he seemed to reach a satisfactory understanding with Sukarno, whom he had not seen in six years. When Sukarno left for Europe the Tunku accompanied him to the airport and told reporters that the talks had been "very, very amiable" (although he refused to reveal details: Sukarno, he said, "might be sensitive").[11] To observers it seemed that the two leaders had agreed to settle their differences peacefully.

As a result of the talks, the foreign ministers of the three countries met in Manila a few weeks later.[12] Those sessions (June 7-11, 1963) probably mark the high point in Malayan-Indonesian efforts to resolve the differences amicably. At Manila it was decided that an "im-

[8] *Straits Times* (April 17, 1963); also see *Malaya/Indonesia Relations* (Kuala Lumpur: 1963), p. 16. Each of the foreign ministers sent his principal assistant to these talks.

[9] Sukarno said: "I am opposed to Malaysia. . . . Malaysia is neocolonialism." From Sukarno's May Day address, May 1, 1963.

[10] Keyes Beech, in *The Washington Post* (May 8, 1963).

[11] *Straits Times* (June 1, 1963). See also *Times of London* (June 3, 1963).

[12] Ganis Harsono, Dr. Subandrio's spokesman at the Indonesian Foreign Ministry, said in an interview early in July 1963 that confrontation "more or less terminated at Tokyo."

partial" authority would endeavor to ascertain whether or not the Borneo peoples wished to join the still unborn Malaysia. It was also at these meetings that President Macapagal won approval for his proposed Greater Malay Confederation that eventually became Maphilindo (for MAlaysia-PHILippines-INDOnesia).[13] Finally, it was agreed that the heads of government would meet in Manila "by the end of July" in order to implement the accords reached in June.

The July meeting, however, almost did not take place. Within days of the ministerial talks, recriminations once again began to fly between Djakarta and Kuala Lumpur. Sukarno charged that the Tunku's insistence that Malaysia be formed on the planned date (August 31) was a betrayal of "promises,"[14] to which the Tunku replied that he had promised nothing. It became highly uncertain whether Sukarno would attend the summit conference. Finally, however, the conference was held (July 31-August 5, 1963), and once again it seemed that confrontation might be terminated.

By mid-August, under the three-nation agreement to accept an "impartial" determination of the wishes of the Borneo peoples, a United Nations team had begun its work.[15] But new arguments arose about how many "observers" each country might send to accompany the United Nations team.[16] The Tunku did agree to postpone briefly the formal establishment of Malaysia,[17] but on September 14, 1963, he announced that Malaysia would come into being on September 16. At that, Indonesia and the Philippines announced they could not immediately recognize the new government,[18] and strong reactions set in: embassies were burned and sacked in Djakarta and attacked in Kuala Lumpur; Sukarno and the Tunku were both burned in effigy. By the end of 1963, the world's major powers were becoming seriously concerned over the worsening conflict. Some feared that the struggle might escalate into war, perhaps even between an Indonesia supported by

---

[13] See "Report and Recommendations of the Conference of Foreign Ministers of the Federation of Malaya, The Republic of Indonesia, and the Republic of the Philippines to their Respective Heads of Government" (Manila, 1963).

[14] *Straits Times* (July 12, 1963).

[15] *Washington Post* (August 10, 1963).

[16] *Straits Times* (August 24, 1963).

[17] Reporting from the talks at Manila, journalists wrote that Malaya no longer "insists on August 31 as the Foundation Date for the federation. . . ." *Straits Times* (August 5, 1963). Later, the Tunku said: "We postponed Malaysia to suit them [Indonesia and Philippines]." *Straits Times* (September 4, 1963).

[18] *Straits Times* (September 16, 1963). See also *Christian Science Monitor* (September 17, 1963).

Communist China and the Soviet Union, and a Malaysia supported
by Britain, New Zealand, Australia and (through SEATO and ANZUS)
the United States.

POST MALAYSIA DIPLOMACY

As a result of these fears, high-level diplomatic efforts to resolve the
conflict were resumed in early 1964. By that time, Indonesian guerrilla
activities in Borneo had intensified, with almost daily incidents between
Indonesians (regulars or irregulars) and British and Gurkha troops
defending Malaysian territory. These events led President Johnson
to ask U.S. Attorney General (now Senator) Robert Kennedy to meet
with the principals.[19] Kennedy traveled to Tokyo, Bangkok, Kuala
Lumpur, Manila, and Djakarta, apparently carrying one message:
there must be a cease-fire in Borneo before there could be hope of
meaningful talks. The Attorney General had met President Sukarno
some years earlier in Indonesia. Moreover, he knew that Sukarno had
often said that only when John Kennedy became President did the
United States begin to understand both Indonesia and its leader.
Against this background, and with his considerable skill in persuasion,
Kennedy apparently was able to convince the belligerent parties to
stop shooting.[20] It was hoped that the cease-fire would be monitored by
Thailand, and it was expected that talks would soon begin in Bangkok.[21]

The talks were held in early February, but they seemed destined to
failure. Only hours after Kennedy left Djakarta, for example, President
Sukarno declared the confrontation must continue. Issuing the famous
call, *Ganjang Malaysia*, he added: "Indonesia may change its tactics,
but our goal will remain the same." [22] The same view was expressed at
the Bangkok talks. An Indonesian official told Thai reporters that "Indonesia's attendance . . . was merely a 'tactical maneuver,' because the
aim of 'crushing Malaysia' remained the same." [23]

Although the talks led to the signing of a cease-fire agreement, a
transcript shows that there was little cause for optimism. The Indo-

[19] *The New York Times* (January 14, 1964).

[20] Sukarno used these words: "In my capacity as Supreme Commander of the
Armed Forces and Great Leader of the Revolution, I herewith instruct all armed
forces to effect a cease-fire." Sukarno press statement, read by Dr. Subandrio,
January 23, 1964.

[21] *The New York Times* (February 6, 1964).

[22] *The New York Times* (January 25, 1964).

[23] *Straits Times* (February 5, 1964).

nesian negotiators stressed the presence of British bases (particularly in Singapore) as one of their main objections to the new Malaysia. The Malaysian delegate retorted, "So what? We have British bases. What about American bases in the Philippines?" When the Indonesian representative answered, "One thing at a time. . . . Later we will tackle the question of American bases in the Philippines," the Malaysian representative warned the Filipinos who were present: "Did you hear that, my friends? Now, it's us; next it's you." [24] The tone of these discussions is evident in this excerpt from the talks, with a senior Malaysian official addressing the Indonesian delegation:

> You accused us of not keeping the spirit of Manila Agreement. But let me tell you this. You, the Indonesians have not adhered to this spirit of brotherliness and friendship. Let me remind you of the Friendship Treaty we have and the Tokyo Communiqué. All these documents emphasized that if there is something which one side is not happy about then the other party can call a meeting and thrash it out in a friendly fashion. There must be close consultation. . . . But on your side what happens? As soon as you were unhappy with us, bang goes the press and all the propaganda machine! You never called a meeting to find out what our explanation was. Instead, you assail us under confrontation and all this nonsense. You called us names. Even here you call us colonial stooges and you said we were rude. But let me say this: of all people, the Indonesians are the people least qualified to blame the British or ourselves of rudeness. Never in the history of diplomatic practice even the wicked British or wicked Germans looted each other's embassies during the two last world wars. But you looted our embassy and have now actually occupied it, while I risked my life to protect yours. And who could be ruder than you when you insulted our national anthem? Deny that if you can! [25]

Thus despite the cease-fire agreement, the Bangkok talks produced few tangible results. Shooting continued, and the Tunku said in March that the breakdown of the "cease-fire . . . was inevitable," for Subandrio had warned in advance that Indonesia might not be able to control its "volunteers." [26]

As the pace of the guerrilla war quickened during the spring of 1964,[27] both President Macapagal and Prince Sihanouk attempted to

[24] *Straits Times* (February 16, 1964). The accuracy of this news item is supported by the records of the conference, cited below.
[25] From the Record of the first meeting of the political committee, Tripartite Ministerial Conference, Bangkok, February 8, 1964. Unpublished.
[26] *Straits Times* (March 5, 1964).
[27] For example, the *Sunday Times* (Kuala Lumpur: May 10, 1964, reported that

bring together Sukarno and the Tunku again. These efforts finally succeeded and, in June 1964, the two men met in Tokyo once more. But the meeting solved nothing. The Tunku had insisted that Indonesian troops must leave Malaysian territory before meaningful talks could be held. President Sukarno, however, had stressed that the purpose of the talks was to find conditions under which the troops might be withdrawn. The two finally met only when Indonesia agreed that troop withdrawal would begin simultaneously with the leaders' meeting in Tokyo.

The Tokyo summit came to an inconclusive close; its only tangible result was an agreement "in principle" to accept a Philippine proposal that a four-nation Afro-Asian commission be formed to resolve the dispute.[28] This proposal has not been implemented, nor have there been further summit talks, for both Indonesia and Malaysia have insisted on conditions unacceptable to each other.

The Other Consequences of the Dispute

Aside from diplomatic difficulties, there were other direct consequences of the dispute over the formation of Malaysia. The most troublesome has been the infiltration of Malaysia by Indonesian armed "volunteers." These "volunteers," who have come overland (in Sarawak and Sabah), in small boats and by parachute (in south and south-central Malaya), and reportedly by submarine as well (on the Malayan east coast), have been acknowledged by the Indonesian government. On several occasions they entered in groups of thirty to sixty, often accompanied by Malaysian Chinese guides. In no case have they met with military success.[29]

Even before this aggressive program was begun, Indonesia—in an effort to end its historic dependence on the entrepôt facilities of Singapore —had severed economic ties with Malaysia. The step hurt Singapore's trade, and adversely affected some groups in Indonesia as well. In Singapore, it meant temporary unemployment for dockworkers and people engaged in rubber-processing, and a general downturn in the

---

security forces in Sarawak smashed "an attempt by two platoons of Indonesian terrorists to set up a 'liberated area' thirty-five miles from Kuching."

[28] See reports, in the *Japan Times* (June 21, 1964); Kyodo Press Service (Tokyo: June 21, 1964).

[29] Almost every intruder was quickly killed or captured, often after having been fed by a Malay peasant who then alerted the police.

economy.[30] In Indonesia, it produced—at least temporarily—the negative effect of slowing down the commercial process by which Indonesian commodity exports are converted into essential hard currency and needed imports. President Sukarno sought to counteract the loss of Singapore's facilities by planning to build an Indonesian "free port," [31] and transferring his exports to the port of Manila and elsewhere. But modern harbor, warehouse, and trading facilities are not built overnight, and the port of Manila is the most corrupt and thief-ridden (slowest and generally the least efficient) in all Southeast Asia.

Moreover, the anticipated pace of the economic-stabilization plan, upon which many of Djakarta's economists had placed such high hopes in mid-1963, was drastically slowed by Indonesia's need to turn its attention to the confrontation with Malaysia. It was evident to these economists—and to others in Djakarta who think in terms of administration and a working economy—that little progress could be made without the direct support and agitational pressures of President Sukarno himself. But his *Ganjang Malaysia!* campaign dashed those hopes. It also proved to wear down what little patience with the Indonesian President U.S. officials had left.[32] By mid-1964, the United States announced that it was ceasing all direct financial aid to the Indonesian government. Despite several warnings by U.S. Ambassador Howard Jones to moderate Indonesia's policies or have aid cease, President Su-

---

[30] The British Board of Trade announced that during the last quarter of 1963 Singapore exports were "18 per cent less than for the last quarter of a year earlier, because of the loss of Indonesian trade." *Straits Times* (May 25, 1964). Dennis Bloodworth reported that Singapore was losing £2 million each month "in net trading profits" thanks to the severance of trade with Indonesia. He reported that numerous small ships were idle, and 121 plants that process coconut oil, rubber, sago, and so on, were faced with the need to lay off several thousand workers. *The Bulletin* (London, January 11, 1964). During 1964, however, Singapore's remarkable economy recouped much of this loss, as new industries absorbed many displaced workers, but some sectors, such as merchants accustomed to shipping numerous Leica cameras and Rolex watches to Indonesia, had not recovered.

[31] See the announcement of Distribution Minister Leimena, announcing plans for a free port at Sabang (a tiny island off the northern tip of Sumatra) and plans for three "free-trade zones." *Christian Science Monitor* (October 11, 1963).

[32] See report in *The New York Times* (January 14, 1964) that President Johnson had already written to President Sukarno pointing out that under the 1963 foreign aid act, assistance to Indonesia must end unless the U.S. President finds specifically that American interests require that it be continued. According to the press report, Mr. Johnson had noted in his letter to Sukarno that "it would be difficult to reach such a conclusion if Indonesia's hostile actions against Malaysia continued."

karno had said publicly: "To hell with your aid!" [33] Simultaneously, Indonesia lost any remaining hopes for financial support from the World Bank for, as its officials explained late in 1964, Indonesia's diversion of energies to projects which do not accumulate money capital was not encouraging.

Finally, the confrontation resulted in failure for Indonesian international diplomacy. Over the past decade, President Sukarno had devoted months to building an image of Indonesia as a leader among Afro-Asian peoples generally, and certainly as *the* leader of the uncommitted states of Asia. He had flown to scores of world capitals, and received world leaders—great and small—in Djakarta. The 1955 Bandung Conference was only the major early manifestation of this effort. After that there were dozens of meetings designed to attract journalists, statesmen, representatives of women's groups and other organizations, to Indonesia.

But, by late 1964, it seemed that whatever support had been built up during the preceding decade could be quickly destroyed. Indonesian prestige suffered a major blow when a United Nations Security Council resolution "deploring" Indonesia's admitted paratroop landing in southern Malaya and calling on both parties to refrain from the threat or use of force "and to respect the territorial integrity and political independence of each other," received nine out of eleven Security Council votes.[34] Not only did Brazil and Bolivia vote for the resolution against the wishes of Indonesia, but so did the Ivory Coast and Morocco—two states which could not be considered within the American sphere and which Indonesia had counted among its friends in the

---

[33] In a major speech early in 1964, President Sukarno said among other things: "But the Tunku is a strange man, brothers. One day he says: All right, all right, let us negotiate. Another day he calls me names. . . . Another day he says: 'To hell with Sukarno.' In doing so he quotes my own words, for the other day I said 'To hell with your aid!' *What I meant was U.S. aid.* What was the reason . . . the United States said it will give aid to Indonesia if Indonesia is willing to stop her confrontation against Malaysia. This means giving aid under conditions . . . Yes, we want to get aid. Who does not want to get aid? Do we accept aid from the United States—we do; from Italy—we do; from France—we do; from the CPR—we do; from the Soviet Union—we do—so long as there are no strings attached to this aid. If there is any country which says: We give you aid but you must stop your confrontation against Malaysia, I will say: 'Go to hell with your aid!'" From Sukarno speech at a general roll call of volunteers (the 21 million volunteers to crush Malaysia), Djakarta, May 3, 1964. Italics added.

[34] Draft Resolution of Norway (Doc. S/5973) reprinted in *Malaysia's Case in the United Nations Security Council, Documents Reproduced from the Official Record of the Security Council Proceedings, September 9-17, 1964* (Kuala Lumpur: Ministry of External Affairs, Malaysia), p. 87.

Asian-African realm. Despite the nine-to-two vote, the resolution failed to carry; Czechoslovakia's vote and the Soviet Union's veto supported Indonesia.

Indonesia's failure to win a majority was perhaps not surprising. Its representative frankly admitted that Djakarta was engaged in small-scale attacks on Malaysia. He sought, moreover to justify these actions —on the scarcely reassuring grounds that no condemnation was warranted, because "to us, 'Malaysia' as a country, as a sovereign and independent country, does not exist." [35] Malaysia, of course, is a member of the United Nations, is recognized by almost all other governments of the world, and has diplomatic relations with many. Indeed, it was the United Nations Secretary-General who reported in 1963 that the people of British Borneo preferred to join Malaysia. For that reason, as U.S. Ambassador Adlai Stevenson commented: "Malaysia therefore is to an unusual degree a child of the United Nations." [36] Nevertheless, Indonesia held that, because it did not recognize or accept the existence of Malaysia, it had every right to launch attacks and "crush" the new nation. This is a novel doctrine, both in international law and in international politics.

In the months after the Security Council meeting, Indonesia continued to land "volunteers"—not only in Borneo, but also on the Malayan mainland and increasingly close to Singapore. The people of Indonesia were told nothing of these events; but, in the foreign arena, President Sukarno's government did not deny them. At a "neutralists'" conference held in Cairo weeks after the United Nations meeting, Indonesia continued its efforts to convince other nations that Malaysia is merely a British puppet. This conference was sponsored precisely by those states among which Indonesia expects to be counted as a leader: United Arab Republic, Yugoslavia, and India. But the signs first evident at the Security Council meetings were not temporary, and Indonesia failed to gain the support of its erstwhile friends. Indeed, the conference members passed a resolution (over Sukarno's vehement opposition) upholding territorial integrity and "peaceful coexistence"— a resolution widely understood to be a criticism of Indonesia's unwillingness to coexist peacefully with Malaysia.

These very negative consequences clearly angered Sukarno and Dr.

---

[35] Statement of Dr. Sudjarwo, Deputy Foreign Minister of Indonesia, in *ibid.*, p. 23.

[36] *Ibid.*, p. 21. Malaya became a United Nations member when she achieved independence in 1957, and the enlargement to "Malaysia" did not alter that status.

Subandrio, for they had done much to court the new nations of Asia and Africa, including the famous refusal to permit Israel and Nationalist China to participate in the Asian Games at Djakarta in 1962. Thus, after the 1964 Cairo Conference, Indonesia let it be known that, if its Middle Eastern "friends" were so untrustworthy, perhaps Djakarta should "reconsider" *its* anti-Israeli policies.[37] In a related move, President Sukarno revealed some of these difficulties to his people.[38] Because they had been exhorted for almost two years to "volunteer" to "crush" Malaysia, perhaps not many were surprised when Sukarno finally disclosed that guerrillas were entering Malaysia because "Indonesia does not recognize that country's sovereignty." But the more important disclosure was Sukarno's announcement that, despite all previous assurances that the new nations backed his policy, "some members of the new emerging forces still could not understand Indonesia's stand on Malaysia." [39]

It was becoming clear that Indonesia's stand was not bringing desirable results. Britain had increased its military assistance to Malaysia; the Australian government announced the remarkable (for it) step of peacetime conscription to guarantee its commitment to defend Malaysia; and the United States sent a military-aid mission to Kuala Lumpur. Malaysia, although torn by racial strife (symbolized by Singapore's secession) was not cracking under *Indonesia's* pressure. It seemed to illustrate the Aesop fable in which the warm sun and the cold wind compete to force the traveler to remove his coat. The threat from Djakarta had helped, in some degree, to encourage a "Malaysian" consciousness: certainly a counterproductive action from Indonesia's viewpoint, and when Singapore later left Malaysia it was not a product of Djakarta's policies.

Perhaps worst of all, Indonesia's image as a model neutralist state was tarnished. The new nations, which might endorse many actions against a colonial power, were reluctant to condone military action by Indonesia against Malaysia, one-tenth its size. Even with its large

[37] This was said by the Indonesia *Herald,* generally regarded as a foreign-ministry organ.

[38] *Straits Times* (December 23, 1964). This may not have been "new" news in Djakarta, for in the tolerant Indonesian society, prohibitions against Western press sources may not count for much, and it is possible to purchase the banned news magazines within blocks of the presidential palace in Djakarta. Similarly, it is difficult to police people's radio-listening habits, though apparently many do not wish to take the risk.

[39] From Reuters and Associated Press dispatches from Djakarta, December 22, 1964, reported in *Straits Times* (December 23, 1964).

British investments, Malaysia is self-governing, and it was the end of British colonialism in Borneo and Sarawak that made possible the formation of Malaysia—a step which the new nations could only welcome. Thus, whereas they might have applauded other Indonesian actions (say, against Portuguese Timor), these nations found it far more difficult even to look the other way as Indonesia confronted Malaysia. In the end, in his frustration at the failure of these nations to support him, particularly in his demand that Malaysia should not be seated in the Security Council, President Sukarno ordered that Indonesia must leave the United Nations altogether.

In this brief chronicle of events, there seem to have been no significant positive results at all for Indonesia. A question must then be raised: Why did Indonesia's leaders decide to "crush" Malaysia?

The Sources of Indonesia's Malaysia Policy

The answer to the question can be found in two aspects of Indonesian politics: a long-standing expansionist sentiment among a number of Indonesian leaders, and certain common elements in the political ideology of leading Indonesians that cut across their otherwise deep divisions.

So much attention has been given to Indonesia's very large Communist faction that a warning is in order: the elements basic to an understanding of Indonesian foreign policies in Southeast Asia have had very little to do with international Communism. Undeniably, Indonesia does occupy an important place within the Communist perspective. For example, it has received important military assistance from the Soviet Union,[40] and the Indonesian Communist party (PKI)—with a membership of between two and three million—ranks behind only those of Communist China and the Soviet Union.

Despite their prominence, it would be misleading to conclude that Indonesian foreign policy is largely the product of Communist-related factors. Indonesia's long dispute with the Netherlands over Irian Barat (West New Guinea), for example, was sometimes pictured as Soviet-inspired. But, although there was firm Soviet support for Indonesia's case (perhaps in the hope of provoking Indonesian-Dutch hostilities in New Guinea), President Sukarno's policy was much older and more fundamental than any Soviet concern. Although Russian arms ship-

---

[40] For a good statement of assistance figures to Indonesia, see Donald Hindley, "Foreign Aid to Indonesia and its Political Implications," *Pacific Affairs* (Summer 1963), 108-109.

ments undoubtedly hastened the success of Indonesia's *Irian Barat* policy, they were not responsible for that policy. On the other hand, both the Soviet Union and Communist China were in the vanguard, along with the Indonesian Communists and their supporters, in attacking the Malaysia proposal. A PKI resolution of December 1961 condemned Malaysia as a form of neocolonialism. Only months later did President Sukarno and his foreign minister decide to criticize Malaysia publicly.

But even before the public criticism, it was not difficult to foresee Indonesia's later hostility as a development quite consistent with the attitudes of the Indonesian elite toward Malaya. When those attitudes are examined, it is clear that Indonesian foreign policies in Southeast Asia have little to do with the Soviet Union or world Communism—except insofar as Russia and China exploit these policies for their own interests. In this respect, the events surrounding confrontation with Malaysia have increased understanding of Indonesia. The abortive Brunei rebellion in 1962, followed by public bitterness between Indonesia and Malaya, and Djakarta's open expressions of fundamental hostility toward Malaysia, have emphasized the need to examine Indonesia's policies specific to Southeast Asia, stripped of its favorite guise as Asia's most prominent neutral. In this perspective, Indonesia's long-standing expansionist sentiment, now infused with a specifically national ideology, commands special attention.

THE BASIS FOR A POLICY OF EXPANSION

Indonesia is perhaps the only Southeast Asian state in which irredentism is openly cited by leading local officials as a possible impetus for governmental actions. Although contemporary leaders in Bangkok, Rangoon, and Phnom Penh sometimes refer to the ancient territorial claims of their imperial predecessors, in none of these capitals is there evidence that serious thought is given to the recapture of these "lost" territories. As Prince Sihanouk has remarked, his anxiety to preserve Cambodia's survival hardly allows any expansionist notions. In Djakarta, however, expansionist goals–known as "Greater Indonesia"—do seem to be very near the surface of today's policies.

Several prominent Indonesians have been identified with these often vague notions of a "Greater Indonesia" destined to be larger than the map now shows. The name that comes immediately to mind is Muhammad Yamin, although attention is now again focused on President Sukarno's own statements on this question. Yamin, who died in October 1962, was a deputy first minister and minister of information—the most vocal and prominent personality to be identified with the "Greater Indonesia" thesis. Although other leaders have chosen not to stress their past actions and statements on this point, Yamin and other "ultra-nationalists," as Guy Pauker has called them, had formulated a vision of Indonesia as early as 1945 that would include what became Malaysia "and perhaps more." [41] And as recently as 1958 Yamin argued that modern Indonesia is the rightful heir to all the former territories of Nusantara (prehistorical Indonesia). Nusantara, he wrote, consisted of "eight groups of islands . . . the Malay peninsular, the islands of Sumatra, of Kalimantan [Borneo], of Java, . . . the group now known as . . . the Southeastern Islands, the islands of Sulawesi, the groups of the Moluccas, and the territory of West Irian." [42]

In today's terms, this would give to Indonesia not only its present territory, but also all of Malaysia (including mainland Malaya and Singapore), and part of Thailand as well. Yamin, at least, was convinced that his vision would be realized: "thanks to the workings of the forces of nationalist independence in Southeast Asia, . . . it is certain that one day it [i.e., Indonesia] will develop again to become the sovereignty of Nusantara, covering the Austronesian people. . . ." A basic question, of course, is: How deeply do other Indonesians and their leaders subscribe to these irredentist ideals? The operational influence of Yamin's thinking has never been entirely clear to students of Indonesian affairs. It is beyond question, however, that Yamin believed that his concept of a "Greater Indonesia" had wide and influential support, and he was firmly convinced that this support forms the basis for potential political action. There is evidence, in fact, that President Sukarno himself has accepted much of Yamin's argument.

"Indonesia Should Extend to Malaya and Papua"—(Sukarno, 1945)

During the early months of 1945 Sukarno and his colleagues, with Japanese support, had reached the final stages of their preparations for independence. In March 1945, Sukarno established a committee of nationalist leaders to express the basic principles of the new state,[43]

---

[41] Guy J. Pauker, "The Soviet Challenge in Indonesia," *Foreign Affairs*, XL:4 (July 1962), 625.

[42] Muhammad Yamin, "A Legal and Historical Review of Indonesia's Sovereignty over the Ages," *Dewan Nasional* (Djakarta: September 1958), p. 19.

[43] The committee was known as BPKI, "Investigating Committee for Preparation of Indonesia's Independence." The deliberations of this group should not be discounted, for from it emerged the "1945 Constitution" and the *Pantjasila*, the

and a special subcommittee to define "the extent of Indonesia's territory." Among its members were Sukarno himself, Hatta, and Yamin. At the first of this committee's meetings Yamin presented his case for an Indonesia considerably larger than it is today.

"The lands which should be associated in the People's State of Indonesia," Yamin urged, included "the former Dutch Colonies . . . Portuguese Timor and North Borneo . . . The Malay Peninsula," and other areas, such as Papua (New Guinea), as well as the four Malayan states which "the Japanese . . . have separated . . . from the rest of the Malay Peninsula by giving them over to Thailand." [44]

In support of his concept, Yamin stressed Indonesia's past history, particularly the Majapahit Era. Some of the independence leaders believed the new state was to include only the lands comprising the Dutch East Indies, but Yamin argued that lands "which have given birth to Indonesian people" should also come within its boundaries. Using this "ethnic" argument, he insisted that the committee members regard themselves as spokesmen for the people of Timor, Borneo, Papua, and the Malay Peninsula, for those territories had "since the beginning of history . . . been inhabited by the people of Indonesia. . . ."

Although Yamin made many references to the book, attributed to the famous Javanese prince Gadjah Mada, in which the extent of Majapahit was described, he also based his argument on a modern "geopolitical point of view" as well. From that perspective, he gave particularly heavy weight to his demand that Malaya must be included within Indonesia:

> Malaya represents a bridge for any power in Indochina to proceed toward Indonesia. Vice versa, the same peninsula has in the past provided a bridge for powers in Indonesia to cross over to the Asian continent. . . . The straits of Malacca provides a passage to our islands while the Malay Peninsula forms the neck of our Archipelago. To separate Malaya from the rest of Indonesia amounts to deliberately weakening from the outset the position . . . of Indonesia in her international relations. On the other hand, to unite Malaya to Indonesia will mean strengthening our position

---

"Five Principles of the Indonesian State" which Sukarno espoused then and which he consistently has declared form the fundament of the Indonesian polity.

[44] *The Territory of the Indonesian State: Discussions in the Meeting of the Investigating Committee for Preparation of Indonesia's Independence,* extracted and translated from the book *Naskah Persiapan Undang-Undang Dasar 1945,* Vol I (Kuala Lumpur: Federal Department of Information, 1964), pp. 2, 6. This translation, though provided by Kuala Lumpur, is accurate, and has not been challenged by authorities who might be "friendlier" to Indonesia.

and completing our entity to accord with our national aspiration and consistent with the interests of geopolitics of air, land and sea. It has been the express and sincere wish of the people there to join with us. I feel that this is a most opportune moment for the people of Malaya to be reunited with the people of the State of Indonesia.[45]

Before Indonesia's confrontation with Malaysia, it was generally held that Yamin's beliefs were the dreams of a visionary, with no influence on other important Indonesian leaders. Indeed, at the committee's second session, Dr. Hatta (who shared with Sukarno the leadership of the independence movement) argued that the new state should be confined to that area "previously ruled by the Dutch." Yamin's views, he said, were imperialistic, and he repeatedly equated Yamin's arguments with those of Nazi Germany. Hatta asked his colleagues to be realistic: "Have we got the capacity to administer the whole territory of our motherland including these new ones?" And, prophetically, he outlined the argument put forward a decade later, when Indonesia was pressing for control of West New Guinea, and questioned Yamin's assurances that the Papuans were the same as the people of Indonesia:

It is quite possible that that is so, but I cannot accept the theory because in science—I always tend to look at things from a scientific point of view—science always begins with doubts. When we have acquired evidence, and plenty of evidence, to say that Papuans are of the same race as us, then I am prepared to accept it, but for the time being I am only prepared to recognize that the Papuans are Melanesians. . . . If we trace back the common origins, we may not find Melanesians but Polynesians instead who are to be found far out in the Pacific Ocean. . . . I am inclined to say that I do not need Papua and that it should be left to the Papuan people themselves. I recognize that the Papuans have the right to be an independent nation and that the Indonesians for the time being —i.e., for decades to come—will not be prepared nor have they the capacity to educate and bring up the Papuans until they can become an independent people. . . . As regards Malaya, let us leave it to the people of Malaya . . . but let us not claim it for ourselves. If we were to do so it would appear as if even before getting independence we were already pursuing an imperialistic policy. . . .[46]

Hatta's moderate and pragmatic approach, like Hatta himself, was rejected by those who were to take hold of the Indonesian revolution.

[45] *Ibid.*, p. 6.
[46] *Ibid.*, pp. 17-19.

Particularly striking was the contrast between Hatta's views and those of Sukarno. Sukarno prefaced his remarks to the committee by denying that he could be considered an imperialist—but, he added:

> At no time during the twenty-five years that I have been connected with our struggle have I declared that *my struggle was confined to . . . the former Dutch-held territory. . . .*
>
> I have never said that Indonesia comprises only those areas that were ruled by the Dutch. In fact, I have on one occasion in my life dreamt of a Pan-Indonesia, which will include not only Malaya and Papua but also the Philippines. . . . But the Philippines is already independent, and we must respect the sovereignty of the Philippine nation. . . .
>
> . . . the Imperial Japanese government . . . has asked us to say what Indonesia shall comprise. For that reason I am in full agreement with the stand taken by my colleague, Mr. Yamin . . . that neither on moral grounds nor on the grounds of international law are we obliged to be the inheritors of the Dutch. . . . I have scores of letters and telegrams which have come from Malaya asking that Malaya be included in Indonesia. . . .
>
> Apart from that, I myself am convinced that the people of Malaya feel themselves as Indonesians, belonging to Indonesia and as one of us. Even if we do not take this reason into account I still say, despite the danger of my being accused as an imperialist, that *Indonesia will not become strong and secure unless the whole Straits of Malacca is in our hands. If only the west coast of the Straits of Malacca, it will mean a threat to our security.*[47]

Sukarno referred, as Hatta had, to New Guinea, but he took a very different tack: he did "not know the wishes of the people there," but would rely on the support of history "and on the territorial limit as described in our history." Following the line Yamin had set, he urged his colleagues to read the Majapahit chronicle, the *Negarakertagama*, and then to add "the question of geopolitics." And, if that were not enough, he invoked the deity:

> God has determined that certain parts of the world should form single units, . . . and when I look at the islands situated between Asia and Australia and between the Pacific and the Indian Oceans I understand that they are meant to form a single entity. For that reason I shall support in this meeting those who advocate that *independent Indonesia should extend to Malaya and Papua. . . . That is my stand and I repeat that I am 100 per cent in agreement with the view held by Mr. Yamin.*[48]

---

[47] *Ibid.*, pp. 20-21. Italics added.
[48] *Ibid.*, p. 22. Italics added.

Other committee members added their views, and it soon became clear they would support Sukarno and Yamin, for as one put it: "If it were not for the British guns which turned the course of its history, I am most certain that Malaya would have been inhabited by no other than Indonesian people entirely. . . ." The committee was asked to choose between "the former Dutch East Indies; . . . the former Dutch East Indies plus Malaka [Malaya], North Borneo, Papua, Timor and the adjacent islands"; and the Dutch Indies without Papua but with Malaya. Of the sixty-six committee members, thirty-nine voted for the boundaries Yamin and Sukarno had outlined, and six more voted to exclude New Guinea but to include Malaya. Thus forty-five of these sixty-six founders of modern Indonesia, with Sukarno in the lead, believed that an independent Indonesia should include all of what became Malaysia.[49]

Their hopes proved irrelevant, for the final determination of these territorial questions was a wartime decision which the Japanese military reserved to itself. At the end of July 1945, because they realized how soon the war might end, the Japanese rushed to complete the final arrangements for Indonesia's independence. At a brief meeting in Singapore on July 27th, regional representatives of the Japanese military administrations "finally decided not to include Malaya along with the former Dutch colonial territories.[50]

[49] In addition to the translation of the 1945 proceedings so far cited here, one should also consult Benedict R. O'G. Anderson, *Some Aspects of Indonesian Politic Under the Japanese Occupation: 1944-1945* (Ithaca, N.Y.: Cornell University Modern Indonesia Project, 1961), p. 29.

[50] Anderson, *op. cit.* There is evidence, moreover, that at a much earlier stage in the war the Japanese had placed British Malaya and the Dutch East Indies in separate administrative categories so far as their readiness for independence was concerned. The Kishi-Nishimura study, made available to this author by Professor H. Benda, shows that the Japanese contemplated in 1943 that when independence came, it would be only for Java and the nearby islands, with Sumatra, Borneo, the Celebes, and so on, not to be included. A Japanese document of August 1943 stated that Java would be the national name, "the name *Indonesia* shall not be taken." By 1945, the "Decision of the Japanese Supreme War Guidance Council" had altered this, but it was still clear that the Japanese authorities *did not contemplate including the British territories in the new state*. The text of the Japanese document read: "The area to be made independent shall be the former Dutch East Indies." That plan was approved by the Japanese cabinet on July 12, 1945. Part of the explanation for the distinction between Malaya and Indonesia made by the Japanese, according to Mr. Kishi's conversation with this author in 1963, was that Tokyo reasoned that the two occupied territories were at different stages and patterns of development. In Kishi's view, "it was never contemplated [by Japan] that Malaya would be incorporated with Indonesia.

Two weeks later, Sukarno, Hatta, and several other Indonesian leaders were called by the Japanese to Singapore and Saigon. Unaware of the Japanese decision, some of them stayed in Malaya for talks with a Malayan group which favored union with Indonesia. This Japanese-supported left-wing nationalist organization was known as the Union of Peninsular Indonesians (KRIS). Its leaders had worked out a plan to declare independence jointly with Indonesia and, when Sukarno's group arrived first in Singapore, they raised Indonesia's flag as their own. When Sukarno went on to Saigon, however, Marshal Terauchi informed him of Japan's decision: Sukarno was to announce Independence within the week, and the new nation would include only the territory formerly known as the Dutch East Indies.

On their way back to Djakarta, the Indonesians again stopped at Singapore, where Ibrahim Yaacob and other KRIS leaders told Sukarno that Malaya wished to join Indonesia in independence. Apparently, Sukarno did not disclose Japan's decision, for when he revealed that Indonesian independence would be proclaimed in a matter of days and Yaacob promised to send a Malayan delegation, Sukarno reportedly shook hands with Yaacob and said: "Let us form one single motherland for all the sons of Indonesia." [51] Once back in Djakarta, however, Sukarno told the independence committee that—despite his own preferences and its intentions and hopes—Malaya, Portuguese Timor, and British Borneo could not be included within Indonesia. He added, however, that he would be "content" with the territory of the former Dutch East Indies.

Yet Indonesia's behavior since the 1962 Brunei revolt strongly suggests that Sukarno was never really "content." No Indonesian leader or group had a voice in the binding and effective decision to restrict Indonesia's sovereignty to the former Dutch territories. As Sukarno himself said at the time: "the Imperial Japanese government will decide what shall form the future State of Indonesia." [52] Japan did indeed make the decision, and it was one clearly not in accordance with the expressed wishes of the Indonesian leadership. If he wished, Sukarno could portray it today as a product of imperialism, and thus open to question.

Indeed, many developments in Indonesia since an independent Ma-

[51] R. Soenarno, "Malay Nationalism, 1896-1941," *Journal of Southeast Asian History,* I:1 (March 1960), 20-21.

[52] *The Territory of the Indonesian State, op. cit.,* p. 22.

laysia was proposed, have tended to confirm Yamin's conviction that his views were accepted in high places. For example, the statements issued since mid-1962 by Indonesia's many "mass organizations" on the subject of Malaysia—to say nothing of later official pronouncements—suggest a very strong and protective interest in almost all neighboring territories. Timor was often the focus of this attention, and Yamin himself commented that the Portuguese colony scarcely merited discussion inasmuch as public support for its eventual "recovery" by Indonesia could be taken for granted: "We must all say nothing now. Not until May 1963. Then we move." [53]

With those words Yamin indicated that not until the United Nations relinquished its temporary administration of West New Guinea would he and other Indonesian nationalists begin to clamor for the return of more "lost" territories. He did not doubt, however, that there already existed in Djakarta an environment conducive to a campaign against Malaysia.

IDEOLOGY AND THE PERCEPTION OF MALAYA

Malaya has been the subject of special attention on the part of Indonesia's leaders, who—for several years before the confrontation—revealed a certain hostility and condescension toward the neighboring government. Essentially, this attitude derived from two elements. The first is the conviction among Indonesia's leaders that Malaya supported the abortive 1958 rebellion, or at least allowed the rebels to use Malaya and Singapore as refuges and centers for their fiscal and informational activities. [54] Included in this suspicion is the belief that Malayan leaders harbored designs on Sumatra, and hoped that it would break away from Indonesia as a result of rebellion. Early in 1963 these elements of Indonesian hostility toward Kuala Lumpur received new stress, as in

[53] Interview with the author, Djakarta, August 1963.

[54] Malaysia denies giving any active help to rebels, but concedes that the rebels, "realising that their cause was bound to fail, escaped to the Federation to seek asylum here. . . . For purely humanitarian reasons the prime minister acceded to their request . . . after obtaining an undertaking from them that they would not participate in any further activities. . . ." Later, Dr. Subandrio proposed an Extradition Treaty between Malaya and Indonesia, and the Malayans responded that they would be favorably disposed except that the Indonesian included an "unprecedented request for an extradition of political refugees." This, Malaya felt, was in opposition to normal practice, and its refusal to sign such a treaty resulted in bitter press attacks on Malaya within Indonesia. *Malaya/Indonesia Relations* (Kuala Lumpur, 1963), pp. 5-6.

Subandrio's remark that in 1958 the Tunku had given the rebels "every kind of support" and that "it was his intention to incorporate Sumatra into Malaya." [55]

The second fundamental element in the Indonesian perception of Malaya is a peculiar dualism: a combination of jealousy and contempt. The seldom-expressed jealousy is aroused by Malaya's undoubted prosperity; the contempt derives from Malaya's failure to expel the British in the process of achieving independence. The most frequently encountered Indonesian criticism of Malaya can be stated simply: Malaya is a "backward" nation because she has not undergone a revolution. Strange as it may sound to Western ears, Indonesia—with full recognition of its deep economic distress—regards itself as historically the more "progressive" and advanced of the two. The expression of such heavily ideologized attitudes among uninformed Indonesians is not surprising, but it is not an exaggeration to say that almost everyone in a position of authority and responsibility in Djakarta describes Malaya in the same grossly distorted and stereotyped terms: *feudalist, colonialist, unrepresentative,* and *infantile.*

Of course, the language (though not always the practice) of politics in Indonesia generally bears a deep ideological imprint. Because government leaders view Indonesia as a nation still in the throes of revolution, the entire official dialogue between the leaders and the people— and much private discussion as well—is conducted in heavily ideologized tones.[56] Familiar slogans and symbols are repeated and new ones are invented. Because the fundamental ethic in this political ideology is a continuing revolution, the people are regularly exhorted to "do more" and "produce more" in the "struggle" against a seemingly endless list of reactionary groups and forces. Sometimes the internal "enemies"

---

[55] *Washington Post* (February 12, 1963), quoting Subandrio press conference. Djakarta Radio broadcast similar comments of Subandrio's several days later, to the effect that "Tunku Abdul Rahman dreamed of annexing Sumatra," and ANTARA, the official Indonesian news agency, reported that anti-Indonesia sentiments in Malaya were "very closely connected with the Tunku's plans of annexing the Indonesian island of Sumatra. Several rebel leaders of the PRRI rebellion are still living in Kuala Lumpur and are preparing a new subversive action." ANTARA, February 13, 1963.

[56] Of course, not everyone swallows the constant propaganda dosage. By late 1964 one of the refreshing developments within the country was the extent to which Indonesians would make it clear that they had long since reached the "saturation point." Yet there are millions who do believe what the government tells them, and almost total control over all information media reasonably assures Djakarta that its message, at the absolute minimum, will be the dominant one.

are the "greedy landlords" and property-owners; sometimes, the resident Chinese; and, most recently, selfishness, official corruption, and the high price of food. Whatever the target, however, the political atmosphere is always dominated by symbols and slogans. Indeed, nothing of potential political significance in Indonesia—not even athletics—escapes ideological characterization. When, for example, Sukarno was rebuffed by the International Olympic Committee for his refusal to permit Israel and Nationalist China to participate in the 1962 Asian Games in Djakarta, he declared his contempt for the action of the Committee, and promptly coined a new Orwellian slogan: Indonesia would be host to new athletic contests—GANEFO, the "Games of the New Emerging Forces."

This illustration is not frivolous, for even GANEFO is symbolic of Indonesia's foreign-policy perspectives. In recent years, an entirely new set of symbols, banners, and wall-scribblings has been in circulation, under the heading of NEKOLIM ("Neocolonialism and Imperialism")—for, as Sukarno and other Indonesian leaders have explained, the world is divided into two spheres: OLDEFOS ("Old Established Forces"), and NEFOS ("New Emerging Forces"), the latter led in Asia by Indonesia and destined to oust the old forces and control the future. Indonesia considers each of its immediate neighbors to be essentially in the camp of the OLDEFOS, while Malaya in particular was for years regarded as a most objectionable illustration of the old, imperialist-dominated world.

An illustration may be taken from conversations the author had (long before Malaysia was established) with one very well-known Indonesian, very well-read, regarded as something of a scholar and historian, and included, by observers long resident in Djakarta, among the most sensible, reasonable, and articulate of all Indonesians. He has since been appointed to an important ministry by President Sukarno. Yet he is as certain as the many less-informed Indonesian officials that Malaya is a British puppet, that "90 per cent of all Malayan rubber is in British hands" (a considerable exaggeration), and that the "British are the real problem in Malaya." This attitude is reinforced, of course, by the public remarks of Indonesia's leaders. In one of President Sukarno's earliest explanations of Indonesia's opposition to the proposed new state of Malaysia, he charged that Malaysia is the "product of neocolonialism," and added, in what must be regarded as neo-Marxism:

Correspondents, mark my words. Malaysia is to protect the safety of tin for the imperialists, Malaysia is to protect rubber for the imperialists and

Malaysia is to protect oil for the imperialists. For this reason we are determinedly opposed, without any reservation, against Malaysia.[57]

These and other comments suggest the depth of anti-Malaya and anti-Malaysia feeling among leading Indonesians. Indonesians, who achieved their independence only at the cost of a bloody and destructive revolution, have understandably bitter memories of the colonial experience. Their understandable concern, however, has been transformed into an eager willingness to pass judgment on the political achievements of other nations. They are also persuaded that Indonesia can cooperate fruitfully only with those nations which have a similar experience of bloody revolution. Many regard free-enterprise states, such as Malaysia and Japan, as horrible examples of chaos; the present prosperity of such nations is considered illusory and transitory, and their economic plenty a sickening waste.

Indonesians of this persuasion—including leaders—feel that it will be almost impossible to deal usefully with the present government of Malaysia. But, because they regard Abdul Rahman's regime as a feudal relic, they seem convinced that a revolution or other major change in Malaysia is inevitable. Indeed, they expect that all the now prosperous (and Western-aligned) Asian states will probably experience a fundamental change in their social and economic structures, by revolution or other means. When the inevitable changes take place, they believe, those states will suffer the same kinds of economic strictures that Indonesia presently endures. Only then will Indonesia be able to "accept" such nations and cooperate with them freely. As Indonesia's Deputy Foreign Minister Suwito said at the 1964 ministerial conference in Bangkok:

Malaysia is not a real Asian creation. We still see very clearly the British element. . . . The intention of Indonesia is we [would] like to welcome Malaysia. But really only as an Asian creation, formed with our help and with the help of the Philippines.[58]

These heavily ideologized notions about Malaysia were well-suited to serve as the "intellectual," semisophisticated foundation for the "Greater Indonesia" implications. In the past, it was possible only to

---

[57] Sukarno's speech of February 13, 1963, at the opening of the Joint Conference of the Central and Regional National Front Committees, Djakarta.

[58] Statement of Deputy Foreign Minister Suwito, from the records of the "Tripartite Ministerial Conference (Bangkok, February 5-10, 1964), second meeting of the political committee, February 9, 1964.

speculate that this would be Indonesia's tendency, but recent developments have removed some of the doubt. For example, at the 1964 summit meeting in Tokyo, Dr. Subandrio told the representatives of Malaysia and the Philippines that the "guerrillas and volunteers [in Sarawak and Sabah] have a deep political consciousness. They are struggling for a political objective. They are fighting for the independence of those people there from colonialism and imperialism." [59] This statement, of course, was made almost a full year after the withdrawal of British rule and long after the establishment of Malaysia. Yet it must not be forgotten that the Indonesian elite consider the peoples of Malaysia to be scarcely more liberated from colonial domination than the inhabitants of Portuguese Timor. As one writer recently remarked: "The Indonesian nationalist thinks that Malayan independence, being tainted by a continued British connection, is far from genuine. . . . The Jakarta appellation for the Tengku is *boneka*, 'puppet'!" [60] In a similar vein, a leading student of Indonesia's internal affairs has written:

> . . . a majority of politically-conscious Indonesians . . . cannot believe that Malaysia is independent. How can she be, they reason and believe, if she gained independence by negotiation, . . . encourages foreign private enterprise, [and allows] . . . military bases on her territory?" [61]

These attitudes, which existed long before an independent Malaysia was seriously contemplated, support the proposition that a base of animosity toward Kuala Lumpur already existed in Indonesia's ideology. Yet some observers—perhaps attributing more rationality to the Indonesian leadership than it possesses—could hardly believe that this animosity might lead to external political action, for they knew full well how severe are Indonesia's internal problems. A well-known observer, attempting to explain (and perhaps justify) Indonesia's arms purchases, assured his readers that Djakarta's military program must be understood only in the light of the New Guinea campaign, for "the Indonesian government continues to declare that it has no territorial ambitions." [62] It was true, he conceded, that the West Irian campaign

---

[59] Dr. Subandrio's statement from the records of the first foreign-ministerial meeting at the official residence of the Japanese foreign minister, June 18, 1964.

[60] Donald E. Weatherbee, "Indonesia and Malaysia: Confrontation in Southeast Asia," *Orbis* (Summer 1962), 339.

[61] Donald Hindley, "Indonesia's Confrontation with Malaysia: A Search for Motives," *Asian Survey* (1964), 904.

[62] Herbert Feith, "Indonesia's Military Hardware," p. 4. Mimeo. Carries the notation that "a slightly shortened version of this article was published in *Nation* [Sydney], November 3, 1962."

had served the purpose of internal groups, particularly the army, but a new "campaign for Portuguese Timor, East New Guinea, or British Borneo would probably have far less appeal. . . . The army leaders would almost certainly oppose an agitational campaign. . . ." [63] Finally, he wrote, Indonesia's need for "functional equivalents" to the New Guinea campaign could be met by tackling internal problems—"nor is external adventure needed to provide targets for aggression." Another writer, summing up the events of 1962, wrote that that year should "have marked the transition from a preoccupation with external affairs [i.e., New Guinea] . . . to domestic efforts focused on the . . . economy"; he found it "therefore surprising that Indonesia is now embarking on a course of action which may further delay the achievement of her people's welfare." [64]

But, against the background of Indonesia's perception of Malaya, it should not have been surprising. Moreover, the private statements of leaders in Djakarta and Kuala Lumpur during 1962 made it clear that relations between the two governments were under strain. Indeed, at the time of Yamin's death in October 1962, developments indicated that some of his beliefs had won wide support among the Indonesian leadership. Malaysia, after all, represented an effort to bring together in one state communities in which the Malay element was dominant, and it was Yamin's view (and not his alone) that any Pan-Malay movement, to be realistic, necessarily required Indonesia's leadership. Yamin had written as early as 1955 that "Greater Indonesia without Malaya is an illusion," and that "Pan-Malaya is dead, while Pan-Indonesia is flourishing." [65] In October 1962, as anti-Malaysia sentiment began to crystallize in Djakarta, an article in the left-wing newspaper, *Warta Berita,* dismissed the Malaysia proposal as "not realistic." Alleging that President Macapagal's proposed confederation and the Malaysia proposal itself were merely new attempts to lure Indonesia into SEATO, the article concluded that the establishment of Malaysia "is contrary to the independent development of the Indonesian state." [66]

[63] *Ibid.*

[64] Guy J. Pauker, "Indonesia: Internal Development or External Expansion?" *Asian Survey* (February 1963), 74.

[65] These comments, which also included Yamin's justification for an Indonesian claim to the entirety of Borneo, are found in Muhammad Yamin, *Sumpah Indonesia Raya* (Djakarta: N. V. Nusantara, n.d., ca. 1956), p. 34, quoted in Donald E. Weatherbee, "Indonesia and Malaysia: Confrontation in Southeast Asia, *Orbis* (Summer 1962), 342.

[66] *Warta Berita,* reported on Radio Indonesia, October 27, 1962.

That notion refers to the widespread conviction among Indonesians that their state, by far the largest in Southeast Asia, must necessarily exercise a controlling influence over its immediate neighbors.[67] Specifically, Indonesian leaders apparently share a belief that they cannot permit, at least without active opposition, transfers of territory which Indonesia may wish to claim or otherwise to influence. And this is no sudden concern, for Sukarno seems never to have given up his conviction, expressed in 1945, that "Indonesia will not become strong and secure unless the whole Straits of Malacca is in our hands." This conviction was reinforced by the 1958-59 Indonesian rebellion, for he and other leading Indonesians still carry a burning resentment that the territory of Malaya was used by the rebels.[68] This resentment should not be underestimated; it may be a major influence in the events which led to confrontation. Alien control over Malaya, and Indonesia's possession of "only the west coast of the Straits of Malacca," as Sukarno expressed it in 1945, "will mean a threat to . . . [Indonesia's] security." [69] In this same context Sukarno, almost two decades later, explained the confrontation with Malaysia:

> The Indonesian nation rejects the creation by the imperialists of a federation near its door, which endangers Indonesia. . . . You may still remember what happened at the time of the PRRI rebellion. At that time, where was the base from which the PRRI rebels operated to destory Indonesia? On the Malayan Peninsula.
>
> . . . Andi Selle committed treason . . . with whose aid? With aid from over there, from the territory now called Malaysia. Therefore, brothers, is it or isn't it right that Malaysia constitutes a danger to us? I say that we have black-and-white proof. . . . The whole Indonesian people feel truly that we must crush Malaysia to the end.[70]

It can probably be agreed that, although the extension of formal sovereignty over adjoining territories is not necessarily Indonesia's precise goal, Djakarta's leaders appear to hope for a dominant influence in Malaya. Of course, there is evidence that some Indonesian leaders also hope that some of the territories concerned, particularly in

---

[67] Hindley, *op. cit.*, p. 906, writes that "Indonesia demands at least consideration in any decisions affecting the political *status quo* in neighboring territories such as Malaysia."

[68] See Hindley, *op. cit.*, p. 907.

[69] *The Territory of the Indonesian State, op. cit.*, p. 21.

[70] From the major speech of President Sukarno "at a general roll call of volunteers to hear his action command," Djakarta, May 3, 1964. Broadcast on Radio Indonesia.

Borneo, might someday request inclusion in Indonesia. This would do away with the "enclaves" against which Yamin warned in 1945. Since 1962, there have been numerous Indonesian statements to the effect that, if the peoples of different parts of Malaysia indicate their desire to join the Indonesian state, Indonesia "would have no objections." Portuguese Timor, for example, has long been mentioned in this connection, and has been the cause of numerous Indonesian disclaimers. Even the Portuguese chargé d'affaires in Djakarta, in an interview early in 1963, remarked that "Indonesia has stated repeatedly that it has no claim over any territory which was not part of the former Dutch East Indies." [71] This accurately reflects the official Indonesian attitude, but it does little to calm those who are told that Indonesia will "support independence movements" in Timor, Borneo, and now, in Malaysia itself. The inspector-general of the Indonesian army commented: "If the people of Timor today or tomorrow started a revolution, . . . we would support them. . . . After independence, if they want to stay independent, fine. . . . If they want to join Indonesia, we will talk it over."[72]

THE GOAL AND ITS JUSTIFICATION

The rationale for these views is that Indonesia is obliged to support "oppressed" peoples. Indonesian Defense Minister Nasution made it clear that he had found plenty of evidence of "oppressed peoples, enslaved peoples," in nearby areas. Naming Timor and Borneo specifically, he went on to say that "every struggle of these oppressed peoples to free themselves from oppression will always find our support." [73] Earlier, the Indonesian army's chief of staff, General Jani, told his troops in Indonesian Borneo that "we give our fullest moral support to our friends [in British Borneo]," and he announced that his men were "awaiting the order" to move in support of those people "struggling for independence." [74] Nasution told Indonesian "irregulars" living near

---

[71] Radio Australia (Melbourne), January 19, 1963.

[72] Statement of Brigadier General Mokoginta, in interview with Warren Unna, *Washington Post* (May 10, 1963). No doubt the ground for "talking it over," so far as Malaysia is concerned, is by now already being prepared: by the end of 1964 Malaysian officials found that Indonesian guerrillas landing not far from Singapore were regular troops of the Indonesian army, whose uniforms had been altered by the addition of a new shoulder patch—bearing the inscription "Malayan National Army." Mokoginta has now become commander for Sumatra.

[73] *The New York Times* (May 9, 1963).

[74] *Washington Post* (February 2, 1963). Jani was among the generals murdered in the attempted coup of September 30, 1965.

the border with British Sarawak: "Remain on the alert, intensify your training, and support our brothers in northern Borneo. . . . You must keep up your struggle until our brothers obtain their independence." [75]

These statements, and the attitudes they reflect, differ strikingly from the norms of Western diplomacy, which is based on the principle of noninterference in the internal politics of other states. States in the West which have abandoned that principle have usually done so with reluctance, apologies, and due references to the "extreme" circumstances warranting the aberration. This rule, of course, suffered its deepest erosion in this century under Hitler: for example, the protection of the German minorities in other states proved to be a convenient disguise for intervention and aggrandizement. Communist ideology, on the other hand, views involvement in the affairs of other nations as a fundamental doctrine, and proudly describes such efforts as "wars of national liberation." This is the rationale that Indonesia has seized, on the pretext that the people of Malaya/Malaysia are not yet independent.

Of course, contemporary world politics are replete with examples of encouragement of "spontaneous" liberation movements, so that Indonesia's behavior is by no means unique. But at least let it be understood for what it is: not the unfortunate by-product of Indonesia's internal circumstances, but the actions of a state the leaders of which appear to have a set of external goals. No doubt, Indonesia's deep internal divisions have contributed to Sukarno's decision to "crush" Malaysia. But the argument that confrontation is the result of Indonesia's need for crisis—to keep together "the various balanced pieces of the governing coalition" [76]—over-emphasizes domestic politics to the point where it ignores a fundamental hypothesis: that important internal groups divided on domestic policies may nevertheless have common external goals. Failure to take that hypothesis into account may lead to near-futile debates on what one or another internal group "really" believes. Thus, while one expert argued that "the army leaders have a vested interest in foreign crisis," [77] another insisted (a few weeks before confrontation) that "the army leaders would almost certainly

---

[75] *The New York Times* (May 9, 1963). Not surprisingly, Nasution announced a few months later that his forces had indeed helped to train "more than 6000 anti-British, anti-Malaysia rebels in the Northern Borneo territories." *The New York Times* (September 3, 1963).

[76] Hindley, *op. cit.*, p. 909.

[77] *Ibid.*, p. 910.

oppose an agitational campaign. . . .[78] Both missed the point, which is that Indonesia's foreign policy is not merely the functional product of internal troubles. If that were so, Sukarno could have embarked upon almost any new campaign to weld together the dissident elements; according to this view he settled on the confrontation with Malaysia largely because that issue best satisfied internal requirements. But the facts seem to indicate otherwise; the decision to oppose Malaysia was made in an environment already conditioned for that goal. The important expansionist element in Indonesian political thought, reinforced by fundamental aspects of Indonesia's ideology and experience had produced a decidedly hostile attitude toward a government in Kuala Lumpur which would be indifferent to Indonesia's leadership.

In consequence, there is at least some ground for skepticism when Indonesian spokesmen stress that the principles of President Sukarno's leadership and policies preclude efforts at Indonesian control or territorial aggrandizement. Significantly, even Yamin stressed the peaceful nature of Sukarno's policies, although he carefully pointed out that the surrounding territories in Borneo, Timor, and Malaya should be regarded, *not* as fields for expansion, but as "lost" territories, so that efforts to restore them to their rightful owner must not be confused with attempts at aggression or aggrandizement.[79]

Nevertheless, even Yamin had counseled patience with regard to Indonesia's long-term goals. He had recognized, as he said, that it would not do for Indonesia to make its intentions known until the New Guinea problem was permanently settled. That affair, of course, had created some enmity toward Indonesia, and some governments wondered if Djakarta's appetite would, in fact, be satisfied by the cession of Irian Barat. Indonesian spokesmen bent over backwards to reassure those governments. At least twice in late 1961, once at the United Nations and once in the press, Dr. Subandrio himself had reminded the world that his government would have no further ambitions once New Guinea was incorporated:

---

[78] Feith, *op. cit.,* p. 5. The full sentence reads: "Indeed, the army leaders would almost certainly oppose an agitational campaign [against Timor or Borneo] because they fear social ferment, which they are generally less capable of handling than are the civilians."

Note the contrast with Hindley's remarks: "The army leaders would hope for far greater Indonesian influence over a number of small, poorer states," and that "To the officer corps the Malaysia 'crisis' must have appeared as a blessing to be cherished. No more talk of reducing army budgets. . . ." *Op. cit.,* p. 910.

[79] Interview with the author, Djakarta, August 1962.

We are not only disclaiming the territories outside the former Netherlands East Indies . . . but . . . when Malaya told us of its intentions to
merge with the three [sic] British Crown Colonies of Sarawak, Brunei, and
British North Borneo as one Federation, we told them that we had no
objections and that we wished them success with this merger so that everyone might live in peace and freedom.[80]

He had made the same point a few days earlier:

As an example of our honesty and lack of expansionist intent, one fourth
of the island of Kalimantan (Borneo) consisting of three Crown Colonies
of Great Britain, is now becoming the target of the Malayan government
for a merger. Of course, the people there are ethnologically and geo-
graphically very close to the others living in the Indonesian territory.
Still, we do not show any objection toward this Malayan policy of merger.
On the contrary, we wish the Malayan government well if it can succeed
with this plan.[81]

Ali Sastroamidjojo, a former premier of Indonesia, vehemently disagreed with Subandrio's professed disinterest in Malaysia. In his view,
Indonesia had a valid claim to all of the Borneo territories and (as he
said in September 1962) a very direct interest in Malaysia. In August
1962, Yamin—who had been counseling patience—called Subandrio's
comments "a stupid mistake."

The Timing and Pace of Confrontation

But events moved more quickly than even Yamin could have realized,
and it became necessary to discard the caution that he had urged. It
seems clear that the catalyst was the revolt in Brunei, which broke
out on December 8, 1962. Before that, Dr. Subandrio had only once
hinted publicly at the anti-Malaya and anti-Malaysia sentiments which
existed in Djakarta.[82] But, in the closing weeks of 1962, the likelihood
of some disturbances in the Borneo territories, particularly in Brunei
and Sarawak, was known to the military and intelligence authorities
of several governments; Djakarta, too, must have known. Indeed, the
British later attempted to explain their apparent surprise at the Azahari

[80] United Nations speech quoted in *Malaya/Indonesia Relations, op. cit.,* p. 12.
[81] *Ibid.,* p. 11, citing Subandrio's letter to *The New York Times* (November 13,
1961).
[82] *Straits Times* (September 27, 1962). Those remarks of Subandrio expressed
apprehension that Malaysian territories might be used by SEATO.

revolt on the grounds that events of this sort had been indicated before but had not come off. The Azahari revolt, more than any other event, signaled Indonesia's open opposition to the Malaysia proposals. It created the flux and instability around the Malaysia scheme that Indonesia needed to justify its open support and covert intervention. After December 8, 1962, restraint was obviously thrown off. Developments in Borneo in the first days after the revolt revealed a situation more susceptible to influence than it might ever be again. President Sukarno may have reasoned (as, the evidence indicates, President Macapagal reasoned) that unless formal objections to Malaysia were raised soon, the new federation probably would be established on schedule. What is certain is that President Sukarno decided at the end of 1962 that the establishment of Malaysia was not in Indonesia's interests and must be opposed.

HYPOTHESIS FOR SUKARNO'S TACTICS

This decision was entirely consistent with views expressed by Indonesian leaders many years earlier and with the then-current political attitude toward Malaya. Nevertheless, Indonesian spokesmen sought to explain the confrontation as something quite different from a desire to dominate or to incorporate Malaysia. Indeed, so many official explanations have been offered that two distinct possibilities arise: first, that President Sukarno has been eager to seize upon almost any pretext to continue the confrontation; and second that he has been seeking some face-saving way to drop a campaign that has proved more difficult than anticipated.

Those two conclusions do not necessarily contradict one another, for there is evidence that, once the confrontation was begun, President Sukarno came under considerable internal pressure to continue and expand it. This suggests the hypothesis that real external goals and an internal environment of hostility toward Malaya led to the decision to oppose Malaysia, but that Sukarno soon concluded the confrontation should be ended because it would not succeed. He found, however, that the campaign had developed a dynamism of its own, and he could not terminate it without exacting dramatic concessions. It is predictable, therefore, that if Sukarno is to cease his opposition to Malaysia, he can do so only under conditions that will persuade other Indonesians he has no other choice.

In that circumstance lies the probable explanation for the strange pace of confrontation, in which Indonesia's willingness—almost anxiety

—to negotiate some solution was accompanied simultaneously by her many demands.

Indonesia's objections to Malaysia have covered a wide range. First it charged that Malaysia would make Borneo a SEATO base,[83] then that it was designed to "encircle" Indonesia, and finally that it represented "colonialism," which it is in Indonesia's overriding interest to oppose.[84] As Sukarno said:

> We do not want to have neocolonialism in our vicinity. . . . Malaysia is the product of the brain and efforts of neocolonialism.[85]

Soon afterward, he added new reasons to oppose Malaysia, and new demands. In his May Day (1963) speech Sukarno stressed that it was the fate of the Borneo territories with which he was most concerned, and that they must be given their independence first. After that, Malaysia could be the subject of negotiation: "friendly talks, brothers— on whether or not we agree with the organization of Malaysia." [86]

Sukarno, however, was even then preparing the ground for talks—and without the prior independence of North Borneo as a condition. In early April, there were subministerial meetings in Manila to prepare for a three-way foreign ministers' conference,[87] and at the end of May

---

[83] *Straits Times* (September 27, 1962), reporting Subandrio's statement that if Malaysia put a military base in Borneo, Indonesia would take "counteraction": "If it is an American base," Subandrio said, "we shall then arrange for a Soviet base in our part of Borneo."

[84] On May Day 1963, Ruslan Abdulgani, the minister of information, spoke to "delegates" from independence movements around the world (including Malaya) and congratulated them on "your coming victory against colonialism in North Kalimantan [Borneo], Vietnam, Laos, the Congo, Angola. . . ." Radio Djakarta, May 2, 1963. And as we saw earlier, General Jani had said that his men were "awaiting the order" to support people "struggling for independence in North Borneo."

[85] From President Sukarno's speech of February 13, 1963, given at the opening of the Joint Conference of the Central and Regional National Front Committees.

[86] Sukarno's speech of May 1, 1963, reported on Radio Djakarta. In that speech Sukarno said "The stand of the Indonesian Republic, . . . the stand of Bung Karno, . . . is give freedom to Kalimantan Utara. After Kalimantan Utara has its independence, after it has its freedom, let us hold talks."

[87] See the joint final Communiqué, issued at the end of the Tripartite Subministerial Meeting, April 17, 1963, Appendix V in *Malaya/Philippine Relations* (Kuala Lumpur: 1964), p. 24. See also Appendix VI, p. 25. the joint communiqué issued by Presidents Macapagal and Sukarno, after their brief meeting on May 23rd. Sukarno, then on his way to Tokyo, "informed President Macapagal that he was ready to meet with the latter in order to thrash out problems existing between the three countries and that Foreign Minister Subandrio was also ready to meet with the foreign ministers of the Philippines and Malaya to lay the groundwork for the meeting of the Malay heads of government."

Sukarno invited the Tunku to join him in Tokyo. Just before he met with the Tunku, Sukarno approved a compromise settlement with the American oil companies operating in Indonesia. The settlement, it seemed, was a victory for reason and moderation—no mean achievement for Indonesia. The Indonesian government had also made a number of organizational changes and shifts in emphasis which seemed to indicate a more realistic concern with the pragmatic requirements of economic stabilization.[88] This willingness to negotiate, and to work toward economic stabilization, gave rise to hope in June-August 1963 that Indonesia might intend to settle down to more sober policies after all.

The Tokyo talks between Sukarno and the Tunku seemed to provide a better atmosphere for communication, and also "cleared the way for a meeting of foreign ministers" which they hoped would then lead to a summit conference in Manila.[89] The June 1963 Manila conference established important agreements, both for President Macapagal's Maphilindo—the loose three-nation confederation—and for Indonesia and the Philippines to "welcome the formation of Malaysia, provided the support of the people of the Borneo territories is ascertained by an independent and impartial authority, the Secretary-General of the United Nations or his representative." [90]

But the optimism was dispelled by new Indonesian demands, suggesting a pattern: "demand, talk, demand again." Early in July, Dr. Subandrio warned publicly that "active confrontation" would be renewed if the Borneo territories were "forced into Malaysia without their agreement by principle of self-determination." [91] He had already made it clear that "a referendum or a plebiscite is the way these things

[88] Indeed, on the Hong Kong and Singapore money exchange, the free-market rate for the *rupiah* began to move downward once again, demonstrating somewhat improved confidence in the government's internal programs and its ability to attract foreign capital.

[89] See the joint statement issued after the Tokyo meeting, June 1, 1963, Appendix XII in *Malaya/Indonesia Relations* (Kuala Lumpur; 1963), p. 44.

[90] "Report and Recommendations of the Conference of the Foreign Ministers of the Federation of Malaya, The Republic of Indonesia, and the Republic of the Philippines." (Manila: 1963), Article 10, p. 3. Mimeo. These recommendations were later incorporated into the Manila accords by the three presidents at their summit meeting in Manila, July 31, 1963. They are published in *Malaya/Indonesia Relations, op. cit.*, Appendix XIV, pp. 47-49.

[91] *Straits Times* (July 10, 1963). This was another occasion when Subandrio said that confrontation actually had its beginnings in 1957, when Malaya "supported" the Indonesian rebels in Sumatra.

usually are done." [92] At about the same time, Sukarno was making it altogether clear that confrontation was "on" again,[93] and Deputy Foreign Minister Sudjarwo charged that the determination of the peoples' will in Borneo "must be a sound and solid one. The usual form understood in the United Nations . . . is a referendum or a plebiscite." Indonesia, he said, would not recognize anything substantially less, and he did not think that U Thant would send a representative to Borneo "just for a week and then make his decision." When asked what Djakarta would do if no referendum were held, he warned that "the Federation of Malaysia will not be a strong one. . . . We will not welcome or support it." [94]

The Manila accords did not, of course, specifically provide for a referendum or a plebiscite, but only that the "support of the people of the Borneo territories [be] ascertained by . . . the Secretary-General." No doubt in recognition that no referendum would be held, and that Secretary-General U Thant's "ascertainment" might not prove favorable to Indonesia, Djakarta's leaders were casting about for a new tactic. In early July, when Foreign Minister Subandrio was asked what Indonesia's reaction would be to an "unfavorable" determination by the Secretary-General, he answered, "U Thant, after all, is only one man. . . . There is always the General Assembly." [95] There, as a result of Indonesia's long courting of the Afro-Asian nations, President Sukarno could still hope to find many friends.

Perhaps Sukarno hoped, through these demands for a plebiscite, to extract this and other concessions from Malaya as the price for his attendance at the Manila summit meeting scheduled for the end of July. Subandrio, of course, had already won considerable concessions at the June conference—most important, the agreement that the Secretary-General would ascertain the will of the Borneo peoples. It

[92] Interview with the author, Djakarta, July 4, 1963.

[93] On July 10 and 11 Sukarno made two speeches which were once again starkly hostile to Malaysia. He charged that confrontation was necessary "to maintain our security," and that Malaysia was itself a confrontation against Indonesia. Sukarno also added that the Tunku had betrayed his promise to Sukarno: "I declare to the world that Tengku Abdul Rahman . . . is a man who does not keep his word." Sukarno's speech to the officers of the West Java War College, quoted in the *Straits Times* (July 12, 1963).

[94] *Straits Times* (July 18, 1963).

[95] Interview with the author, Djakarta, July 4, 1963. In this implied threat to go "over the head" of the Secretary-General lies an early hint of that frustration with the United Nations that led later to Indonesia's withdrawal.

seemed inevitable that that must lead to another concession: at least a postponement of the date on which Malaysia might come into existence. This would be evidence of Indonesia's power to shape events in Southeast Asia. Moreover, in his address at the opening ceremony of the conference, Subandrio said he had come to Manila "because we felt it is our main responsibility to keep the peace, the security and stability in this region." It was no accident that, when the conference closed, the first operative article of the *Report* said the same thing: "that the three countries share a primary responsibility for the . . . security of the area." [96] It was no small accomplishment to have the Philippines (a SEATO member) and Malaya (a British Commonwealth nation) agree that neither America nor Britain had "primary responsibility" for the security of Southeast Asia.

But this was not enough for President Sukarno, who went to Manila to gain further concessions. Thus, when Sukarno left Manila at the close of the summit meeting, the joint statement now stipulated that foreign military bases were "temporary," and that none of the three countries would allow "arrangements of collective defense to serve the particular interests of any of the big powers." [97] Because Indonesia has long been a bitter critic of SEATO generally, and the British base in Singapore particularly, no one need doubt which country pressed for the inclusion of these stipulations. It was this provision that led Guy Pauker to conclude that the Manila accord "constituted a diplomatic triumph for Indonesia." [98]

Sukarno had extracted one further concession: postponement of the date on which Malaysia would come into existence. Sukarno had asked

[96] "Report and Recommendation . . . ," p. 1. The text of this article reads, in part: "The ministers were of one mind that the three countries share a primary responsibility for the maintenance of the stability and security of the area from subversion in any form or manifestation. . . ."

[97] The text of Article 11 is as follows: "The three heads of government further agreed that foreign bases—temporary in nature—should not be allowed to be used directly or indirectly to subvert the national independence of any of the three countries. In accordance with the principle enunciated in the Bandung Declaration, the three countries will abstain from the use of arrangements of collective defense to serve the particular interests of any of the big powers." Appendix VIII, in *Malaya/Philippine Relations*, p. 29. See also *Straits Times* (August 2, 1963), where Subandrio's dislike for the British Singapore base is reported—something he had pressed in Manila and June.

[98] He states there "it was no mean achievement for Indonesia . . . to have two of her neighbors who are tied to Western powers by military alliances state officially that Western bases were 'temporary in nature.'" Guy J. Pauker, "Indonesia in 1963: The Year of Wasted Opportunities," *Asian Survey*, IV:2 (February 1964), 689.

the Tunku for a delay when they met in Tokyo, and had been refused;[99] indeed, the Tunku said again on the eve of the summit talks that no change in the date would be made: "If this does not come about on August 31, we will be admitting defeat." [100] But midway through the summit talks, reports circulated that Kuala Lumpur was no longer insisting on that date,[101] and when the Tunku returned home he conceded that he was prepared to postpone the date for a few days "if necessary." [102]

Thus Sukarno had done much better in Manila than Subandrio had —even the establishment of Maphilindo might be seen as a victory for Indonesia, for it provided a potential framework for Indonesia's leadership of the Malay peoples—and some observers expected that these new concessions would make it possible for Sukarno to back away from the confrontation.

But although Maphilindo was given great public emphasis in Indonesia, it was never taken very seriously by the Indonesian leadership.[103] Of the three nations involved, only the Philippines ascribed real potential or importance to the new group (largely because of the North Borneo claim).[104] Yet from Djakarta's viewpoint, there seemed little to complain about in Maphilindo. The tone of the Manila proceedings suggested that they had been dominated, almost dictated, by Sukarno. The joint statement is replete with concepts generally identi-

---

[99] *Straits Times* (June 6, 1963). The Tunku said that Sukarno had asked him repeatedly not to mention this August 31st date, "but I told him I could not do this. The other territories concerned had all agreed to August 31."

[100] *Straits Times* (July 26, 1963), reporting the Tunku's remarks a few days before his departure for Manila.

[101] *Straits Times* (August 5, 1963).

[102] *Straits Times* (August 7, 1963), quoting the Tunku.

[103] This statement is based on a number of conversations with officials in Djakarta, all of whom saw Maphilindo as a "nice idea" but without substance for the present. Dr. Subandrio said that the notion of a practical Malay Confederation was at least ten or twenty years premature, and would have to wait until Malaya and the Philippines developed to the same level of "national consciousness" that Indonesia had, or at least was striving to achieve.

[104] Aside from domestic political capital, the Philippines extracted a concession from Malaya: an agreement, to which all three governments subscribed in the Manila accords, "to exert their best endeavors to bring the claim to a just and expeditious solution by peaceful means, such as negotiation, conciliation, arbitration, or judicial settlement. . . ." *Malaya/Indonesia Relations*, p. 48. This is the paragraph that has continued to plague relations between Malaysia and the Philippines, because Manila insists on "judicial settlement" as the only means of settling the dispute, while Kuala Lumpur points to the Manila accord and says that several other techniques were agreed upon, such as "negotiation, conciliation," and so on.

fied with Indonesia: in its one page there are two major references to
the Bandung Conference and the Bandung Declaration (by which
the three signatories were "inspired") ; a reference to "the spirit of
Afro-Asian solidarity"; a pledge to hold regular consultations to be
known as "Mushawarah Maphilindo," and finally, an acknowledgement
that the three nations are "new emerging forces." [105] These acknowl-
edgements, relatively new to Kuala Lumpur, and only slightly less so
to the Philippines, had to be considered as victories for Sukarno, and
they were presented as such to the Indonesian public.

But it soon became clear that at least some groups in Indonesia
were not yet satisfied. While Djakarta's press reflected the tone set by
Merdeka's comment that even the June ministerial talks were a "great
success," the pro-Communist *Bintang Timur* and the PKI's *Harian
Rakyat* "published no news at all about the talks." [106] This is not
surprising, for—from the Communist viewpoint—both Subandrio and
Sukarno had brought home nothing but words. Sukarno had not, after
all, persuaded the Tunku to agree to a referendum or a plebiscite for
the Borneo territories. But it is doubtful that any concession would
have satisfied the Communists, and they probably hoped that the
fragile understanding between Sukarno and the Tunku would be
broken by new demands. From their viewpoint, the very establishment of Malaysia was a setback in Southeast Asia. The PKI had always been in the vanguard of the anti-Malaysia campaign, [107] and had
criticized any actions which seemed to permit Malaysia's establishment
—though avoiding direct attacks on Sukarno. Thus, only days after the
summit conference, new demands were heard, and Sukarno, though he
had been given much of what he asked for, responded. Again, the demands concerned the "method" of ascertainment.

Djakarta may have wanted to call into question the wisdom of the
Secretary-General himself, but Sukarno chose a far less prestigious
target: the personnel and procedures of the United Nations team. It

[105] See *Malaya/Indonesia Relations,* Appendix XIII, pp. 45-46.

[106] *Merdeka* wrote: "The achievements attained in Manila constitute a mile-
stone in bringing the nations concerned closer toward the ideal of independence."
Other papers at least published the text of the foreign-ministers' statement on
their front pages. *Straits Times* (June 14, 1963).

[107] A PKI party resolution as long back as December 1961 attacked the Malaysia
proposal as "neocolonialism" and an effort "to suppress the democratic and
patriotic movements of the peoples in these five countries [Malaya, Singapore
Sabah, Sarawak, and Brunei] which aim at the attainment of genuine national
independence and freedom from imperialism." See *Malaya/Indonesia Relations*
Appendix XI.

soon became obvious that the "ascertainment" that U Thant agreed to undertake would not be a referendum, and thus there would be no justification for demanding from Malaya a very long delay in Malaysia's establishment. It should not be overlooked, of course, that Kuala Lumpur was certain enough of its position to allow two foreign governments to prescribe the conditions under which they would "welcome" the new federation, and those two had agreed that whatever satisfied the Secretary-General would satisfy them too. This was a striking concession for a state to make, and one that it was certainly not obliged to undertake.[108]

Nevertheless, as soon as the United Nations team arrived in the Borneo territories, Indonesian opposition began to mount. The first charge was that there was insufficient time to undertake a "proper" ascertainment—though Malaya had already postponed its "birthdate" by two weeks to allow the United Nations mission more time. Then there arose the question of "observers." The Manila agreements had not specified that there *must* be observers, let alone how many. It was agreed merely that the three governments "deem it desirable to send observers to witness the carrying out of the task [by the United Nations]," [109] and that Malaya would ask the British to cooperate and admit observers. During the last weeks of August, however, Indonesia —and also the Philippines (which seemed now to be quite under Djakarta's influence in this affair)—demanded thirty "observers" each —while there were only eight members of the United Nations team! The British pointed out the difficulty even of finding accommodation and making suitable transport arrangements for so many on short notice, and added that Manila and Djakarta could reasonably be satisfied with a number of observers equal to the United Nations team. In the end the British announced that they would issue visas for four observers from each country, each of whom was to be accompanied by a "clerical assistant." Foreign Minister Lopez of the Philippines promptly

---

[108] Malaya was, in fact, obligated to no authority outside Britain (which was relinquishing its colonial control in Borneo) and the projected Malaysia territories, to "prove" that the people there favored the new arrangement. By a series of elections and other steps, these requirements had been met. Whether or not they were the best-run elections in the world is really beside the point—if one accepts the principle of noninterference in the internal affairs of other, even neighboring states.

[109] It was Subandrio who asked for the "observers" in the first place, but U Thant stated that "I wish to make it clear that the working teams working under supervision of my representative will be responsible directly and exclusively to me."

retorted that he did not care what they were called, but his clerical assistants "were also expected to carry out the task of observers," [110] and the Indonesian contingent reportedly included an army colonel as one of their "clerical assistants."

Nevertheless, President Sukarno launched a series of bitter attacks on the entire United Nations operation, maintaining that it was not "democratic." Lawrence Michelmore, the international civil servant to whom U Thant had entrusted the thankless task, was attacked consistently by Indonesian spokesmen as a tool of OLDEFOS—for Michelmore is an American. It did not matter that the United Nations team included representatives of the "neutral" nations, as well as of the Soviet bloc (U Thant's deputy representative was G. Janacek, a Czech national), nor even that the leader of the Indonesian "observers" had pronounced the task well done.[111] Finally, of course, it did not matter that the mission fulfilled the terms of the Manila accords—for Secretary-General U Thant announced that the survey's results indicated the Borneo peoples wished to join Malaysia. For Sukarno decided he could not agree to the establishment of Malaysia, "in spite of the announcement made by the . . . Secretary-General, because the procedures agreed upon in Manila . . . were not followed properly." [112] It was difficult to tell from Sukarno's remarks exactly what aspects he disagreed with—the Tunku's public announcement that Malaysia would be formed on September 16th,[113] the number of Indonesian observers, the fact that the United Nations team had not talked with everyone in Borneo, or the fact that the entire ascertainment could have taken longer. But what he wanted became clear enough a week after Malaysia was established:

> Please *reascertain* the wishes of the Kalimantan Utara people. *Do it over again,* because the procedures followed before were not in line with the Manila agreement. Please do it over again. And let me repeat it here:

[110] *Straits Times* (August 24, 1963).

[111] In Singapore, on his way back from his "observations" in Borneo, the leader of the Indonesian observers, Brigadier Otto Abdul Rachman, stated that the United Nations team had conducted its survey "impartially."

[112] Sukarno's speech in Jogjakarta, September 25, 1963.

[113] By a provision in Malaya's laws, it was a statutory requirement that any new date for the formation of Malaysia be proclaimed before August 31, 1963. The Indonesian government was informed of this when a special representative was sent from Kuala Lumpur to meet Dr. Subandrio. In accordance with this requirement, and with the Secretary-General's agreement that he would complete his survey by September 14, Malaya changed its law at the end of August and fixed the new date at September 16.

If after the procedures agreed upon in Manila have been followed and it is proven that the majority of the Kalimantan Utara people is pro-Malaysia, we shall say O.K. But if the procedures are not followed, we shall not accept Malaysia.[114]

Later, President Sukarno elaborated on his complaints:

Thus, what Michelmore did in behalf of the United Nations was not according to democratic procedures; not in conformity with [United Nations] Resolution No. 1541; not in conformity with sub-Article 9 of Article 2, which had been agreed upon by Macapagal, Sukarno, and Tunku Abdul Rahman Putra.

Something else happened which really pained us. Before Michelmore completed his work—which took only a few days, to boot—even before Michelmore completed his work, on 16 September [sic], Britain and the Tunku proclaimed Malaysia. They did not even wait for the outcome of the Michelmore mission. Even before Michelmore completed his work, they proclaimed Malaysia on 16 September. This was the greatest humiliation of Indonesia and the Philippines, brothers and sisters.

There was an agreement signed by the Philippines President, Macapagal; an agreement signed by the President of the Indonesian Republic, which has a population of 103 million. This agreement was torn up, like a scrap of paper, by the British on 16 September; even before Michelmore had completed his survey work which was undemocratic, Malaysia was proclaimed.

This was the reason why Indonesia said: "We do not want to recognize such a Malaysia." We said plainly, "We do not want to recognize it." [115]

These and many other "explanations," ranging from fundamental political objections against Malaysia to disagreements over trifles,[116]

---

[114] Sukarno speech of September 25, 1963. Italics added.

[115] From Sukarno's speech at volunteer roll call rally, April 13, 1964. It should be noted that there is one quite major inaccuracy in President Sukarno's charge against Malaysia. It is not true that the Tunku formally proclaimed the formation of Malaysia before the United Nations team's work was known. U Thant's letter to the Tunku is dated September 13, 1963. It states: "I attach herewith the conclusion which I have undertaken to communicate to your government on the basis of the report of the United Nations Malaysian Mission." The Tunku announced formally, one day later (September 14th) that Malaysia would come officially into existence on September 16th.

[116] Thus, in Sukarno's speech just quoted, certain minor details (the procedures of the Michelmore mission and the date of the Tunku's public announcement) are cited: "This was the reason why Indonesia said: 'We do not want to recognize such a Malaysia.'" Compare that with one of Subandrio's remarks, going to more fundamental issues: "The Indonesian attitude . . . constitutes a matter of principle, because Indonesia is against imperialism and colonialism." Subandrio, in an interview with Australian Television, Ltd., on October 3, 1963.

might suggest that Sukarno will seize upon almost any pretext to continue the confrontation. But there is, simultaneously, much other
evidence which suggests that he *does* want a settlement. This apparent
contradiction led to the hypothesis suggested earlier: that President
Sukarno decided to end the confrontation some months after it began,
but found he would not be able to do so until he could convince the
more rabid opponents of Malaysia that he had extracted every concession and exhausted every approach, and that Indonesia faced no
other choice.

The evidence to substantiate this hypothesis unfolds once we examine events after late 1963, when Sukarno began more openly to use
"volunteer" troops in Malaysia. The steps were the Robert Kennedy
mission, with the resulting cease-fire request, and Sukarno's quick
agreement; the talks at Bangkok, where again Indonesia was seeking
a basis for settlement; and finally the 1964 summit in Tokyo, where
Sukarno grasped at the first suggestion for a settlement that came
along. The content of those steps suggests that Indonesia's Malaysia
policy since June 1963 is explicable if seen as an exercise in building
and drawing upon political support. Sukarno's task has been to impose, on certain of his recalcitrant supporters, his intention to end the
confrontation, but he apparently perceives that he can no longer do
this by fiat alone. Thus he must achieve real gains which show that
Indonesia *can* cease confrontation, and he must present convincing
evidence that "larger forces" tend to *require* that action.

The real concessions Sukarno won early in the Manila talks of June
and July 1963 demonstrated that Indonesia's will had been effective,
and that the "diplomatic triumph" achieved there established a
"larger force." For Maphilindo meant a rationale, larger than Indonesia, within which to accept unpalatable decisions.[117] Yet, it is now
clear, President Sukarno needed more.

[117] The *Indonesian Herald* (a mouthpiece for the foreign ministry)—comment-
ing on Indonesia's willingness to end confrontation and on Subandrio's willingness
to go to Bangkok to talk with Thanat Khoman—stressed first that Sukarno's
policies were effective: "The confrontation policy itself is beginning to achieve
the desired results. The influences of colonialist interests [read *Singapore*] in the
foreign-trade economy of Indonesia are rapidly being uprooted and new avenues
for fair trade with other countries [read *Philippines*] of the world are being
opened."
    Then the *Herald* pointed to the "GANEFO movement" as evidence that Indonesia
was being given the overwhelming support of the new emerging forces; and denied the "British myth" that Indonesia is a "cornered rat."
    "The fact that [Subandrio] has shown willingness to help re-establish a normal

The first opportunity to try for more was offered by Robert Kennedy's appeal for a cease-fire. This, Sukarno could accept—citing the larger appeal made to him by all that Kennedy represented and thereby absolving himself from much of the responsibility for the cease-fire.[118] Thus, a few weeks later, talks began in Bangkok to provide a "political settlement" which, it was hoped, would solidify the cease-fire. During the course of those talks, Sukarno's dilemma was made exquisitely clear by Deputy Foreign Minister Suwito:

> So we now come to a new step. We have agreed to stop firing. I hope it can be understood the serious effort on our side to take this new step, that is, to stop firing. I hope you realise our President, being the Supreme Leader of the Revolution, has used all his influence to bring about a cease-fire despite so many difficulties. We have taken many steps to come together. *I must be frank to you all. This coming to Bangkok was not entirely agreeable to many groups in Indonesia.* Yet our President agreed. . . . So now, we expect our friends from Kuala Lumpur to make things easier for us to welcome Malaysia. *As we said in Manila, to make our task easier.*[119]

The day before, Suwito had spoken in a similar vein:

> We have explained in Manila last year that *the implementation of the Manila agreement was meant to provide us with evidence to convince* our people in Indonesia that Malaysia was really wanted by the people of Sarawak and Sabah. . . . We know that Malaysia will come one day but *we would like to have proof which we can show to our people to convince those who are not very happy with the project* that Malaysia is really according to the wishes of the people . . . but . . . [shortcomings in the ascertainment made it] very difficult for our people to believe that Malaysia was really wanted.[120]

---

state of affairs in Southeast Asia *at a time when events are turning in favor of Indonesia* . . . is a commendable attitude. Magnanimity in the sight of . . . victory is an attribute of greatness." Finally, the *Herald* pointed to the framework for settlement: "Now the problem appears to be with the leaders of 'Malaysia.' . . . Has Britain shown any indication that it would welcome a *revitalized Maphilindo, a collective expression of self-determination of the Malay peoples?*" *Indonesian Herald* (November 15, 1963). Italics added.

[118] Of course, as noted earlier, Kennedy was hardly out of the country when Sukarno made one of his fire-eating speeches and promised that, although there might be a cease-fire, Indonesia's goals had not changed. Confrontation, he stressed, was still on. This action is not surprising, given the difficult requirements of Sukarno's task: to give in without appearing to.

[119] From the records of the Tripartite Ministerial Conference, February 9, 1964. Mimeo. Italics added.

[120] *Ibid.*, February 8, 1964. Italics added.

Thus, the Bangkok talks should be seen as part of a continuing effort to bring an end to the confrontation. President Macapagal and his "special emissary," Lopez, worked hardest to bring Indonesia and Malaysia together, and it is clear that Indonesia was willing to have the effort made. But Kuala Lumpur continued to insist that no real progress could be made toward a solution and a new meeting until the Indonesian guerrillas were withdrawn from Malaysian soil. Finally Lopez's visits to Djakarta and Kuala Lumpur achieved some success: at the end of May, Sukarno dropped his insistence that he would order only a "token" withdrawal, and the Tunku dropped his insistence on a "complete" withdrawal. The summit meeting then met (June 18, 1964) on the vague agreement that some withdrawal would take place "simultaneous" with the beginning of the leaders' talks in Tokyo, and the last round of high-level diplomacy on the Malaysia dispute began.

THE LAST SUMMIT

The Tokyo summit was characterized by two important developments: Indonesia's acceptance of additional checkpoints in Borneo, so that Malaya could be satisfied that more than a mere "token" withdrawal was being undertaken; and the acceptance in principle, by both sides, of President Macapagal's suggestion that the solution to the Malaysia problem be entrusted to a four-nation Afro-Asian commission. These achievements were preceded by several important statements which not only illustrate the fundamentally different approaches taken by Malaysia and Indonesia, but also help to substantiate the hypothesis that Sukarno was eager, under certain conditions, to end confrontation.

The Malaysian approach was characterized by traditional Western concepts of international relations. Indonesia's arguments, on the other hand, were altogether different—particularly in the willingness to regard the threat and use of force as a legitimate political instrument. At the first session, Deputy Premier Tun Abdul Razak of Malaysia outlined the basis of the problem: "There are troops in our country which have no right to be there. So, if these troops are removed and withdrawal takes place, . . . it will be very easy to resolve our dispute and we can surely live in peace as neighbors." [121] Subandrio immediately answered:

[121] This, and all following quotations, come from "Records of the First Foreign Ministerial Meeting held at Official Residence of Japanese Foreign Minister on June 18, 1964" (13 pp.); "Record of the Meeting of Heads of Government held

. . . Tun Razak in his speech said that the only issue between Indonesia and Malaysia is the presence of guerrillas [in Borneo]. According to Malaysia, if the guerrillas are withdrawn, then there will be no more trouble and our problem will be solved.

But I hope Malaysia will try and understand why it is not so easy for us to say "withdraw" and to expect the guerrillas to obey our command. . . . The guerrillas and volunteers have a deep political consciousness. They are struggling for a political objective. They are fighting for the independence of those people there from colonialism and imperialism.

. . . So even if we wanted to treat this question of withdrawal as a simple matter of physical, military withdrawal, we cannot succeed. The only basis for this question is to regard it as a political problem, not a military one.

Razak, adhering to the traditional concept that states are either at peace or at war with one another, seemed almost unable to understand Subandrio: "I cannot see how we can hold a summit if there is not going to be a genuine withdrawal and a genuine intention to withdraw." The word *genuine* was apparently the key, for a few moments later Subandrio announced: "I have talked to General Yani who is now prepared to issue an order for three additional checkpoints [to verify withdrawal]. But . . . this does not mean there can be complete withdrawal before the summit." Tun Razak answered: "That's good. We want to see a genuine effort made."

On that basis the meeting could continue, and the discussion turned to the question of an agenda. Subandrio hinted what Indonesia's position would be:

It is the fault of the British who interfered with the procedures laid down in the Manila agreements.[122] Any difficulties which may have arisen between us are due to a breach in the spirit of the Manila agreements. Therefore, we have to return to the spirit of the Manila agreements. This is our principle.

When the three heads of government met two days later, Sukarno took the same position, and suggested that the "real" reason for his opposition to Malaysia was that Britain had humiliated Indonesia, "threaten-

on June 20, 1964, at 9:30 A.M." (9 pp.); "Record of the Meeting of Foreign Ministers held on June 20, 1964, at 3:30 P.M." (5 pp.); and "Record of the Meeting of Heads of Government held on June 20, 1964, at 4:45 P.M." (4 pp.). Mimeo. In author's possession.

[122] Presumably Dr. Subandrio meant Britain's refusal to grant visas to the thirty Indonesian "observers" in September of the previous year.

ing us and making all sorts of obstacles." A clearly important factor in Sukarno's decision-making is his concern with Indonesia's national image. And indeed, if the hypothesis is correct (that Sukarno wants a settlement, but must avoid any impression that he has been bested), Indonesia must not allow any "humiliation." Thus there appears to be a fundamental importance in Subandrio's striking admission during these talks that ". . . *the outcome* [of the United Nations ascertainment] *is immaterial but don't make us a laughing-stock.*"

At this point, the session began to flounder in a sea of charges and countercharges. Indonesia insisted on a return to the *status quo ante* Manila. President Macapagal, whose efforts had brought about the meeting, acknowledged that "there is now a difference of opinion on the implementation of the Manila agreements. But . . . Asian nations . . . find a way to solve their own problems." For a few agonizing moments, both Sukarno and the Tunku urged Macapagal to be more specific. Finally, he announced:

> Each of us will select an Asian or African nation. Then these will unanimously elect one more. The four-man commission will be given a time limit. That is my humble way of perpetuating and expanding the Manila agreement.

The Tunku replied that, although he had to consult with his colleagues, he accepted the Philippine proposal "in principle." The session ended with Sukarno saying: "I accept."

The last session of the summit meeting proved to be the most interesting. It was clear that Malaysia was still unwilling to accept the presence of foreign troops on its soil, but it was not at all clear how the proposed Afro-Asian commission would resolve that problem. Kuala Lumpur wanted an end to confrontation "in all its forms." And Subandrio once again stressed:

> You say Malaysia is a *fait accompli.* . . . From our point of view we have a conflict about the formation of Malaysia. Our guerrillas and volunteers are helping to liberate the people there. This is a political problem and not a physical or military problem.

The drift of the Indonesian argument soon became clear: Indonesia was willing to withdraw its troops, but President Sukarno was not willing to take the responsibility for that action. His immediate—indeed, eager—acceptance of the Afro-Asian commission had already hinted at that. The debate over the connection (if any) between the proposed commission and the problem of troop withdrawal revealed Sukarno's goal: to be able to cite and draw upon the larger, external authority of a four-nation commission—which, he knew, would recommend troop withdrawal anyway. In the meantime, Indonesia was prepared to continue its clearly futile incursions in Borneo[123] because Sukarno was unwilling to return to Djakarta and announce that *he* had agreed to withdraw the troops. The records of the meeting support this theory.[124]

The Tunku, opening the session, asked once more: "How can we have peace and look into this question of Malaysia when all these acts of aggression are taking place?" Macapagal, attempting to mediate, explained that "before the commission reports there must be good conditions." The Tunku, taking *good conditions* to mean *troop withdrawal,* answered: "that must be done before the formation of the commission." Subandrio disagreed:

Subandrio: We must start from the existing conditions of the conflict. A commission is appointed to find a solution to the problems arising from the existing conditions.

Macapagal: What do we do before the commission completes the report?

Sukarno: We wait. It is the job of the commission to find ways to stop the conflict quickly.

Tunku: Then everything goes on—confrontation and conflict?

Subandrio: We are confronting because of the formation of Malaysia. . . . The commission is to sort out our differences. . . .

Tunku: The aggression is always against us, which amounts to nonrecognition of our sovereignty and our right to secure our own territory from trespass and aggression. It is not just political. It is an act of war. . . . Whatever political differences we may have, you have gone further by attacking us. . . .

Sukarno: It is for the commission to suggest the pulling-out of guerrillas.

Tunku: That is not their work. It is to be expected that . . . [nations] should not attack their neighbors. The commission is to suggest how to be friendly again.

Subandrio: It is *not* an act of aggression. The commission is to recommend on *all* [sic] aspects as they go along.

Razak: There are only two ways open to us: peace or war. You cannot have it both ways. You can't have both methods at the same time.

---

[123] In November 1964, the author asked a senior spokesman in Djakarta to explain what could be accomplished by the continuing losses of Indonesian young men, as soon as they landed in Malaysia. With remarkable cynicism, he answered: "We can lose twenty, thirty every month . . . so what . . . what does it matter?"

[124] Except as noted, all italics in the following added by author.

If Indonesia does not like Malaysia—all right—but there is no justification for aggression. We are under a threat to agree to a solution. An independent country cannot accept that.

Macapagal: As I see it, withdrawal will continue under the supervision of the commission.

Razak: The Thais should be told how long this withdrawal should take.

Macapagal: The idea is that the commission will not be formed until the withdrawal is completed?

Razak: Yes, there is no time [to be lost]. We can work out the terms of reference later.

Tunku: We can't go on now with all these troops in our country. We shall have given in under pressure. We would rather be crushed and perish.

Subandrio: We are not aggressors, since Malaysia is not in existence. But how can you impose on Indonesia conditions without some political solution? We accept President Macapagal's plan.

As the meeting drew to a close, the Tunku began to make clear his prime objection to the proposed commission: although the idea was a good one, he could not justify in his own country an agreement permitting foreign aggression to continue indefinitely. Sukarno recognized the crux of the issue: "So you have come here willing to talk *after* guerrillas have gone out?" The Tunku responded that he had come to talk for peace, but that what Sukarno was asking was too much: "Only *I* am giving in. And I can't give in on this military question." Then Sukarno, in a remarkable statement revealing that peace is not enough for Indonesia, said to President Macapagal: "You have told me to find a *solution* and not just peace." Macapagal suggested that withdrawal might be completed "at the same time as the report of the commission is submitted." But this was not enough for Sukarno: "No, no. All withdrawal is in conformity with the progress of the political settlement. We stick to that."

It now became altogether clear that Macapagal's proposal would provide innumerable opportunities for confrontation to continue, should Sukarno deem that necessary, whatever the recommendations of the commission. President Macapagal suggested that the commission could work under a deadline—say, three months—during which time "withdrawal takes place and the commission will be able to work out something." This, Indonesia refused to accept:

Sukarno: So the commission reports to us? No. The idea is that *after the commission has submitted its various recommendations,* when I

OK one recommendation and Rahman OK's it, *I pull out some. Then some more.* That is my standpoint.

Tunku: And all the time your guerrillas are in our territory? The question of withdrawal is part of the condition of this meeting and not to be treated as a concession in this dispute. . . .

Sukarno: Whatever decision or suggestion the commission makes, I shall accept. But I won't prescribe [for] the commission.

Tunku: There must be terms of reference and procedure, otherwise it will cause a lot more trouble than we have bargained for. *Cease all acts of aggression; then I shall agree to the appointment of a commission.*

Sukarno, announcing now that he understood the two conflicting positions, left for a television interview. Thus, the final session of the summit meeting on the Malaysia dispute came to an end.

Two fundamental patterns of Indonesia's policy were explained and developed at this summit meeting. The first pattern was President Sukarno's willingness—indeed, eagerness—to seize upon the notion of an international commission to settle the dispute, although there was no reason to think that its recommendations would differ from those President Macapagal might make or any of the three parties themselves could develop within the framework of Maphilindo. After all the years of Indonesian emphasis on the Afro-Asian bloc, however, it was reasonable for President Sukarno to hope that a solution recommended by such a commission would be acceptable *in Djakarta.*

The second clear pattern was Sukarno's hope that he could continue to apply the threat and use of force as a weapon against Malaysia. The device would demonstrate to Djakarta extremists that Indonesia was continuing to "chew" Malaysia (and that any settlement would be on the insistence of friendly Afro-Asian forces). Also, Sukarno's veto on troop withdrawal would continue to provide him with latitude to extract new concessions from Malaysia—even as the Afro-Asian commission did its work. It is clear, of course, that Indonesia feels no need to apologize for its use of force. As Subandrio said: "We are not aggressors, since Malaysia is not in existence." This doctrine, later expounded with awful clarity in the Security Council debates—combined with Indonesia's expansionist sentiment and its modern self-imposed obligation to support "oppressed peoples"—provides a formidable basis for any aggressive action.

After the Tokyo summit meeting broke up in June, there were no further negotiations, but Indonesian incursions into Malaysian territory continued and increased. In September 1964, Malaysia took its case to the United Nations Security Council. There, although the Soviet veto prevented the Council's resolution from being adopted, Malaysia clearly won recognition that its sovereignty had been violated. The nine-to-two vote, which indicated that Indonesia had overestimated its support among the newly emerging forces, must have infuriated President Sukarno. Moreover, although he had promised that he would "crush" Malaysia by "the time the first cock crows on New Year's Day 1965," nothing particular happened on that day. It had never seemed likely that Indonesia would launch full-scale aggression against Malaysia, and yet Sukarno had to do something to demonstrate to his people that Indonesia was not standing still. Thus, immediately after New Year's Day, President Sukarno announced that Indonesia was leaving the United Nations and all its agencies. It seemed, as Guy Pauker had suggested earlier, that Indonesia's policies "got out of hand, and . . . she [found] herself incapable of terminating an understandable but unfortunate episode." [125]

Conclusions

Because Indonesia is potentially, and perhaps already, the most important state in Southeast Asia, the main elements in its foreign policy should now be recounted. As we have seen, certain goals, related to a position of Indonesian dominance in the region, have been common to the attitudes of its leaders. Clear evidence of the "Greater Indonesia" thesis is found in the statements of Sukarno himself, and its crudest manifestation is the willingness of some Indonesian leaders to accept certain expansionist goals. Frequently, the adoption of policies in pursuit of these goals has been justified by charging that the territories in question are, in fact, Indonesian, though separated from the motherland by "historical accident." One product of these attitudes is that within the Indonesian leadership there are objective, or real, foreign-policy goals.

Moreover, the Indonesian political environment contained important anti-Malayan sentiments long before the Malaysia concept was seriously proposed. These sentiments derive from several sources, among them, the notion that Indonesia is the "natural" leader of the Malay peoples and is culturally "superior" to present-day Malaya. A more mundane source of hostility was Indonesia's conviction that a component of the newly-formed Federation—Singapore, with its banking, com-

[125] Pauker, "Indonesia in 1963: The Year of Wasted Opportunities," *op. cit.*, 691.

mercial, and commodity-processing facilities—had been largely responsible for the economic "bleeding" of Indonesia. Indonesia's belief that both Malaya and Singapore shielded rebels during the 1958-59 Indonesian revolt strained its diplomatic relations with Kuala Lumpur, and reinforced Sukarno's conviction (expressed as early as 1945) that his country could never be strong until it controlled both sides of the Straits of Malacca. Additionally, Malaya's economic prosperity and its relative political stability have led Djakarta to fear that some Indonesians (particularly those on Sumatra) might attempt to emulate their neighbor's example in Indonesia. Thus there is some concern regarding secessionist notions for Sumatra, leading either to its independence, an association with Malaysia, or simply a revolt aganst the present Djakarta regime.

The final element in Indonesian attitudes toward Malaysia derives from parts of the heavily ideologized political atmosphere. The Indonesian view is that the world is divided into two camps: the old established forces, and the new emerging forces. Indonesians consider Malaysia to be one of the old established forces, and it is part of the fundamental Indonesian political ideology to work for their dissolution. Because Indonesian leaders have maintained that they have an obligation to help and support national liberation movements—particularly those on their own borders—they have been perfectly willing to give overt and covert support to measures designed to disrupt the government of Malaysia and replace it with one more inclined to the views of the present Djakarta government.

Taken together, Indonesia's real foreign-policy goals (including perhaps expansionism or, at least, dominance over Malaysia) and its long-standing anti-Malaya attitudes provided a political base for its efforts to disrupt Kuala Lumpur's plans for a new state. The opportunity for such action arose in December 1962, as a direct result of the abortive Azahari revolt in Brunei. Indonesia then dropped any restraint it had previously shown with regard to its ultimate goals, and launched the confrontation. The thesis that Indonesia's decision was mainly the product of internal forces operating on President Sukarno—that "components of the Indonesian ruling group were eager to embrace some new foreign crisis"—must be rejected. Had a "foreign crisis" been required, Indonesia had plenty of targets from which to choose. Portuguese Timor, surrounded by Indonesia, is an ideal candidate for "liberation." Portugal has one of the world's most negative national images, and certainly no important group—inside Indonesia or out—would have effectively opposed a campaign to "liberate" Timor. On every conceivable ground—economic, military, diplomatic, ideological, ethnic, and political—a confrontation of Portugal over Timor would have served Indonesia's "need for a foreign crisis" better than the confrontation of Malaysia. Indonesia's decision resulted, not from this alleged "need," but from its external goals and internal political environment, and the Azahari revolt triggered the confrontation itself.

It seems clear that Indonesia believed its opposition to Malaysia would lead with relative ease to important changes in the nature of the proposed new state. Djakarta's immediate goal was probably at least to delay the formation of Malaysia. Its middle-range goal was probably to assure that Malaysia—when and if it came into existence—would be only a loose federation of the component states. This would have meant a relatively independent Malaya, Singapore, Sarawak, and Brunei, perhaps in loose and *separate* confederation with Indonesia and the Philippines. Such an arrangement would have provided a far greater opportunity for Indonesia to incorporate all or parts of the new nation. Singapore—a hated symbol in Indonesia—would have been the only "pill" difficult to swallow, but it could have been effectively "sugar-coated" by the other, far more clearly "Malay," communities.

Malaysia, however, proved to be a concept far more difficult to undermine than President Sukarno at first believed. The difficulties in achieving success for the goals of confrontation became starkly apparent during the last half of 1963. Sukarno's ensuing behavior strongly suggests a recognition that the price of confrontation—the decidedly negative economic and political effects within Indonesia—might be too high. The political effects, more readily perceived by Sukarno, were themselves in part a consequence of the economic cost of confrontation. Therefore, Sukarno resolved (probably by June 1963) to attempt to end the confrontation. But by that time confrontation had developed a dynamism of its own within Indonesia, particularly among Indonesian Communists and their associates. To the PKI, confrontation combined all possible advantages short of an actual Communist takeover of Indonesia. First, confrontation meant that effective economic stabilization in Indonesia—the one thing the PKI cannot readily tolerate—would be delayed. Second, the PKI was opposed to the concept of Malaysia, because it clearly represented, from any Communist perspective, a backward step: Malaysia reduced an easy opportunity to apply the pressure of national liberation movements to the last remaining colonial territories in the region; and, worse, Malaysia promised to bring—especially to the Borneo territories—a stable government and economy. Finally, confrontation placed the PKI once again at the forefront of an Indonesian movement championed by President Sukarno. Thus, it held out the possibility of further reducing Indonesian fears that the Communists are more concerned with international Communist goals than with Indonesia. Confrontation, by associating the PKI with a new nationalist crusade, helped erode those fears, and contributed as well to Sukarno's increasing conviction that Indonesia's Communists can be trusted in the future.

In this environment, Sukarno has found it exceedingly difficult to call a halt to confrontation, which he *has* been willing to do. Because of the internal pressures exerted by the PKI and other groups, he can end confrontation only under conditions that would convince those groups that he had no other choice. This is his dilemma: how to give in without appearing to.

Whatever the outcome of this confrontation, its genesis in Indonesia's objective goals and subjective attitudes must be stressed. Those goals and attitudes will not cease to exist should confrontation end. Thus, should another opportunity arise under circumstances again susceptible to a catalyst, Indonesia may be expected to resume a foreign policy tending toward regional dominance.

CHAPTER IV: PERSONALITY IN
SOUTHEAST ASIAN
INTERNATIONAL POLITICS

Personalities, even personal disputes, play a large role in Southeast Asia's international relations, generally a larger role than in the international politics of Western nations. This is one reflection of the three types of society that Professor Riggs described: "fused," in which traditionally a very narrow elite dominates all things pertaining to authority; "refracted," in which many persons, groups, and institutions comprise the political system and shape policy by their interactions; and, in between the two, combining features of both, the "prismatic" society.

The nations in Southeast Asia fall into the "prismatic" category; some, like the Philippines, strikingly so—its free press and competitive party system are very suggestive of a "refracted" society, while many other of its internal political practices are more evocative of "fused" society. The same tension between old and new forms is evident in the other Southeast Asian states, though only the Philippines has so many features of the fully refracted model. Nevertheless, no Southeast Asian state fully fits the fused model, either; they are all in-between. Thus, while in Malaysia and Indonesia many evidences of traditional society are still important (kinship ties in the Indonesian bureaucracy, and the significance of the sultans and old nobility in Malaya, for example), those states also possess important features of modern, refracted politics (the disciplined, mass-based PKI in Indonesia, the competitively-entered, efficient civil service in Malaya).

In the shaping of their foreign policies, Southeast Asian states exhibit features in much the same range, or continuum. They are neither so complex in making foreign policy as the "refracted" United States, where numerous veto-holding groups are the rule, nor are they so simple that any one leader can simply dictate policy, as might be so in the "fused" model. Instead, in their shaping of foreign policy, these nations fall between the two poles, and the policy latitude of their leaders varies accordingly. In the Philippines, for example, President Macapagal was not able, despite his preference, to gain acceptance for close ties with Indonesia; nor was he able—again, despite his personal desires—to generate wide support for his claim to North Borneo. Sukarno and Sihanouk, on the other hand, have had much greater latitude for impressing their will on their respective nation's foreign policy. At times, the imprint of personality on the foreign affairs of both Cambodia and Indonesia has been so great that the very whims of leaders seemed to be the determinants of policy.

Sihanouk and Sukarno

Because this personal imprint has been so heavy, it will be helpful to sketch roughly some aspects of the style and characteristics of certain leaders, especially the more colorful. The sketch may also help explain why sometimes politics among Southeast Asian states resembles a series of personal feuds.

President Sukarno and Prince Sihanouk, for example, are both fun-loving men. They reportedly lead colorful private lives in which women and music play a large part, and Prince Sihanouk does not mind speaking of his "past." Once, to deny that his politics were influenced by a Chinese mistress, he explained:

> Now I swear before the dear Venerables and the children that if I was truly in love with a Chinese girl, as alleged by Thanh, I would be condemned in hell for five hundred lives. I am absolutely not the kind of man described by Thanh.
>
> Being a nationalist, I prefer only girls of Khmer nationality. It is true that I had many Khmer girl friends. . . .
>
> When I was king, I was a good-looking boy. I was not potbellied as I am now. Because I was a handsome young king, I was loved and chased by girls who were also eager to take me as their lover. It is always the girls who wanted to make love to me, dear children. . . .[1]

Sukarno, on the other hand, avoids public reference to the more hilarious aspects of his private life, and seeks instead to convey the impression that his sole passion is for the Indonesian revolution. Nevertheless, even the school children of Djkarta must doubt Sukarno's advertised image as a devout Muslim. Stories of his escapades, and the private comments of foreign diplomats (who must make "arrangements" during his overseas trips) ring too true.[2]

[1] From Prince Sihanouk's speech of October 9, 1963, at the inauguration of two primary school buildings in Kampot Province.

[2] An American police official tells of Indonesian requests to find hostesses for the visiting President, and of his indignant refusal. This was "culture gap": in Southeast Asia police channels would have been correct for this request.

Both men, however, share a conviction that they are loved by their people. Sukarno, who has surrounded himself with as much pomp and as many titles as ever any sultan on Java or Sumatra, also suspects that most of his opponents are inspired by base motives, primarily the desire to gain for themselves the material satisfactions of high office. Yet Sukarno does, in fact, "embody" the revolution. He has been the only Indonesian in public life able to command enough support among the many diverse elements in Indonesian society to prevent Indonesia from breaking apart. He is almost the model of charismatic leadership and possesses immense personal magnetism; one foreign diplomat, after a day with Sukarno, commented: "He's a warm and lovable human being. If only the *S.O.B.* weren't the president of the Republic of Indonesia!" [3]

Sihanouk, who may lack Sukarno's charisma, is nevertheless able to draw upon the aura that goes with kingship (which he relinquished). Moreover, he is daring, and has stood up to France, China, and the United States. With courageous persistence, his delegation succeeded at the 1954 Geneva Conference in wearing out even Molotov,[4] and Cambodia was as a result permitted to ask later for American military assistance. Earlier in the campaign for independence, he succeeded in embarrassing the French, with steps that included self-imposed exile. Demonstrating that continued French presence was facilitating Communist success, he obtained through skillful, if slightly bizarre, diplomatic methods what Son Ngoc Thanh was unable to achieve through clandestine activities.[5]

But it also appears true that Prince Sihanouk is a man whose vanity is easily wounded, and he sometimes delivers extended tirades against those who are critical of him, or by whom he believes he has been insulted. Early in 1964, when he was the subject of a "cover story" in *Time,* he fired off a sharply critical letter to the editors, complaining about the things that had been said about him and his country. (This is something which few, if any, other governmental leaders would have

---

[3] Statement to the author in Djakarta, June 1962.

[4] According to Anthony Eden: "The Cambodians skillfully held out till last, when we were exhausted. . . . At two o'clock on the morning of the 21st, after hard bargaining and some surprising last-minute concessions by Molotov, we succeeded in resolving the remaining differences. . . . *Memoirs of Anthony Eden: Full Circle* (Boston: Houghton Mifflin Company, 1960), p. 159. Cited in Roger M. Smith, "Cambodia," in George Mct. Kahin (ed.), *Government and Politics in Southeast Asia,* 2nd ed. (Ithaca, N. Y.: Cornell University Press, 1964).

[5] Leifer, *op. cit.,* p. 19.

done.) Sihanouk's vanity seems to be of a different sort than that of Sukarno, who rarely appears in public without his small black hat for fear that the considerably less distinguished appearance accompanying his baldness will become too familiar to his people.[6]

Both men seem to have strange decision-making techniques: Sihanouk consults an astrologer, and Sukarno has sometimes avoided responsibility during a domestic crisis by going abroad. This method at least insulated his prestige while allowing him to provide the appearance of a solution. Yet on numerous other occasions Sukarno's ability to sway men's minds may have been all that held the country together. Whether cajoling a small group of powerful dissidents or exhorting an audience of thousands, Sukarno's repeated and successful use of his oratorical skills, as well as his own estimate of his reputation, must reinforce his conviction that only his will preserves and sustains Indonesia.

In a political environment where even a colorless leader would have great policy latitude, it is clear that Sukarno and Sihanouk are probably exceptional persons. Given these conditions—and the added fact that in some cases the leaders identify themselves with the state—a deep impact of personalities on politics among these nations is not surprising.

PRINCE SIHANOUK
AND DIPLOMACY BY PERSONAL ABUSE

Personality disputes are but one reflection of the impact of personality on politics, and several have been of political significance in Southeast Asia. Probably the best examples revolve around Prince Sihanouk. Cambodia's many disagreements with Thailand and South Vietnam have so often been reflected in personal recriminations among leaders that aspects of Cambodian foreign policy have on occasion seemed to be no more than verbal fireworks. In 1961, for example, Sihanouk was very upset because, he claimed, he had been called "a pig" by the prime minister of Thailand, Marshal Sarit. It happened that Sarit, referring to Sihanouk's statement that Cambodia would more likely have to defend herself against her pro-Western neighbors than against the Communists, had observed that Thailand, so much

---

[6] Sukarno too, of course, has been the subject of a "cover story" by *Time*; and he too was most disturbed. But Sukarno was upset about the *picture* of him that was used on the cover, complaining bitterly that it made him appear "like a monster." See Louis Fischer, *The Story of Indonesia* (New York: Harper & Row, Publishers, 1959), p. 150.

more powerful than Cambodia, would exercise restraint and would take "consolation in the old proverbial tale of a pig challenging a lion to a fight. . . ." [7] Sihanouk took the reference to "a pig" as a personal affront,[8] and promptly severed relations with Thailand.

This event reopened a period of mutual vilification, but it was by no means the cause of the personal animosities that have characterized Thai-Cambodian affairs in recent years. Thai officials believe that much of this hostility can be traced to 1953, when, to embarrass France, Sihanouk sought asylum in Bangkok and was treated less diplomatically than protocol requires. The Thais, who maintain that there was an honest misunderstanding regarding the type of welcome he expected, suspect that he has harbored a deep bitterness over an imagined slight ever since;[9] and while they concede that their protocol arrangements could have been better, they also point out that the event took place a long time ago. In their view Sihanouk's vanity prevents him from forgetting the affair, and it is this element in his personality, they stress, which impedes better relations between the two countries.

The importance of this personal irritant was underlined to the author in 1962—even as Thailand and Cambodia were emerging from the settlement of a substantive difference. The World Court had just awarded the ruins of Kao Prah Viharn to Cambodia (see Ch. II), and Thai officials were asked to describe the impediments to good relations with Phnom Penh. Their answers discounted the usual issues—Cambodia's flirtation with China, for example—and ignored even the frustration caused by the loss of the temple. Instead, all stressed Sihanouk's verbal war with Thailand, and one official, a principal advisor to the Thai Foreign Minister, said that nothing stood in the way of better relations except "the personality of a spoiled man." Describing Sihanouk as emotional, selfish, and vain, the advisor concluded that as long as the Prince ruled Cambodia, Thailand had little hope that relations with Phnom Penh could be put on a satisfactory basis.[10] Since that conclusion is so widely shared among Thai leaders, it raises a question: Might Thailand take steps to "speed" Sihanouk's exit?

---

[7] Leifer, *op. cit.*, p. 28, citing Thai documents.

[8] *Ibid.*, p. 29.

[9] This judgment, based on numerous conversations the author has had with Thai foreign-ministry officials, is supported by Leifer's study as well. "It is likely," he says, "that Sihanouk has not quite forgiven the Thais for the cool reception he received. . . ." Leifer, *op. cit.*, p. 19.

[10] Author's interview with Mr. Anand Panyarachun, Foreign Ministry, Bangkok, July 1962.

Sihanouk, on his part, regularly charges that Thailand and South Vietnam (he has recently added Laos and generally includes the United States) are involved in a conspiracy to depose him. Without question, there is—and has been for years—an active opposition to his regime, and a rebel radio regularly broadcasts anti-Sihanouk propaganda. More concretely, a major plot against Sihanouk, known generally as the "Dap Chhuon affair," was discovered in 1959. The same year there was also a bomb explosion in the palace.

It was alleged then, as it is now, that the purpose of these efforts is to replace Sihanouk with his major rival of preindependence days: Son Ngoc Thanh. Sihanouk has been quite specific in his public disclosures of these efforts, and in 1963 he even named the American official (Victor Matsui) whom he accused of complicity in the Dap Chhuon incident.[11] He also implicated a former minister in the South Vietnamese government of Ngo Dinh Diem: Mr. Ngo Trong Hieu. (There is no doubt about Hieu's involvement, for in mid-1962 he made it quite clear that the "Dap Chhuon affair" had indeed been one of his activities.[12])

There has been very little evidence of a renewed plot against Sihanouk in recent years, but in late March 1964, he warned that his overthrow was planned for April, and reported that a "secret meeting" had just been held in Dalat, a resort town in South Vietnam:

> The participants were General Khanh [then Premier of South Vietnam], Son Ngoc Thanh, and Phoumi Nosavan of Laos. The meeting was held in Dalat from 12 to 15 March. Its aim was to draft a strategic plan to attack us and destroy our neutrality. Because I have warned Khanh, Son Ngoc Thanh, and Phoumi Nosavan that if they mistreat us we will contact the Communists and establish friendly relations with them, the South Vietnamese government sent a delegation to Phnom Penh to pretend to negotiate with us lest we open negotiations with Hanoi and Peking. For this reason, General Khanh has become gentle . . . by trying to compliment me and flatter me. . . . In other words, he tries to lull us to sleep and keep us from drawing ourselves close to the Communists.[13]

Of course, Sihanouk has for years accused South Vietnam of plotting his overthrow, yet this address may have been the first occasion on

[11] Sihanouk made these charges, though not for the first time, in an editorial in the Cambodian magazine, *Nationalist* (October 9, 1963).

[12] I would not report this interview with Ngo Trong Hieu, which took place in Saigon in July, 1962, were it not for the fact that he was executed in the wake of the overthrow of the Diem regime late in 1963.

[13] Sihanouk's speech of March 27, 1964, in Stung Treng province.

which Sihanouk named the new Vietnamese leader, General Khanh, casting him in the same evil light as former President Ngo Dinh Diem, and probably destroying the brief "honeymoon" between Cambodia and South Vietnam that began after the overthrow of the Diem regime. The speech also differed from earlier ones in that Thai leaders were excluded from the allegations and Laotian leaders accused in their stead.

One thing that remains unchanged, however, is Sihanouk's conviction that the United States either inspires these plots, or at least gives them lavish support. In a recent typical remark, a journal that reflects Sihanouk's views claimed that "we have for many years been aware of the existence of an American plot against the person of the Chief of State." The "Khmer Serei ["Free Cambodia"] movement, it went on, "could not survive for an instant without the subsidies and support of the Americans." [14] These claims, repeated over the years despite exasperated American denials, seldom caused damage to Cambodian-American relations. But in one instance Sihanouk's lack of restraint, which has so often strained his relations with his neighbors, severely jolted those with the United States. The occasion was the assassination of President Kennedy. Initial reactions in Phnom Penh were perfectly proper, and included the announcement of a three-day mourning period.[15] A few weeks later, however, when Marshal Sarit died of a kidney ailment, Sihanouk called for rejoicing in the streets of Phnom Penh, the better to mark the death of the Thai leader. The government ordered that all public buildings must continue to fly their flags as usual, and all "compatriots are asked to pin a red ribbon on their shirt" [16]:

> We beg to inform compatriots that during the past few days . . . our man in whom we place our confidence has sworn to the children that if Sarit Thanarat, who mistreated us, dies, civil servants throughout the kingdom will be given a one-week leave. But because our country is achieving economic reform, this leave is cancelled.
>
> However, . . . Prince Sihanouk authorizes all government services and civil servants throughout the kingdom to have two-hour leave every day

---

[14] "Pentagon at Work," editorial in *Réalités Cambodgiennes* (May 23, 1964).

[15] All public buildings were ordered to fly their flags at half-mast, and the people were further told that "during this period all newspapers published in Cambodia will observe an absolute truce and refrain from all polemic arguments against this great friendly country." Phnom Penh Radio, November 23, 1963.

[16] Information Department communiqué, December 9, 1963.

. . . for a period of two weeks so as to permit the children to dance and amuse themselves. Beginning tonight, there will be musical programs in the . . . Square, and the celebration will be recorded and broadcast by the national radio.[17]

The Cambodian government communiqué then went on to link Marshal Sarit's death with the earlier murders of Ngo Dinh Diem and his brother, Ngo Dinh Nhu, and added one further comment: *"Moreover, the great boss of these aggressors shared the same fate. . . .* People from all walks of society . . . feel elated, not out of enmity but simply at the end of persons who mistreated us." [18]

Sihanouk had for years referred to the United States as the "boss" of Thailand and South Vietnam, so the reference to the recently slain President Kennedy seemed altogether unmistakable. President Kennedy had been murdered only two weeks before, and the memory of his tragic death and funeral was still starkly present in the minds of Americans.

Ambassador Yost was that day Chief of the United States Mission to the United Nations. He expressed his disgust at these remarks, and called them "barbarous." In turn, Sihanouk took great offense at the word, and construed it to mean that the United States was referring to him—and to all Cambodians—as barbarians. Sihanouk demanded an apology from Yost (none has ever been given) and then went on to terminate all American aid programs and to condone a number of anti-American demonstrations in Phnom Penh. Despite a number of mediation efforts, particularly by President Macapagal of the Philippines, Cambodian-American relations seem not to have resumed even the precarious state they were in before these events.

Leading Thai officials regarded these events as a corroboration of their belief that it is impossible to have normal dealings with Prince Sihanouk. Sihanouk's decision to decree national rejoicing over their premier's death, they declared, "is, to say the least, unusual and represents an unprecedented practice among civilized nations, even among those who are bitterest enemies." [19] In what Sihanouk may have regarded as yet another threat, the Thais added that the "songs and music" he ordered "may prove to be the swan songs announcing the

[17] *Ibid.*
[18] *Ibid.* Italics added.
[19] Royal Government of Thailand, Department of Information, Ministry of Foreign Affairs, *Press Release,* December 11, 1963.

end of Prince Sihanouk. . . ." Similarly, General Praphat, second in power only to the prime minister of Thailand, declared:

> We must . . . put an end to the most vile acts of Sihanouk, for a country which is concerned about its future cannot allow itself to be continually harassed by another country, *one that considers it all a stage play, to be conducted as it pleases.*[20]

Similar sentiments have been voiced by the Foreign Minister, Thanat Khoman, who seems now to have become Prince Sihanouk's major target. Thanat has accused Sihanouk of selling his country to Communist China and sometimes also suggests that his behavior exceeds the bounds of rationality. According to one report, the Thai Foreign Minister said that "judging from his recent statements, Sihanouk is not mentally stable." [21]

Further illustrations of this personal vilification among leaders would be amusing, but of little value. Three points, however, should be stressed: first, it is not only Thailand and Cambodia that have engaged in this sort of exchange; second, attempts have been made to curb these personal attacks; and finally, this aspect of communications among leaders in the area—bitter though it has been—is a symptom as well as a cause of tension among the states involved.

It is not surprising that Cambodia's relations with South Vietnam too have been characterized by bitter, personalized recriminations. Sihanouk did, after all, uncover a conspiracy, which clearly involved high Vietnamese officials. Moreover, Cambodia has for years accused South Vietnamese troops of crossing over into Cambodian territory in their search for Viet Cong guerrilla forces. Despite these problems, the dialogue between these two countries has seldom approached the level of publicly expressed bitterness that exists between Cambodia and Thailand. This may in part be a recognition, on Sihanouk's part, that

---

[20] From a press conference statement of General Praphat, reported by the Cambodian government, March 20, 1964. Italics added. This was the same conference in which Praphat was quoted as saying: "The actions of Prince Sihanouk do not differ from a toad who sits in a coconut and dreams of immense deeds" (see Chapter II).

[21] Report of Thanat's press conference, broadcast by Philippines Radio, "Call of the Orient," November 20, 1963. Sihanouk immediately responded: "That fellow Thanat insults me by saying that I am crazy; a man who has lost his mind. . . . . Thamat Khoman says I am a barbarian and a fool. . . . Moreover, he insults me by calling me a 'beastly subhuman.' . . . You see, such is the way he insults me." From Prince Sihanouk's statement at the sixteenth national congress, Phnom Penh, December 31, 1963.

a break with Thailand entails little material loss, but that some sort of regular relationship with South Vietnam must be preserved as long as Cambodian trade on the Mekong River depends on access to the port of Saigon. It was notable, after all, that Prince Sihanouk "broke relations" with President Diem's regime only when that government was losing the support even of the United States and was clearly about to fall. Even then—and this is crucial—Cambodia severed only "political relations"; its economic ties with Saigon were not disturbed.[22]

This sort of restraint indicates that even Prince Sihanouk recognizes some limits on what he ought say about other nations' leaders. (He once denied, for example, that he had "prayed to the spirits of his ancestors to bring about Ngo Dinh Diem's destruction." [23]) And there have been attempts, both in Saigon and Phnom Penh, to impose a moratorium on public criticism of the other nation's leaders. These efforts reinforce the widespread conviction that press comments often inflame an episode that might otherwise have been passed over. But, in each instance, some minor misstep seems to have killed the agreements very quickly.[24] The fact that a press moratorium was attempted should not be overlooked, however, because these efforts reflect some willingness to reduce the tensions complicated by personality disagreements.

SUKARNO AND THE TUNKU

Another major example of the impact of personality clashes is in the relationship between President Sukarno and Prime Minister Abdul Rahman of Malaysia. Rahman is Sukarno's opposite in almost every conceivable manner: Sukarno is flamboyant and ostentatious, while Abdul Rahman is almost retiring; Sukarno's speeches are fiery, im-

---

[22] South Vietnam recognizes how dependent Cambodia is on access to Saigon. On September 21, 1964, it was reported that General Kanh, in retaliation for Sihanouk's alleged contacts both with Hanoi and with exiled South Vietnamese leaders in France who support De Gaulle's "neutralization" proposals, was considering a decision to block this access. South Vietnam's leading naval officer declared that an end to this Cambodian trade on the Mekong could be accomplished without delay, and it was assumed that this would be regarded as no light threat in Phnom Penh. *Straits Times* (September 21, 1964).

[23] Editorial in *Dépêche du Cambodge* (October 24, 1962).

[24] The same has been true of attempted "press moratoria" between Bangkok and Phnom Penh. Once, when Sihanouk made remarks about Thailand which Thais felt were more abusive than their truce permitted, the Prince responded that "as far as he was concerned the truce had gone overboard." *Far Eastern Economic Review* (April 4, 1963), 9.

passioned, demagogic, while Rahman's are marked by quiet appeals
to reason, and delivered in a manner that is almost pedantic.

The two men come from extremely different backgrounds: Rahman
is a Prince (Tunku) of the old Malay nobility, and represents traditional authority transplanted to a democratic environment. He was
educated in England; he is a pipe-smoker; and he greatly enjoys golf
—in Malaysian politics and business the golfcourse is a prime milieu
for important transactions. The Tunku even looks somewhat British,
in much the same manner (as C. Northcote Parkinson once remarked)
that General Ayub Khan of Pakistan looks like most British generals
would *like* to look. None of this applies even remotely to Sukarno.
His background was decidedly lower-middle-class (his father was a
lower-level civil servant in the Dutch colonial bureaucracy), and his
rise to power was the result of achievement, not ascription.

And yet the early meetings of the two men were not unpromising.
It was indicative of the Tunku's makeup, though, that on his first
visit to Sukarno in Djakarta (November 1955), he carried a camera
over his shoulder—as if, in Willard Hanna's words, "the center of
photographic interest on the trip would be somewhere outside his own
periphery." [25] When he arrived in Djakarta, he was fêted lavishly by
Sukarno, and reportedly was much impressed at the hundreds of
thousands of citizens who greeted Sukarno and himself on the tour of
Indonesia that followed. In general, the Tunku found that not all Malay
leaders are so retiring as he.

Whatever goodwill was created by that visit (and there is reason to
believe that it made a good impression on Rahman) has, of course, been
dissipated in recent years. Part of this deterioration derives from Sukarno's obviously patronizing attitude toward the Tunku and his country, for Indonesian leaders certainly are aware that many Malays in
Malaysia have long regarded Sukarno as a heroic figure.[26] Rahman and
other Malaysian leaders are also aware of this attraction (which Indonesian propaganda organs constantly stress) to the far larger Malay
nation, and are very sensitive to any element of patronization in their
relations with Indonesia.

But until 1960-61, whatever mutual suspicions existed among the
leaders of these two Malay communities seldom erupted into public

---

[25] Willard A. Hanna, "Indonesia and the New Malayan States," *American Universities Field Staff, Reports* (New York: AUFS, 1956), 17.

[26] In Malayan *kampongs* it was not unusual, at least before Sukarno launched
confrontation, to find pictures of Sukarno on the villagers' walls.

comment. A façade of ethnic Malay brotherhood was presented instead, while privately, nasty comments about the Tunku became increasingly common in Djakarta. It had long been common, for example, for Indonesian leaders to question the Tunku's role as a "spokesman" for Malays. They have argued that he is not a Malay at all. He is, in fact, half-Thai in extraction and, as one Indonesian official said in 1962, "How can he pretend to speak for Malaysia or Malays? He is simply a façade."

Leaders in Kuala Lumpur returned the "compliment" both privately and publicly. Today, of course, and since the beginning of confrontation, both the Tunku and Deputy Prime Minister Tun Abdul Razak make no effort to speak moderately about Sukarno in public. But even before Indonesia's open hostility to Malaysia was declared, those two leaders had answered his mild insults with backbiting of their own, often focusing on the many rumors and reports of Sukarno's unconvential private life. All this is to say that even before the torrent of public invective was unleashed between Kuala Lumpur and Djakarta by the establishment of Malaysia, personal animosity existed among the leaders.

The causes of this animosity were many, of course, but one event which rather immediately preceded the Malaysia proposals particularly helped impede easy communications between Sukarno and the Tunku. This was the reaction of Sukarno and Foreign Minister Subandrio to Malaya's suggestions on the Indonesian-Dutch dispute over New Guinea. Kuala Lumpur had, in fact, supported Djakarta, but at one point offered to mediate the dispute and made public proposals for a settlement. The Malayans were met with a stinging rebuff from Djakarta, administered, it seems, by Subandrio. As it turned out, the Indonesians, while pointedly ignoring the Malayan suggestions, soon afterward accepted a similar proposal from Ambassador Ellsworth Bunker, who served as the United Nations mediator. A man who knows both Sukarno and the Tunku well, and is regarded as an extremely knowledgeable observer, expressed the general consensus on this development: that Dr. Subandrio's behavior infuriated the Malayan leaders, and "left Rahman out on a limb." [27]

These developments widened and reinforced the derision with which the Indonesian leaders may already have been regarded in Kuala Lumpur, and they certainly eroded any confidence in President Su-

[27] Mr. Thomas Critchley, Australian High Commissioner to Malaysia, in an interview with the author, Kuala Lumpur, July 1962.

karno that Rahman might have had. Rahman himself, in attempting to assess his difficulties with Indonesia in the immediate wake of Sukarno's policy to "crush" Malaysia and his support for the Brunei rebellion in 1962, summed up the entire problem this way: "I still believe the whole trouble is a personality thing. He doesn't like me."[28]

Analyzing the Personality Factor: Tentative Suggestions in Theory

Rahman was exaggerating: the "whole trouble" is not "a personality thing," and it is clear that there is considerably more to Malaysia's difficulties with Indonesia than Sukarno's feeling toward him. Nevertheless, more significance should be attached to disputes among leaders of developing countries, such as those in Southeast Asia, than to those among leaders of the advanced nations. The question is: How much more significance? Without suggesting extreme precision, certain generalizations can be offered.

SUBSYSTEMS AND PERSONAL LEADERSHIP

Personality factors—such as the easily wounded vanity of a Sihanouk or the I-am-the-nation attitude of a Sukarno—have played the largest role in the foreign policy of those states with only one dominant subsystem in their political systems. These factors will play a correspondingly smaller role as the states become institutionally more varied—i.e., as the number of major subsystems increases.

Cambodia, for example, might adopt almost any foreign-policy tactic to ensure survival, as long as Prince Sihanouk's internal position is only weakly challenged. To see why this is so, first consider the state as an over-all system, which—in response to stimuli, or inputs—produces certain foreign-policy decisions, or outputs. Obviously, inputs vary in size (i.e., importance) both objectively and in relation to the system affected. For example, an objectively large input would be a warning by State *A* that it is about to invade State *B*, accompanied by the threat that if State *B* does not welcome the conquerors, it will be destroyed in a thermonuclear attack. Conversely, an objectively small input would be the refusal of State *A* to accept the credentials of State *B*'s ambassador.

Though these two inputs objectively seem poles apart, their real

[28] Quoted in the *Washington Post* (March 3, 1963).

magnitude will be that attributed to them by the *system*'s perception.[29] That perception is a function of the system's over-all sensitivity— which, in turn, is a function of the number, kinds, and relative dominance of the subsystems within a system.

Thus we can say, on the basis of what we already know of Prince Sihanouk, that what he perceives as a personal insult will be as large an input into the foreign-policy-making system of Cambodia as a direct military threat would be to a nation with a more complex institutional structure. Sihanouk's behavior in response to an insult is, then, not an aberration, but a quite probable and predictable outcome of the system in which he is the dominant subsystem.

President Sukarno has less latitude than Sihanouk because he must contend with at least three subsystems in addition to himself: the army, the PKI, and the bureaucracy and parties (they are much the weakest). Yet until the attempted coup of September, 1965, which initially weakened the PKI severely, Sukarno came close, for a time, to achieving the position of dominant subsystem within Indonesia. This was the case so long as the army and the PKI remained internally fundamentally at odds with, and organizationally distinct from, one another, and as long as neither was substantially weakened or reduced in size. To that extent, Sukarno's latitude in foreign policy matters thereby increased. It seemed especially wide when the PKI and the army subscribed to the same immediate or tactical goals. This was true initially in Indonesia's confrontation with Malaysia, and certainly in Sukarno's earlier drive to expel the Dutch from West Irian.

Assume, however, a PKI revival and a series of the crises which lead to exercises in army-PKI harmony—campaigns not only to "crush" Malaysia, but to "liberate" Portuguese Timor, to bring "self-determination" to the Australian half of New Guinea, to further nationalize certain industries and estates under army control, and perhaps to defeat another internal revolt. Assume that this drama might require ten years

---

[29] Consider the likely effect if Nigeria refused to accept Nkrumah's ambassador from Ghana; or if the United States refused to accept credentials from the ambassadors of either of those two, or of Cambodia. The reactions in each of the small countries would be large. If, on the other hand, Burma or Cambodia insults the American ambassador (which has happened) it is simply an item duly to be noted, although it irritates. The same input but not the same result.

Then consider the thermonuclear threat, a "large" input. If the Soviet Union voiced such a threat to, say Egypt, it is very likely that capitulation would be almost immediate. But if the threat were aimed at the United States, it is much more difficult to predict the reaction. The time could come when such a threat might be regarded a new twist at "spoofing."

to play out. The regular and extended exercise of mutual tolerance between the army and the PKI could eventually reduce the mutual suspicion between those two subsystems. That development, it is suggested, would narrow the foreign-policy latitude of Sukarno—or of any successor who sought, as Sukarno has, to reply upon his acceptability to the presently incompatible camps. The camps, that is, would have ceased to be warring camps; *their* perception of stimuli would determine the magnitude of inputs affecting the system—and, to that extent, their leadership, rather than the president's, would set the limits of Indonesian foreign-policy decisions.

This is apparently not yet the case in the Indonesian political system. Although mutually tolerant of one another as far as the campaign to "crush" Malaysia and other tactical problems are concerned, the army and the PKI are still in disagreement about fundamental domestic- and foreign-policy alternatives. Thus they remain powerful and distinctive subsystems, striving for the adoption of their separate views, and as a result, Sukarno's foreign-policy latitude is wider than it might be if their mutual tolerance were deeper or more permanent. Nevertheless, Sukarno's latitude is narrower than Sihanouk's. For example, Sukarno cannot adopt, as Sihanouk conceivably might, either a pro-West or a pro-Communist stance as circumstances require.

In accordance with the thesis that the personal imprint of a leader in foreign-policy decisions will be less as the number of subsystems increases, one would expect President Macapagal of the Philippines to have less latitude than Sukarno and far less than Sihanouk. The Philippine political system, insofar as foreign-policy decisions are concerned, is not simple, and it is not dominated by any one internal element. Thus in the Philippines, if an input is to enter the decision-making system as a factor which might result in a policy change, it will have to reach and overcome the threshold of perception of several distinct subsystems. Each of these subsystems—the President, congressional leaders, the press, political parties, the military, and so on—has its own perspective. To become politically significant in the Philippines context, therefore, an input will have to be both intense and multifaceted. One would expect, therefore, that an input of objectively small intensity (such as a calculated personal insult to the chief of state) will produce a much less significant reaction in the Philippines than in Cambodia. Among the states of Southeast Asia it is probably in the Philippines that personality factors are least likely to become a significant element in important foreign-policy decisions.

Two Types

The states in Southeast Asia, insofar as the influence of personality factors on the making of foreign policy is concerned, are of two relatively different types: those in which, because of a larger number of powerful subsystems participating in foreign policy, the influence of any one personality factor on foreign-policy decisions is negligible; and those in which, because there is only one or a very few subsystems, the influence of a personality factor is likely to be significant.

The Philippines might be regarded as a model of the first "negligible personality" (*NP*) type; Cambodia comes closer to being a model of the second, type (*P*), where personality is not so negligible. Obviously, most states will not conform to these ideals.[30] Thus there is a range of examples, and in Southeast Asia this range might be expressed along something like the scale in Fig. IV-1.

IV-1

THE PERSONALITY FACTOR IN INTERACTION: FURTHER SUGGESTIONS

Is it possible now to discern any patterns in the interactions *among* these types of states? Of course, the nations dealt with here are few, and most of them have been in charge of their own foreign affairs for only a few years. Consequently, any pattern that might be detected will be based on very slight evidence indeed. Nevertheless, there do seem to be some general tendencies, and these should be pointed out—if only to see how constant they may be over time.

For one thing, in instances of two-nation contact where *both* nations are *P*, the *P* factor seems to have functioned as the major medium of contact, and as a result the quality of the relationship—hostile or friendly—has been intensified. Of course, a given *P* nation might be quite friendly in its attitudes and behavior toward one state, but may exhibit quite hostile (even personally insulting) behavior when dealing

---

[30] The imprint of a single leader's personality is only total or near-total under exceptional conditions, and it is probably also exceptional to find states in which there are so many large and well organized subsystems that the leader is merely one among numerous forces.

with some other nation. In that first instance, the designation of the P nation would become $P+$, in the second instance, $P-$. The three modal types then, are $P+$, $P-$, and NP. In Fig. IV-2, all possible two-nation combinations of these entities are expressed:

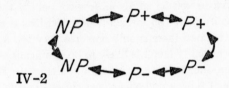

IV-2

Under this format, Cambodian-Thai relations might be expressed as

$$\text{IV-3} \quad P- \times P- = P--$$

$P--$ indicates a further worsening of relations where the contact between the two states has been along personalistic lines. Thus if two nations, both personality-subsystem-dominant, are engaged in already unfriendly relations, the outcome is likely to be more and more personal recrimination. This has, of course, been the case with Cambodia and Thailand, and the negative personal relationship seems to have added to the difficulties of reaching an accommodation.[31]

The same pattern, but with a different quality to the personalities (and, hence, to the outcome) has characterized Thailand's relations with Burma since General Ne Win assumed power in Rangoon. These relations can be expressed as

$$\text{IV-4} \quad P+ \times P+ = P++$$

In this instance the personality element appeared to be decisive, and the actual outcome of the contact seemed to depend upon whether or not the leaders involved "got on" with one another. The personalities involved were those of General Aung Gyi (at the time the second most influential man in Burma) and General Dawee of Thailand. The two

---

[31] Although no one personality dominates Thailand's foreign policy to the extent that Prince Sihanouk controls Cambodian foreign affairs, it is nevertheless true that Marshal Sarit (and his successor, General Thanom) seems the decisive element. The Thai premier takes foreign-policy counsel only from a very small group immediately around him, including especially the foreign minister and one or two generals, including General Praphat.

were on very good terms, and between them they settled to a remarkable degree a number of long-standing Thai-Burmese disputes. As in the Thai-Cambodian case, in this instance a P factor (in this case, $P+$) was intensified.

These formulations raise the question of combinations in which there seems to be no P factor at all, or in which one of the two states is NP.

Such cases have arisen recently in Southeast Asia, and two formulations will express these combinations and what seems to be their product:

$$P \times NP = NP$$

$$\text{IV-5} \quad NP \times NP = NP$$

In both instances the outcome is designated as NP; that is, the relationship was characterized by the relatively nonpersonal methods already familiar in politics among nations: bilateral diplomacy through usual diplomatic channels, third-party mediation, threat and/or use of violence, arbitration, resort to the United Nations, and so on.

Three Illustrations

An example of $P \times NP = NP$ is the relationship between Indonesia and Malaysia. The dispute between the parties has not been escalated by the mutually interacting personal animosities of the two leaders;[32] but neither has it been settled on the basis of warm personal ties between them. Instead, more traditional methods have been followed, in-

---

[32] As is generally the case between Cambodia and Thailand, i.e., a $P— \times P—$ relationship. In the case now being discussed, where Indonesia (Sukarno) appears as $P—$, it might even be said that President Sukarno has attempted to deal with Malaysia *as if* the relationship between the two countries were $P— \times P—$. Thus, he has made a number of direct personal attacks on the Tunku, and his propaganda organs, as pointed out earlier, attempt to reach the Malay portion of the Malaysian population by ethnic—even racist—and historic appeals. But the Tunku, operating in a different political environment from Sukarno's, is not readily able to respond in kind to these attacks. He cannot, for example, freely play on the sentiments of his own Malay population, in efforts designed to counter Sukarno's appeals, because he must constantly be aware of the internal communal (racial) divisions in his own country. Thus, retorts in kind to Sukarno's appeals could lead readily to even greater Malaysian Chinese disaffection from his leadership than at present. As a result of these and other considerations which have to deal with the nature of Malaysian politics, the relationship between Indonesia and Malaysia has not been $(P— \times P—)$, but $(P— \times NP)$.

cluding both the threat and use of force, resort to parliamentary diplomacy in the United Nations, and the mediation efforts of such third parties as Thailand, the Philippines, and even Cambodia.

The same equation—$P \times NP = NP$—expresses the relationship between Cambodia (P) and South Vietnam (NP). Despite President Diem's emphasis on *personalism* (the term he chose to express the nature of his rule), it is apparent that since 1961—as internal divisions markedly increased and the role there of the United States grew in significance—South Vietnam has been characterized by the presence of several important subsystems. These included a disaffected population, some portions of which cooperated with the insurgents; military groups; religious groups; and the United States itself. The fall of President Diem in late 1963 made these divisions even more apparent, and the number and significance of active subsystems increased. As a result, restraints have increased, and it is certainly clear that no South Vietnamese leader has the foreign-policy latitude of a Sihanouk, or even that of a Sukarno. Consequently, South Vietnam is characterized as an NP state, and its relations with Cambodia expressed as $P \times NP = NP$. The equation indicates that the method and outcome of relations between two such entities will be NP, and that appears to have been the outcome in fact.

For one thing, relations between the two countries during the past several years have not been characterized by a heightening of mutual recriminations. A major subsystem in South Vietnam—the United States presence—has acted as a restraining influence on Saigon's relations with Cambodia. Moreover, whatever many South Vietnamese think of Cambodians in general and Sihanouk in particular, this much is clear: Sihanouk's numerous personal insults to President Diem after 1960-61 did not make relations any worse than they had already been.[33] This is not to say that relations between the two have improved, but the method of communication between Cambodia and South Vietnam is not head-on personal vilification between their respective leaders.

The explanation seems to be that, since only one of the two states

---

[33] In relation to the hypothesis that an increase in subsystems decreases the scope and likelihood of personal latitude, it is significant that the major South Vietnamese personal attack against Sihanouk (the Dap Chhuon affair) came in 1959. That year also marked the high point of President Diem's control over his country and its brightest prospects. After that, in the wake of the renewed Viet Cong insurgency, and the Diem regime's increasingly repressive measures partly in response to the civil war, the heavily personalized nature of the regime began to dissolve, this becoming most apparent from 1962 on.

(Cambodia) can be characterized as P, it has not been possible for communications between them to follow a personalistic path. Cambodia has attempted to find satisfaction in its complaints against Saigon by two methods: resort to the United Nations, and requests for a large-scale multilateral conference (probably comprised of those states that attended the 1954 Geneva Conference). In neither method has Cambodia met with any real success. Saigon, for its part, has seemed largely to ignore Cambodian initiatives. South Vietnamese military units continue to cross into Cambodian territory when their officers feel that the search for Viet Cong troops warrants it, and South Vietnamese leaders have made it clear that—along with the United States—they oppose any multilateral conference which has as its prime goal the "neutralization" of the area. Consequently, relations between Phnom Penh and Saigon have reached a certain level of hostility or estrangement, but change very little. This seems to be one result of the nondirect communications between the two capitals.

A third illustration of a relationship in which the outcome is characterized as NP is in the dispute between the Philippines and Malaysia over North Borneo. The relationship between these two states is expressed as $NP \times NP = NP$. Here, too, there is no common denominator of leading personalities which might lead *either* to increased hostility or accommodation along personal lines. The Philippines has pressed its claim in a more or less gentlemanly manner, indicating on numerous occasions that its first preference is to resolve the dispute by resort to the World Court, and no responsible Manila official has *publicly* charged Rahman or his leading associates with bad faith or other reprehensible behavior. Indeed, the Philippines has taken many opportunities to show that it did not want to cause any severe deterioration in relations with Malaysia, including the despatch of leading Filipinos to Kuala Lumpur from time to time.

Malaysia, for its part, expressed disappointment that the Philippines should see fit to raise this issue, but refrained from making statements that might exacerbate the dispute. Thus, after first behaving as if they hoped that the dispute would somehow "go away," Malaysian leaders eventually concluded that they would first prefer bilateral talks with Manila in order to determine whether it "really had a claim." Both parties relied upon a third party—Thailand—to act as mediator and communications link, and decided that Bangkok probably would be the ideal locale of further talks on the subject. The inescapable conclusion in this particular dispute (and only as far as the methods are concerned), is that both parties acted in a manner that revealed they did not want the affair to get out of hand. Both seemed at pains to preserve a public state of calm, avoiding any official actions or statements which might jeopardize their nonhostile relationship.

Conclusion

The number of cases available in Southeast Asia for analysis of personality influence on foreign policy is very small, but certain patterns and generalizations are discernible. The one that seems most clear is that only in a combination where both states can be designated as P is it likely that personalities may play a major role, leading either to a settlement or an intensification of disputes. This seems to be the result of the presence of a common denominator, whether it is a $P+$ or $P-$.

In combinations where one or both states may be designated as NP, the relationship will be characterized by the nonpersonalized method of communication, and the substance of the dispute is not likely to be much affected by personalities.

Because only a certain—and increasingly rare—kind of state is likely to be designated as P, most contacts between states in Southeast Asia are likely to be $P \times NP$ or $NP \times NP$. In most combinations, therefore, a personalistic factor will not be decisive. But there is probably a risk in offering even these tentative conclusions, aside from the difficulty involved in testing them, because it may be thought that we have suggested that in some cases personalities are by themselves the causes of tension among states. That proposition must be rejected, for no persuasive evidence supports it, and it discounts the existence of objective foreign-policy goals which may be masked by flamboyant behavior and personal recriminations.

Instead, it must be stressed again that, in Southeast Asia, personalized disputes have sometimes reflected long-standing tensions among the states—and, in some instances, these personalized disputes have aggravated the sore spot that already existed. Less often, a personalized axis of communications does seem to have contributed to a lessening of tension. But there are also conflicts among nations in Southeast Asia which have nothing whatever to do with personalities or the personal preferences of leading political figures. There are cases in which a state has one or several real and definable foreign-policy goals; in such instances, the role of personality becomes most apparent and important mainly as it affects the style, the timing, and the tactics adopted in pursuance of those goals.

Part Two: Cooperation in Southeast Asia

CHAPTER V: AN ENVIRONMENT FOR
REGIONAL COOPERATION

Readers may reasonably now wonder whether international relations in Southeast Asia consists of all conflict and no cooperation. Admittedly, a bleak picture has been painted so far, and any potential for cooperation among states in Southeast Asia must be considered against that background. The statesmen and other leaders of the region do, of course, reckon with the conflicts discussed here, both as those conflicts shape the immediate pace and nature of developments, and as challenges to be overcome—particularly if new patterns of international politics are to develop in Southeast Asia. In that sense, earlier parts of this book provide an essential introduction to the subject to be discussed in these final chapters: the environment and prospects for regional cooperation in Southeast Asia. That topic is especially important today, because among leaders in the region there is a consistent, perhaps remarkable, interest in the potential for forms of cooperation among their states.

Two questions come immediately to mind: Why does this interest exist? And how important is it? When leaders in Southeast Asia refer to the goal of "regional cooperation," what, specifically, do they have in mind? Are they merely voicing familiar hopes for peace or are they thinking in more concrete terms? Finally, even among those who favor cooperation, and do think in specific terms, is there agreement on what should be done?

From the perspective of many leaders in Southeast Asia, a number of unsatisfactory conditions—elements of the economic and political environment for cooperation—have given rise to this contemporary interest in regionalism. The political environment, as we have seen, is heavily infused by distrust, and certainly not marked by any important sense of community among the nations of Southeast Asia.

Yet, even in the absence of "community," there has been increasing contact among these states. An intensive communications pattern exists today, although admittedly it derives largely from conflicts and efforts to resolve them. Indeed, the states of Southeast Asia know far more of one another today than at any time in the past, precisely as a result of the region's many troubles. But this mutual awareness also reminds leaders that, despite the vague dreams of regional "unity" expressed from time to time, the states of Southeast Asia are in some respects as divorced from one another today as they were in the colonial period.

The Economic Environment for Regionalism

The economic environment cannot be so readily characterized. Although there is some good information about the economies of each of these nations taken separately, very little attention has been devoted to the economics of the region as an entity. Much needs to be known concerning the area's present and potential interactions, involving not only intraregional trade—which has tended to be a favorite focus of attention—but other forms of economic relations as well. There are, however, two important political features of states in Southeast Asia that help make the potential for economic cooperation susceptible to analysis: the major role played by governments in the economies of the region, and the fundamental commitment of these governments to the goal of rapid economic development.

In Southeast Asia, matters that relate to the economy are subjects of high governmental priority. Compared to the leadership of the already developed nations, national elites in Southeast Asia devote relatively more of their attention to economic problems, and to those things that affect economic development specifically. Indeed, this results from the fundamental commitment to economic development that is so characteristic of the new nations. From the vantage point of our discussion, this commitment to development is a decided analytic advantage, for economic problems are more readily translatable into elements of the political environment. It is in that perspective that the interest in regionalism needs to be judged. This interest touches governmental leaders at a sensitive point: their dedication to economic development, and their relative willingness to use government to achieve that goal.

Within that perspective, it becomes more understandable that many leaders in Latin America, Africa, and Southeast Asia, have devoted so much of their attention to the goal of regionalism. For regional cooperation is more often today than before seen instrumentally—as a means by which to speed the primary goal of national development. For example, in Latin America and in Central America, the subject of regional cooperation has occupied priority attention for almost a decade. But especially since the Montevideo Treaty of 1961, the possible benefits to be derived from a Latin America Free Trade Association (LAFTA), and related forms of regional economic cooperation, have begun to attract increasing attention.[1] Similarly, in East and Central Africa, comparable economic considerations have led leaders in those countries to plan for the adoption of an African common market. They have, for example, proposed agreements for regionwide industrial "rationalization."[2] Generally speaking, the nations of the developing regions do share at least three fundamental economic features which have led to an interest in cooperation with other states: dependence on one or a few raw materials and agricultural commodities as major exports; widespread poverty; and, in many cases, a relatively small population.

There is, of course, plenty of loose thinking by local leaders on the implications of these features. Often they seem preoccupied with mere population size, as if by suddenly tripling their markets they might at the same time become major actors in world economic competition. Consider the proposed economic union for East and Central Africa. Officials in the seven countries concerned claimed, for example, that "by regional planning for a total population of more than 50 million, they can . . . leave themselves less at the mercy of world prices."[3] The very next day, from the other side of the world, newspapers reported that in Cambodia Prince Sihanouk had proposed a "league of Indochinese States." "We would," he said, "be Indochina, a mass of 40 million citizens, representing a not negligible economic potential and natural resources."[4]

Whether the number is 50 million or 40 million, there is no denying that leaders of the developing countries are impressed with what they believe to be the disadvantages of their often relatively small populations. One reason is that the end-product of many manufacturing industries—say, a major petrochemical complex designed also to produce fertilizers—would be unreasonably costly for a market of 10 million

---

[1] See Miguel S. Wionczek, "Latin American Free Trade Association," *International Conciliation*, 551 (January 1965).

[2] See *The Washington Post*, February 28, 1965, for a report of economic integration plans for an area in East and Central Africa larger than India. A major element of this proposal has been to provide for joint industrial licensing, whereby one factory would be given a monopoly in the region for several years.

[3] *Ibid.*

[4] *The New York Times* (March 1, 1965).

people, but might be a much more attractive proposition in a market of 40-50 million. In some cases, economies of scale might result, but there are said to be other potential benefits of cooperation which do not necessarily derive from expanded markets. Thus some have urged that, planning together, small nations could pose more attractive investment conditions than could any one of these states operating alone. Similarly, other leaders from small states, who have little voice when speaking separately, have thought in terms of commodity-producers' agreements, hoping that these would enable the small nations, acting jointly, to extract better trade terms from the large, industrialized nations with which they must deal. For their problem, essentially, is that of a currency squeeze. To implement their national plans, the developing nations need increasingly expensive capital imports—and the hard currencies with which to buy them. These currencies are earned primarily by the sale of the rubber, oil, sugar, tin, and so on, that are the mainstays of the developing nations' economies. Unfortunately, the prices received for these commodity exports have seldom kept pace with the rise in price of the needed capital imports,[5] to say nothing of the imported consumer goods which generally are needed and desired.

The answer, it has seemed to most leaders, is to industrialize as quickly as possible—emphasizing imports of machinery and plant, sometimes to the neglect of agricultural production. That, in turn, reduces the relative availability of hard currency. It is a terrible dilemma, and one that is felt throughout the world. It has led to increasingly insistent demands by the developing countries for "better" treatment by the advanced countries. The 1964 United Nations Conference on Trade and Development was the most striking manifestation of the recognition by the developing nations that their problems are remarkably similar. It helps explain, in part, the new pattern of thinking with which we are concerned here: the revived attention by many leaders to the idea of regional economic cooperation as a means of helping to resolve developmental problems.

In Southeast Asia, moreover, there are elements that reinforce and suffuse the contemporary interest in regionalism. One is the belief that the period of European colonialism gave rise to "artificial" separations

---

[5] See, for example, the conclusion of a recent survey: "The balance of trade of the developing ECAFE countries [by and large, this means Southeast Asia] as a group worsened substantially during the 1950s. . . . By 1959-1961, while the value of exports had remained practically unchanged, *that of imports had risen by 28 per cent.* United Nations, *Economic Bulletin for Asia and the Far East,* XV:1, (June 1964), 2. Italics added.

among peoples who have had much in common. From the beginning of the independence period—say, from 1945—there have been regular exhortations by leaders of the states in Southeast Asia for these states once again to "come together." Men such as Burma's Aung San, and Quirino of the Philippines, complained, as so many others have, that Southeast Asians knew far more about Europe and America than they did of their nearest Asian neighbors. Almost all links, whether of trade, education, communications, and so on, were with the metropole powers or others among the advanced states.[6]

It must be said, however, that there is little historical support for the contention by some Asian spokesmen that Southeast Asia had any important meaning as a region in the precolonial period. Yet what matters is not whether this was ever true, but that some leaders have persuaded themselves that it was. Even more important, however, is that this vaguely expressed desire to establish some sense of community in Southeast Asia now has the potential of a practical and pragmatic basis. This practical basis lies in the priority concern each of these nations attaches to rapid economic development. It makes the concept of regionalism, which was before relatively un-related to national goals, more immediately attractive because of the economic gains that regional cooperation might contain. Their understanding of economics, particularly the economics of development, and their several years of experience with independence, have brought home to leaders in Southeast Asia the possibility that what was before a vague dream may now be both feasible and necessary.

The "case" for regional economic cooperation revolves essentially

---

[6] Several years ago, ECAFE asked three of Asia's senior economists (K. B. Lall, of India's finance ministry; Luang Thavil, former Under-Secretary of Economic Affairs in Thailand; and the prestigious Saburo Okita, Director of Japan's Planning Bureau) to undertake a study of the prospects for regional economic cooperation. Among the statements in that report, which came to be known as that of the "three wise men," was this:

"Asia's pattern of trade is largely an heritage of old political ties which naturally helped to promote close economic links between metropolitan countries in Europe and their dependent territories in Asia. Preferential arrangements in tariffs and trade had been worked out to promote exchange of manufactured goods from metropolitan countries for raw materials. . . . Transport and communication facilities . . . were geared to service this channelled pattern of trade. . . . The trade links . . . left little scope or incentive for trade to be developed across these channels with neighboring countries of the region. In the circumstances, it is not surprising that production, consumption and trading patterns in Asia are extraregionally oriented." Report of the Consultative Group of Experts on Regional Economic Cooperation in Asia" ([formerly "strictly confidential"], December 17, 1961), 14-15.

around the belief that economic cooperation with neighboring countries can smooth the road to growth that is now impeded by their special economic circumstances—their poverty, shortage of capital generally and hard currency in particular, shortage of skills, and dependence on a very narrow range of primary commodities for export earnings. For some, this has meant efforts toward greater regional trade, perhaps developing through stages ultimately into a common market. Others have emphasized the need for an Asian Payments Union, or other steps designed to alleviate relatively short-term currency deficiencies. Most recently, a number of specialists have urged that the most meaningful forms of cooperation will center around an Asian Development Bank, allied perhaps with a plan for regional industrial planning and related programs, designed to develop industrial specialization among the countries of Southeast Asia. Taken together, it is hoped that cooperation will enable these countries to satisfy common needs, and realize economies, through the collective utilization of their separate national resources and skills.

ROLE OF PRIMARY COMMODITIES

A major point relating to the potential for regional cooperation among the nations of Southeast Asia is the heavy dependence on primary commodity exports that is characteristic of their economies. This is seen in Table V-1, which shows the commodities that figure most heavily in the export earnings of Southeast Asian countries. Using monthly averages during 1960, Column (4) shows the percentage of *total* export value that just three commodities represent. Column (5) shows, moreover, how important exports generally are to these countries. It presents the value of exports as a share of their Gross Domestic Product.

Three commodities at most account for the overwhelming bulk of the value of exports of Southeast Asian countries. In some cases, the dependence is extreme, as in Malaya, where rubber exports alone generally account for 60 per cent of the total (and also for 30 per cent of all employment). In others, the proportions are not much smaller —as in Thailand, where rice exports represent more than half the total value, and the Philippines, where one third of all export values are accounted for by sugar.[7]

[7] See, for example, "Annual Report on the Economies of the ASA Countries, 1961-62" (Manila: November 21-24, 1962), Table 17. Mimeo.

This great reliance on an extremely narrow range of export products is not only fundamentally descriptive of Southeast Asia's economies, but is also a major restraint in the logic of their development plans. Whereas many other elements of their economic environment appear to

TABLE V-1

ROLE OF PRIMARY COMMODITIES
IN SOUTHEAST ASIAN EXPORTS

Exports of Three Major Commodities
1960 Monthly Averages

Country	Commodities	Value (in millions of local currency units)	Percentage of Total Exports	Total Exports As Percentage of Gross Domestic Product*
Burma	Rice and rice products, teak, rubber	71 (kyat)	78.9	18
Cambodia	Rice, maize, rubber	173 (riels)	85.2	11.4
Malaya	Rubber, iron ore, tin metal	206 (dollars)	84.4	41.8
Indonesia	Rubber, petroleum and products, tin ore	2,447 (rupiah)	77.6	8.9**
Philippines	Cocoanut and preparations, sugar, logs and timber	33 (U.S. dollars)	70.2	9.0**
Thailand	Rice, rubber, tin ore and concentrates	475 (baht)	66.2	16.6

Source: Adapted and computed from United Nations, *Economic Bulletin for Asia and the Far East,* XV:1 (June 1964), 9 (Table 13), and "Asian Economic Statistics," in *ibid.,* pp. 77, 87, Tables 6 and 7.

* 1959-61 averages, except for Malaya and Indonesia (1958-60) and for Cambodia (1958-59).

** The figures of 9 per cent for Indonesia and the Philippines are misleadingly low, largely as a result of unrealistic exchange rates. "If more realistic exchange rate valuations were used, . . . the resulting ratio of exports to total product in the late 1950s would appear to be in the neighborhood of 14 per cent for both countries. . . ." Douglas Paauw, "Economic Progress in Southeast Asia," *Journal of Asian Studies* (Fall 1963), 81. (For comparative purposes, note that among all developed countries, income from exports accounts for about 8 per cent of gross domestic product; in the United States, of course, the share is perhaps 3 per cent.)

be dynamic, the income from the rice, copra, rubber, and so on has tended to be relatively fixed and unchanging. "By 1959-61, while the value of exports had remained practically unchanged, that of imports had risen by 28 per cent." [8] Thus, the dependence on commodity exports is readily seen as a variable which comes under great pressure, for it must bear the cost of meeting two basic demands: the requirements of rapid population growth, and the increasing quantities and higher costs of needed capital imports. This is a losing battle.

Most studies of economic problems in Southeast Asia point to this dilemma, and note with some distress that, although Asia's populations continue to grow at a high rate, its production of the basic commodities which supply foreign currencies has not kept pace. Often the production of the basic commodities is insufficient to meet even the domestic requirements of a nation's population growth, to say nothing of the additional burdens taken on as a result of its commitment to rapid economic development. One of the earliest examinations of trade patterns among these countries, with a view to analyzing their potential for regional cooperation, noted that "the rate of growth in the region's exports amounted only to 2.6 per cent during 1953-61. On the same basis, the rate of growth of imports was 5.0 per cent." [9] Other studies show that much of the apparent growth rate of Southeast Asia's economies is wiped out by the rise in population, so that in some instances there has been a decline in the over-all ability of the economy to meet national needs.

At best, there is a static quality to much of economic "development" in Southeast Asia.[10] The causes, and some of the suggested remedies,

---

[8] *Economic Bulletin for Asia and the Far East, op. cit.,* p. 2.

[9] *Ibid.,* p. 1. Also see ECAFE, "Report of the Consultative Group of Experts on Regional Economic Cooperation in Asia," p. 11, where this statement is made: "One of the important factors limiting economic growth in many countries of this region is the widening gap between export earnings and import requirements. The less-developed countries in the ECAFE region rely largely on export of their primary products—mainly foodstuffs and industrial raw materials; and external demand for these has been rising less rapidly than the increase in world income or world trade."

[10] Noting that "one can hardly view with equanimity the rising rate of population growth," Douglas Paauw has concluded: "Confronted with this drag on raising per capita real income, no Southeast Asian country has succeeded in raising the rate of growth of aggregate real product over the course of the postwar period. On the contrary, it appears that there has been a perceptible retardation of growth rates in all Southeast Asian countries, and where new growth has occurred it appears that incremental capital output ratios have risen sharply. In short, there has been a tendency for the slow-growth economies to become stagnant and

are probably better argued by economists; it will be sufficient here to note that Asian economists concerned with the problem are increasingly turning to regional cooperation as a major framework for improving the economic environment. And although there is no agreement concerning just what specific forms "cooperation" should take, most would subscribe to this judgment by the Secretary-General of ECAFE, the one institution which looks at the economy of Asia as a whole:

> Recent international economic developments have perhaps brought home one lesson more vividly than any others: *singly and separately* the developing nations of the ECAFE region cannot hope to attain reasonably satisfactory rates of economic growth which would support their fast-growing populations at decent levels of living as envisioned by the United Nations in this development decade. All the prognostications and projections made of the future international trade of the ECAFE developing countries point to the large and growing trade gap with which the region will be confronted in the coming years. On the one hand, the prospective increase in export earnings from traditional export commodities is fairly limited for a variety of technological and other reasons, and on the other, their import requirements for the minimum living needs of their peoples and for executing their programs of economic development are growing steeply.[11]

The conference at which those remarks were made (in Manila at the end of 1963) marked a high point in the evolution of thinking about regionalism among many of Asia's economic elite. The point to stress is that so many recommendations urged cooperation as a major weapon in the drive for development. Governments agreed, for example, to "make coordinated efforts in the planning and execution of agreed industrial, mineral, [and] agricultural projects"; to "promote the growth of intraregional trade"; and to begin work on an Asian Development Bank, which could be an instrument to ease the problems caused by the relative scarcity of hard currency. These, and related actions, should all be regarded as tentative and groping steps taken by the developing countries of Asia. They point up the fact that cooperation

---

for the growing economies to grow less rapidly—both in terms of aggregate and per capita product . . . [plans and policy] have failed to reverse the trend toward a narrowing gap between growth of output and growth of population." "Economic Progress in Southeast Asia," *op. cit.*, p. 90).

[11] Statement by U Nyun, Executive Secretary of the United Nations Economic Commission for Asia and the Far East, Manila, December 1963, ECAFE Doc. E/CN.11.641, January 6, 1964. Italics added.

among states is increasingly seen as a main technique in support of developmental goals.

Trade and Cooperation

One problem, however, has continued to plague the thinking of the leaders concerned, whether they have been government officials and economists, academic specialists, or ECAFE officials: the role of trade in regional cooperation.

Some have argued that greater regional trade is the main *path* to regionalism, while other specialists argue that greater regional trade will be one of the main *results* of cooperation (which should concentrate first on such things as joint industrial planning). Very recently, senior members of the ECAFE secretariat have themselves become sharply divided on this question,[12] though in the past ECAFE's advocacy of cooperation generally tended to stress trade. Indeed, until recently, most advocates of regional cooperation seemed to share a fundamental preoccupation with trade—almost to the exclusion of other potential forms of economic interaction and cooperation. Today, however, it is widely recognized that very little has been accomplished as a result of those urgings, and regional trade in particular remains at a depressingly low level.

The disappointing efforts to increase regional trade, by ECAFE and others, have confirmed the suspicions of some who believe that all regionalism is impractical. This appears to be particularly true of political leaders, but many of their economics advisors are also beginning to lower their estimates of the role that trade alone can play in achieving cooperation. Nevertheless, to the extent that political leaders believe that regionalism is impractical, they of course do much to fulfill that prophecy.

Yet the early focus on trade may have been unavoidable, for most of the world's practical experience with economic cooperation has been with various forms of trade agreements, and also because Asia's econo-

---

[12] This difference is amply illustrated by the stark divergence between the views of Mr. R. Krishnamurti, Chief of ECAFE's trade division (which emphasizes trade) and Professor Hiroshi Kitamura, acting chief of the research and planning division. The differences between the two men symbolize the split, between Japanese and Indians, that seems to divide ECAFE generally. Krishnamurti's position seems so far to have been the dominant one within ECAFE. It may be instructive that when Secretary-General of ECAFE U Nyun convened a "Working Group of Experts on Regional Economic Cooperation" in 1963, the secretariat for the group was comprised exclusively of members of the international trade division.

mists undeniably have been greatly influenced by Western analyses of economic cooperation, which also emphasized trade.[13] Trade, moreover, may appear to be a relatively easy form of cooperation,[14] and it is also quantifiable. Thus those who have wanted to show how much potential there is for greater interaction in the region have had plenty of data to demonstrate the very low level of intraregional trade. The literature is now full of studies, both by ECAFE and by independent economists, that describe this low level of trade, and suggest means for intensifying it.[15] Generally, what they show is that, over the past decade Asia's intraregional trade has been in a steady decline. This is seen in Table V-2, which focuses on the "developing ECAFE countries" (i.e., excluding Australia, Japan, and New Zealand).

As Table V-2 shows, the intraregional trade of the developing ECAFE countries in 1960-62 was smaller than one fourth of their total trade.[16]

[13] Thus when ECAFE adopted in 1960 a resolution favoring "regional economic cooperation for trade and industries," a major study published as a result was entitled "Regional *Trade* Cooperation." (*Economic Bulletin for Asia and the Far East*, XII:1 (June 1961). Dutifully, it examined the various forms of cooperation, such as customs unions, free-trade areas, preferential tariff agreements, and so on—all of which have long been favorite subjects of analysis and effort in the West.

[14] Among Southeast Asian countries at least, when leaders have wished to symbolize a new era of mutual cooperation, they have often begun with promises to buy more of each other's products. The most recent example was in the far-reaching (on paper) agreements between the Philippines and Indonesia, signed in Djakarta on May 27, 1963. Several agreements were signed at that time, as a result of the visit to Djakarta of the "Hechanova Mission."

[15] See "Regional Trade Cooperation," *op. cit.*, and "Measures for Economic Cooperation in the ECAFE Region [Report by a Working Group of Experts], in ECAFE, "Report of the Ministerial Conference on Asian Economic Cooperation." Also see Lim Tay Boh, "Regional Trade Cooperation Among Asian Countries," in *Pakistan Development Review* (Summer 1962), 543-57, and other articles in that issue, particularly that by D. T. Lakdawala, "Trade Cooperation Within the ECAFE Region." Also see A. D. Goseco, "Underdeveloped Countries: A Multilateral Trading Scheme," *The Eastern Economist* (September 1, 1961); and Donald B. Keesing, "A Proposal for a Small Common Market," *Malayan Economic Review* (1965). I am also indebted to Professor Clair Wilcox for an unpublished paper on trade and cooperation in Southeast Asia.

[16] For some countries, including some of the largest, trade within the region is at even lower levels. Thus of Indonesia's total reported imports of almost $800 million in 1961, only $317.5 million represented imports from *all* of Asia. Of even that figure almost one half—$142.3 million—is represented by imports from Japan alone. This means that if Indonesia's transshipments from Singapore are excluded, Southeast Asia provides a negligible portion of Indonesia's imports. Only Burma occasionally ships sizable quantities of goods (rice) to Indonesia, and President Sukarno has promised to send rice imports. These figures are adapted from ECAFE "Intraregional Trade Statistics" (December 27, 1963), Table 9. Mimeo.

TABLE V-2

INTRAREGIONAL TRADE OF ECAFE COUNTRIES,
1952-54, 1956-58, and 1960-62: ANNUAL AVERAGES
(In millions of U.S. dollars)

	Exports			Imports		
	1952-54	1956-58	1960-62	1952-54	1956-58	1960-62
Trade of developing ECAFE countries						
(1) With World	5,920.1	6,988.3	7,919.7	6,718.2	8,388.5	9,386.6
(2) With Developing ECAFE Countries	1,553.1	1,718.4	1,778.4	1,579.8	1,879.2	1,878.8
(3) With All ECAFE Countries	2,259.7	2,579.4	2,866.9	2,384.1	2,984.4	3,393.5
(2) as percentage of (1)	26.2	24.6	22.5	23.5	22.4	19.1
(3) as percentage of (1)	38.2	36.9	36.2	35.5	35.1	34.5

Source: Table I, ECAFE, "Approaches to Regional Harmonization of National Development Plans in Asia and the Far East," E/CN.11/CAEP.2/L.5 (September 25, 1964), 10. Mimeo.

If the trade with Australia, Japan, and New Zealand (i.e., all ECAFE) is included, this proportion was just over one third.

The table indicates some general trends. For example, exports of the developing ECAFE countries to the *world* increased from 1952-54 to 1960-62 by 33.8 per cent, while their exports to all ECAFE countries increased by only 18.6 per cent during the same period. Thus, within the developing ECAFE countries as a region from 1952-54 to 1960-62, both exports and imports decreased as a percentage of total trade to the world: for exports, from 26.2 per cent to 22.5 per cent; imports, from 23.5 per cent to 19.1 per cent.

The low level of intraregional trade, and its decline in relation to total trade, is a fact of the economic environment in Southeast Asia. Its causes have been analyzed by several economists, and the reasons for the decline given in an ECAFE study can be repeated here:

They are mainly the countries' foreign-exchange difficulties and their self-sufficiency drive. . . . Foreign-exchange shortage in the past has necessitated changes in the developing ECAFE countries' import structure. . . . Exchange and import restrictions usually reduced the imports of consumer and other "nonessential" goods and gave priority to the imports of capital goods . . . mostly supplied by the developed countries outside the region. To some extent, P.L. [Public Law] 480 aid from the United

States, tied loans given by the developed countries outside the region and the national self-sufficiency drive . . . were other factors that explain the decline in the intraregional trade of the ECAFE countries.[17]

Even more important, regional trade is not likely to improve. As this study found: "Likely future trends, if left to the natural course of development, do not seem to encourage expansion of intraregional trade."

It is difficult to argue with that conclusion, because the present national plans of these countries show that they intend to continue their present import-substitution policies, and also to export roughly the same basic commodities that they do now.[18] The reason is that only the earnings that come from those exports can provide the capital essential for industrialization, which, in turn, makes it possible for these countries to substitute for as many imports as possible. In the early stages, at least, that policy of import-substitution will emphasize precisely the products that other developing countries are also able to produce, for they are the relatively least sophisticated manufactured goods. Over-all, these development plans will mean a continuation and intensification of the present direction of Southeast Asia's trade to the industrialized world (which, aside from Japan, means the non-Asian world).

Within this perspective, it becomes clear why the efforts by ECAFE and others to intensify regional trade have accomplished so little, for the barriers to greater intraregional trade have not been governmental policies (such as tariffs) designed to inhibit trade, but the present stage of development of Southeast Asia's economies. This fact is now increasingly recognized among economic specialists in the region, both as an explanation of past trade patterns, and as an indication that regional trade is hardly likely to improve. This recognition has two consequences: one negative; the other positive.

The negative consequence is that, regional cooperation, to the extent that it has become associated with regional trade, is regarded as unrealistic. Trade, as an avenue to cooperation, has not worked, and agencies connected with the effort—like ECAFE—have not gained in

[17] ECAFE, "Approaches to Regional Harmonization of National Development Plans in Asia and the Far East," *op. cit.,* p. 9.

[18] The source for this statement is in the several national development plans, and also United Nations, "Foreign Trade Aspects of The Economic Development Plans of ECAFE countries," *Bulletin for Asia and the Far East* (June 1963). It should be pointed out that the phrase used by ECAFE—*the developing ECAFE countries*—includes all the states of Southeast Asia.

reputation as a result. More important, it has become clear that the improvement of regional trade would not in itself have great impact, at least in the short term, on the fundamental goal of rapid national economic development.[19]

Regional "Harmonization" of Development

The positive consequence is that those leaders who continue to attach importance to the goal of cooperation, recognizing that trade may not now be the route, have begun to focus on other means of strengthening economic interaction in Southeast Asia. Because one of the main drawbacks of the approach through trade is that it may not contribute initially to the goal of national economic development, they have turned their attention to means by which to work toward the two goals simultaneously: national development *and* regional cooperation. This approach stresses cooperation in production, and links this closely to the nations' developmental goals. Although this approach gives an important place to trade, it recognizes that existing production and trade patterns are not such "that the mere lifting of trade barriers . . . would considerably increase the intraregional trade flow.[20] This view, for which one of the foremost spokesmen is Professor Hiroshi Kitamura, emphasizes that "mutual cooperation among the countries of the region will have rather to be extended to the sphere of *production,* with a view to changing the composition and magnitude of investment." [21]

The issue should not be seen as a simple dichotomy between trade efforts on the one hand, and developmental efforts on the other. Instead, it is the view of some of Asia's most experienced economists that these two aspects are complementary. They urge that the time has come for the nations of Southeast Asia to combine their efforts in such a way as to benefit from agreements on specialization in production, with increased regional trade as an ultimate result. They seek to put into practice the principle of comparative advantage on a regional basis, reasoning that the task of development is so big, and the problems so commonly shared, that there is enough for each of the nations

---

[19] This is the view expressed by, among others, Professors Kyoshi Kojima, Lim Tay Boh, Noboru Yamamoto, Dr. Puey Ungphakorn, and Saburo Okita, as stated in interviews in Tokyo, Singapore, and Bangkok during 1962, 1963, and 1964.

[20] ECAFE, "Approaches to Regional Harmonization of National Development Plans in Asia and the Far East," E/EN.11/CAEP.2/L.5 (September 25, 1964), 14.

[21] *Ibid.*, p. 16. Italics added.

to specialize on different sectors of production. Greater regional trade, they believe, will be a natural outcome of concentrating first on specialized production.

It is clear that, although the ultimate goals of these perspectives are similar—i.e., greater economic cooperation in the region—there are differences of timing and emphasis. The newer approach urges specialization in production now, so that greater intraregional trade will be generated by the economic complementarities that result from specialization.[22] "The task of policy," Kitamura has suggested, "is not to expand the trade flow along the traditional lines, on which the existing trade barriers are of a marginal significance, *but rather to create deliberately a new pattern of complementary production, on the basis of which alone new lines of trade can be developed.*"[23] Dr. Puey, Governor of the Bank of Thailand, and another of Asia's most competent economists, has spoken frequently in similar terms. In conversations, he has stressed that the effort to intensify intraregional trade has been misplaced; as he sees it, the need is to attract capital—which is lacking locally but available worldwide—to "good-risk" production ventures in Southeast Asia.

These views have major implications; put into practice, they would require cooperative agreements on a single pattern for regionwide industrialization. This, in turn, suggests the need for an agreed-upon format for attracting investment capital to the region. Dr. Puey has suggested, for example, that the economic planners of the countries concerned develop a single "investment prospectus," presenting the industrialization and development plans of the nations involved as a regional entity, and appealing to world money markets on that basis. To avoid redundancies, an intensive analysis of the countries' separate plans would be involved in preparing such a prospectus; indeed, the

[22] In contrast, those whose primary emphasis has been on trade have expected that *specialization* would be the beneficial by-product. To some extent, that was the pattern in the already-developed world and, in orthodox economic terms, removal of trade barriers should indeed enable the countries involved to concentrate on those lines of production in which they have a comparative advantage. This thesis assumes, however, great mobility of internal resources and great supply elasticity, elements which were present in Europe but are not in Southeast Asia. Economic growth in Southeast Asia, in Kitamura's words, "has been inhibited mainly by the factors on the supply side," and efforts to provide economies of scale—as through trade liberalization alone—would have little effect on those factors. For the problem in Southeast Asia, as many have pointed out, is to increase saving potential and to attract larger investment.

[23] *Ibid.*, p. 14. Italics added.

prospectus would be the anvil on which the agreements for regional economic cooperation and development would be hammered out. For a given nation, this might mean deferring or canceling altogether, plans to establish, say, a major paper-and-pulp industry, because one of the other countries in the regional agreement was going to develop that facility. Yet, once completed, this prospectus would provide a paramount advantage: it would allow potential investors to commit capital without fear of competitive enterprises being established during similar time periods and in nearby locations.

Without doubt, the major statement for this thesis is found in the detailed ECAFE study already cited.[24] Prepared under Kitamura's direction, this study makes a dramatic proposal for the "harmonization" of the separate national development plans. Its rationale is that, through harmonization or agreements to specialize on different industrial sectors, the developing countries can achieve the level of investment effort which will allow them to exploit economies of scale. The core of the argument is that, although such investment levels probably are beyond the reach of any one of the nations, opportunities do arise through "deliberate planning of joint efforts . . . for establishing efficient plants of economic size in some of the key industries."[25] In his analysis for ECAFE, Kitamura outlined seven major sectors of industrial activity, each related to the economic development plans of Asian countries, in which he believes there are major opportunities for such "harmonization."

For example, aluminum would seem to provide a natural area for cooperation among Southeast Asian states: the metal will be in heavy demand; the nations of the region have the natural resources to produce it; the capital requirements of this industry are very large; and at some phases of its production there are significant economies of scale. In the developed world, aluminum, because of its special qualities and low cost, "has now come to compete both with other metals such as steel, copper, zinc, tin, and lead and with ceramic and plastic products."[26] Demand for the material, because of its unique qualities,

---

[24] ECAFE, "Approaches to Regional Harmonization of National Development Plans in Asia and the Far East," *op. cit.*, Prof. Kitamura, presently chief of ECAFE's planning and research division, has been professor of economics at Tokyo Metropolitan University. Those readers who have a further interest in the subjects touched on here should certainly consult this remarkable and cogent document, particularly the theoretical analysis (pp. 3-30).

[25] *Ibid.*, p. 15.

[26] *Ibid.*, p. 67.

shows every sign of expanding dramatically among Asian countries: in India, by 1966 aluminum consumption will have tripled in ten years; in Taiwan, consumption doubled in only three years; and in Japan, "the projected consumption of 262,000 tons in 1965 was already exceeded in 1961." [27]

In Southeast Asia, moreover, there is plenty of bauxite (Japan is already heavily dependent on producers in Indonesia and Malaysia), and both Indonesia and the Philippines presently have plans to establish major aluminum-producing facilities.[28] Because market size is an important factor in determining relative profitability in this industry, a case may exist for cooperative specialization among several of these neighboring states. Economies of scale seem especially important in the labor-intensive bauxite-mining phase; it was found in Ghana, for example, that labor input decreased by 40 per cent (from 3.4 to 2.0 man-hours per ton) when the scale of operation increased from 400,000 tons to 1 million tons.[29] In the later stages of alumina and aluminum production there are again economies of scale, and particularly heavy investment requirements as well.[30] Generally, the factors that most affect cost (such as the price of electric power) point to strong incentives for cooperation among states which do not by themselves possess all the necessary production ingredients. For example, cooperation among those states producing cheap electricity, and those which can produce bauxite, seems indicated, and as Kitamura concluded: "Any step in the direction of cooperation for a larger market is welcome." [31]

[27] *Ibid.*, p. 69.

[28] Indonesia's plan is to establish, with considerable Soviet assistance, an integrated alumina-aluminum industry, and the Philippines proposal also depends on foreign capital.

[29] We cannot be precisely certain, of course, of the exact extent to which improvements in technology also accounted for the man-hour reduction, and to what extent true scale economies have been responsible for this saving.

[30] The economies of scale in aluminum production which we cite as relevant for developing countries would not apply to the United States. In the United States reduction in production cost is today not so much a factor of scale economies as it is a function of technological improvement and innovation. In general, it might be said that (1) there is a certain minimum output point below which aluminum production makes little sense to anyone; (2) that above that point and up to a higher level of production, scale economies do exist; and (3) beyond a certain magnitude of production scale economies are of little or no importance. As we are dealing with the subject here, it is the middle range that is being discussed.

[31] ECAFE, "Approaches to Regional Harmonization of National Development Plans in Asia and the Far East," *op. cit.*. p. 72.

Another field that would seem to call for cooperation is fertilizer production. The ECAFE region now accounts for only about 10 per cent (3.5 million tons) of world consumption of this product, yet one study estimated that, if farm acreage remains constant, 20 million tons will be needed annually by 1980. Recognizing this problem, all the states in the region do plan to increase vastly their production and use of fertilizers, but this effort requires a massive investment of technological skills, machinery, raw materials, and capital. Indonesia, alone, for example, has programmed more than $225 million for this purpose; if the needs of the entire region are to be satisfied, an equipment expenditure approaching $5 billion will be required.

Would cooperation on production aid in the realization of these goals? Although the question has never been thoroughly investigated, preliminary signs do point in that direction. The areas calling for agreement concern the production of the specialized machinery and plant involved, as well as production of the different types of fertilizers. One thing is certain: if the nations of Southeast Asia are to satisfy their requirements for fertilizers with purchases from the industrialized world, very heavy foreign-exchange costs will be incurred. Another strong likelihood is that the region probably possesses the raw materials from which chemical fertilizers can efficiently be produced, but that considerable geological research and exploration is necessary before major local production can be undertaken. These requirements may themselves provide a suitable opportunity for joint ventures.

There are, of course, additional developmental goals shared by many of the nations in Southeast Asia, which seem, on initial analysis, to be likely candidates for regional specialization and cooperation. Probably the best-known industrial categories are the production of rubber, juice, rice, and paper and pulp—to say nothing of iron and steel. Insofar as they have been examined, they all appear to provide illustrations where cooperation or coordination could permit the achievement of developmental goals sooner and more efficiently than would be possible for any one nation acting alone. In some cases, this is because of the economies of scale that would develop, or because the sheer amount of the investment required is too great for any single state, or because several of the needed resources for a given industry are located in different countries.

Under such a system, most of the nations would not possess *all* the industrial facilities they may now contemplate, but the system holds out a major advantage over present single-nation planning: it makes the achievement of certain of their goals practicable much earlier than would otherwise be possible, and it brings forth the likelihood that those major industrial ventures which are established in Southeast Asia will be of such size and efficiency that they can reasonably be called economical. That is no mean advantage, because the long-term economic goals of the Southeast Asian countries can be realized only when the products of their industries can compete in world markets.

What should be stressed, therefore, is that the industrial-harmonization concept may alter the essentially economic aspects of the environment for cooperation. The regional environment can be seen as a field in which both disincentives and incentives to cooperation come into play, and the industrial-harmonization proposal appears to give rise to certain incentives. In large measure, this is because of the linkage it may provide between national development goals on the one hand, and cooperation on the other. Some aspects of the economic environment that purportedly are related to regionalism—the emphasis on intraregional trade in particular—have not seemed to show this linkage. That absence of close articulation contributed to the sense of unreality, or impracticality, that many Asian leaders have associated with the concept of regional cooperation. Thus, as long as the political hurdles to cooperation seemed too high, and insofar as the economic aspects of cooperation appeared so slightly related to their national goals, it is not surprising that among Asian leaders there has been a disbelief that regionalism could be considered a matter of practical politics. On balance, there were few important incentives to regard regional cooperation as serious business, while the disincentives were all too clear.

Important aspects of the industrial harmonization concept, however, are in direct support of indigenous development goals, and it is, in that sense, appropriate to regard harmonization as an incentive for regional cooperation. This would be especially clear in those instances where harmonization may encourage a nation to establish an industrial facility for which its government has already established a priority in its national plan. Moreover, certain clearly extranational ideas which have long been regarded as impractical or unworkable (such as an Asian Payments Union) carry much more practical meaning when tied to a regional plan for industrial specialization. This is the case regarding an Asian Development Bank, an often proposed step which now has formal ECAFE backing and which is also supported by the United States. Such a bank has for years been urged by a number of economists in

Southeast Asia,[32] and it is now, for the first time, seen as a practical matter.

This is the fundamental contradiction that must follow from every examination of the scope and potential for regional cooperation in Southeast Asia. The goal of cooperation continues to attract the attention of Southeast Asian leaders. What has altered, for the first time since Asian leaders began to talk of regionalism in the immediate postwar period, is that some of the steps in support of cooperative proposals are now seen to support basic national goals as well. This gives to the previously vague and perhaps idealistic notion of regionalism a practical basis and meaning. Moreover, it is once again clear that the United States, which has long given at least vocal support to regionally cooperative economic efforts in several parts of the globe, may now be prepared to give concrete assistance to such efforts in Southeast Asia. As President Johnson announced in his famous Baltimore speech of April 7, 1965: "The first step is for the countries of Southeast Asia to associate themselves in a greatly expanded cooperative effort for development. . . . For our part, I will ask the Congress to join in a billion-dollar American investment in this effort." [33]

[32] See, for example, the speech and article by P. Sithi-Amnuai, "A Regional Bank as a First Step Towards an Asian Common Market," *Bangkok Bank Monthly Review* (March 1963), 76.

[33] Lyndon B. Johnson, *The New York Times* (April 8, 1965). The United States does even now give material aid to certain cooperative efforts though these are not of major proportions. One illustration is in the annual foreign-aid payment given to the Asian Productivity Organization, an intergovernmental and intergroup organization with headquarters in Tokyo. The purposes of the A.P.O. include training and other forms of assistance to national "productivity" organizations, with the emphasis on improving industrialization and manufacturing techniques particularly in small- and medium-scale enterprises. Similarly, through its financial contribution to ECAFE, and its specific contribution to the Mekong River project, the United States has given support and encouragement to that intra-Asian development project. The Mekong project, designed eventually to transform the valley of the Mekong, by a series of projects in dam-building, agricultural improvement, and electric-power generation, figured prominently in President Johnson's Baltimore speech on Southeast Asia.

The major earlier U.S. effort to support a regional approach to Asian development, however, led to a widespread disappointment among U.S. officials. It was at the conference at Simla, in India in 1955, at which the United States apparently offered to make its foreign-aid assistance available on a multilateral, or "regional basis," as one part of an effort to improve regional contact and regional economic cooperation. The recipient countries were apparently not very much interested, partly, it is reported, for fear that they would receive less aid from the United States if that aid were part of a regional "pie," than if each were to approach Washington separately. This is reported in most detail in L. P. Singh, "Asian International Organizations: The Politics of Regional Economic Cooperation in

It is apparent from President Johnson's words that any effort in which the United States participates will be dependent on Southeast Asian initiatives. It is no doubt recognized by now that, along with the many other difficulties which can impede an effort to bring about regional cooperation in Southeast Asia, any suspicion that the idea is generated from outside of Asia can be the kiss of death. Thus the American expectation is that, if practical advances are to be made in the direction of economic cooperation, they must come largely from internal efforts. Such a conclusion is not only consistent with American interests, but it will probably also be regarded as the correct policy by those who desire greater regional cooperation, for regional cooperation must be an essentially indigenous effort.

Asia." Unpublished doctoral dissertation, Australian National University, Canberra, 1965, pp. 9-12.

CHAPTER VI: ASA: THEORY AND PRACTICE
IN SUBREGIONAL
COLLABORATION

The Bangkok Declaration of July 31, 1961, established the Association of Southeast Asia, known usually as ASA within the region but barely known at all outside the area. Yet, unlike the better-known "regional" organizations in Southeast Asia (e.g., the Colombo Plan, SEATO, and ECAFE), ASA was inspired and organized by Asians. This alone may give it a promise for the future the others cannot match[1] and also suggests one important reason to understand ASA: it is a substantive illustration of an indigenous effort toward regionalism.

Of course, with its limited membership—Thailand, Malaysia, and the Philippines—ASA is, more accurately, a subregional body. As an ECAFE study reasoned, the entire Asian region, or even Southeast Asia, is simply too big and diverse for intensive regional cooperation, but some procedures—such as reciprocal tariff reduction—could be contemplated on a subregional basis:

> . . . the Foreign Ministers of the Association of Southeast Asia, for instance, decided in April 1963 that each member government should "explore the possibility of establishing among the ASA countries a free trade area initially in respect of certain commodities as a basis for future discussions. . . ."[2]

ASA is also an example, in Asia, of the general conditions involved in any environment for collaboration among nations. In today's international relations integrative steps and other efforts toward cooperation

---

[1] But a warning must be given at the outset. Although ASA was established as an organization for cooperation, primarily in economic and "cultural" fields, it can show few major material achievements. Indeed, it has been in a state of limbo ever since Malaya and the Philippines broke relations a few days after Malaysia was established in September 1963. ASA's present status is that it is inactive, although all three governments insist that its activities will be resumed soon.

[2] "Measures for Economic Cooperation in the ECAFE Region," Report by a Working Group of Experts, Appendix 2, pp. 21-22, in "Report of the preparatory Meeting for the Special Conference on Asian Economic Cooperation," Appendix V in ECAFE, "Report of the Ministerial Conference on Asian Economic Cooperation," E/CN.11/641 (January 6, 1964). Italics added.

are among the most interesting patterns of political behavior. As Ernst Haas has noted, the study of regionalism challenges the theorist because of its "potentialities . . . for insights into the process of community formation at the international level."[3] Haas himself, and another student of politics, Professor Harold Guetzkow, have separately studied the politics of integration (particularly in Europe), and both authors have attempted to generalize upon the conditions under which nations may collaborate. Their findings, and their subject matter, parallel in many respects the steps toward regional cooperation in Southeast Asia.

The Conditions for Collaboration: Observations on Theory

Haas, for example, was concerned with the background against which collaboration has developed in postwar Europe, and found that an important element was a dissatisfaction among elites with present conditions. There was among some, he writes, a desire to establish "a new way of life," and among all a "dissatisfaction with European international relations of the interwar variety."[4] Guetzkow has written along similar lines: "past experience factors," he suggests, are among the critical elements that will determine whether an environment will be conducive or inimical to collaboration.[5] He suggests that past experience with successful intergroup relations produces a tendency toward collaboration and that, conversely, consistent experience with satisfactory "internal or self-reliant measures" produces a tendency to avoid collaboration.

Heavy emphasis on past experience may have only limited utility in Southeast Asia, for the states there have barely more than a decade of modern independent existence and experience. Yet, one of the major themes stressed by all Asian leaders and statesmen who have urged various forms of cooperation is that some degree of "Asianness," though

---

[3] Ernst B. Haas, "The Challenge of Regionalism," in Stanley Hoffman (ed.), *Contemporary Theory in International Relations* (Englewood Cliffs, N. J.: Prentice-Hall, Inc., 1961), p. 223.

[4] *Ibid.*, p. 231. Haas based much of his findings on data in Karl W. Deutsch, *et al., Political Community and the North Atlantic Area: International Organization in the Light of Historical Experience* (Princeton, N. J.: Princeton University Press, 1957).

[5] Harold Guetzkow, "Isolation and Collaboration: a Partial Theory in Internation Collaboration," in James N. Rosenau (ed.), *International Politics and Foreign Policy* (New York: The Free Press of Glencoe, Inc., 1962), pp. 152-63.

not unity, existed in the region before it was carved up by the European colonialists. They argue that the colonial period emphasized and deepened such divisions as already existed in Southeast Asia, and added some new ones as well. Many also complain that the impact of the Cold War intensifies the region's divisions, robbing Asians of their capacity to make an Asian contribution to contemporary problems.[6] Thus, what Haas points to as European "dissatisfaction" with previous political patterns is sometimes underscored in Asia; there it appears as a desire to break completely with certain aspects of the political past. Perhaps this reaction against the colonial period does reinforce contemporary interest in closer intra-Asian cooperation. If true, Asians' knowledge of their past history does contribute to collaborative tendencies, and Guetzkow's hypothesis is in part supported.

Guetzkow has also suggested hypotheses which bear closely on the perspectives, especially the economic condition, of newly independent states. Some of the fundamental problems of trade and economics found in most of the developing countries come to mind here: the "squeeze" between low-priced exports and high-priced imports; foreign-exchange problems; commitment to rapid development and industrialization, and so on. Many of Asia's economists and other leaders believe that these problems require regional cooperation for their effective resolution. This is a conclusion strongly evocative of what Guetzkow has called "the nature of the task hypothesis." In his words: *"by their very nature the group's unsatisfied demands may or may not necessitate relations with other groups for their realization."* [7] For example, he points out that:

A small state with neither the quantities nor the range of raw materials to supply its own needs will seek trading relations with other units far more often than will a large continental power with a wide variety of resources within its own borders.[8]

---

[6] For many in Southeast Asia, of course, the desire to see Asians act together, and speak with a common voice, finds expression in the Afro-Asian movement generally, and specifically in such widely applauded (in Asia) efforts as the Bandung Conference of 1955. That was in many senses an effort at cross-national collaboration in Asia, though clearly the forces that brought Bandung into being were not sufficient to provide for continued existence. It might even be argued that the forces that eventually dissipated the "spirit of Bandung" were themselves a product of non-Asian influences imposed on indigenous desires.

[7] Guetzkow, in Rosenau, *op. cit.,* pp. 156-57. Italics in original.

[8] *Ibid.,* p. 157. Applying this to contemporary Southeast Asia, Professor Guetzkow is probably right, for somewhat the wrong reasons. That is, economists and planners in the newer nations are far more likely to perceive trade as a stimulus to growth and development, rather than in the more simplistic and somewhat

Haas, in his analysis of ten historical cases and in his own research on the EEC, also found that "expectations of economic gain are constituents of the process of integration found to recur with monotonous regularity."[9] In Southeast Asia the economic incentives may indeed be the critical factors; far more than in Europe, the potential economic advantages of regional cooperation have so far been its paramount attraction.

At least one other of Haas' major findings bears directly on the Southeast Asian environment, and gives rise to some optimism about the eventual outcome of contemporary Asian interest in regionalism: the ease with which cooperative steps could be taken varied inversely with the breadth of political responsibility in a state. In the European integration experience, cabinet ministers and planners had to bargain extensively with well-organized, articulate, and powerful special-interest groups (including labor unions, parties, industrialists, and trade associations). Clearly, European leaders have considerably less decision-making latitude in this sphere than do key elites in Southeast Asia, where economic planning is taken more for granted, and where special-interest groups are generally far less organized—where, indeed, they exist at all. Haas concluded that "government negotiators and high civil servants working in isolation from political pressures and democratic accountability achieve mutual responsiveness more readily than groups resting on mass support."[10] If this is true, and preliminary experience in Asia indicates that it is, those who hope to bring about cooperation in Southeast Asia will have at least one lower hurdle to overcome than did their European counterparts.

Haas and Guetzkow raised other provocative suggestions, and as ASA is examined, we hope to show how these hypotheses bear on Southeast Asian data. Four major problems will be examined concerning ASA: the reasons for its establishment; its goals; its accomplishments; and the lessons it may contain about the process of cooperation.

The Establishment of ASA

The first occasion on which responsible officials of Southeast Asian governments met together, in the series of events which led eventually to the formation of ASA, was the Tunku's visit to Manila in early

---

old-fashioned autarchic terms that Guetzkow's emphasis on "limited resources" implies.

[9] Haas, *op. cit.*, p. 239.

[10] *Ibid.*, p. 236.

January 1959. The Malayan premier did not intend to launch a formal effort at the time; instead, he hoped simply to familiarize President Garcia with ideas that he and other officials in Kuala Lumpur had been considering for months.[11] Specifically, what Rahman had in mind was a new organization, under a "Southeast Asian Friendship and Economic Treaty"; privately, his advisors were already referring to the proposed group as SEAFET.

SEAFET, they planned, would be a "nonpolitical" group, including not only the Western-affiliated states but also such "neutralist" nations as Burma and Indonesia, and functioning largely in the fields of economic and cultural cooperation. Clearly, Kuala Lumpur did not envisage defense or mutual-security measures, or avowedly political consultation.

But it is also clear that a fundamentally political interest moved Rahman to propose regional cooperation. His major concern was to develop a program to forestall the Communist movement in Southeast Asia, where, he was convinced, poverty is its major ally. He believed that, by increasing economic well-being in the area, regional cooperation could help defend against Communist expansion. He also admitted to a vague feeling (as he told some of his foreign-ministry personnel) that "we cannot live alone," even though Malaya's own immediate economic and security situation did not then require any special ties to the region.[12]

President Garcia, however, seemed to have had a project of more immediate impact in mind. Manila officials told Rahman's party that SEAFET, as originally conceived, was "too broad and grandiose" (which was another way of saying that, in 1959, Manila preferred to associate primarily with the Western-oriented nations of Southeast Asia). Nevertheless, Garcia felt sufficiently certain that he and the Tunku were thinking along similar lines, for he announced that they had agreed on the need for a new regional group. Although Rahman reportedly felt that Garcia's public announcement was premature, a train of events had been set in motion.

One unfortunate consequence, however, probably did come from that first step: Garcia's specific and public association of Rahman's

[11] As early as 1958, when the Tunku made a brief visit to Ceylon, he had spoken publicly of his belief that regional cooperation might bring considerable benefits to the nations of Southeast Asia.

[12] These paragraphs are based largely on extensive interviewing among foreign-ministry personnel, including ministers, in Manila and Kuala Lumpur in 1962, 1963, and 1964. Departmental documents were also consulted.

proposals with both countries' dread of Communism.[13] Since then, despite all ASA disclaimers and its actions to the contrary, leaders in other Southeast Asian countries—particularly in Indonesia, Cambodia, and Burma—have maintained that ASA is a "political" group. Some, like Indonesian Foreign Minister Subandrio, have not attempted to conceal their conviction that ASA is merely a front for SEATO.[14]

Later in 1959, Thailand and Malaya took steps to bring the still-vague proposals for cooperation closer to fruition. Thailand's foreign ministry prepared a proposal for regional collaboration, a "Preliminary Working Paper on Cooperation in Southeast Asia," which it circulated to other governments in July.[15] In October, Rahman sent letters to the leaders of every Southeast Asian state (except North Vietnam),[16] soliciting their comments on his regional proposals, and suggesting that they meet to discuss them.

THE THAI PROPOSALS

The Bangkok proposals are important both because they were so widely circulated, and also because of what they emphasized and evidently sought to discount.[17] Thailand, too, wanted to attract the "neutral" nations of the area, but felt that to exclude "politics" would be unrealistic and narrow:

It has been proposed by some countries (Philippines and Malaya) that the scope of the organization should be limited to the economic and cultural fields. However, in view of recent developments in the region, it is felt that such a scope would be too limited and unnecessarily so. Therefore, it is submitted that SEACOR[18] should be allowed to take up and consider any concrete and practical problem affecting the Southeast Asian

[13] See *The New York Times* (January 4, 1959).

[14] Subandrio interview with the author, Djakarta, July 4, 1963.

[15] Interview, Ministry of Foreign Affairs, Bangkok, July 1963. Except for Hanoi, all regional capitals were contacted by mid-August 1959.

[16] Hamilton Fish Armstrong, "The Troubled Birth of Malaysia," *Foreign Affairs* (July 1963), 861-82.

[17] Moreover, compared with the cooperative proposals which had so far come from Manila and Kuala Lumpur, the Thai paper illustrates a far more hard-headed approach. In part this is probably the result of a larger, more experienced, and highly trained staff in Bangkok, and they prepared a sophisticated, detailed document.

[18] The Thais wanted to call the group "Southeast Asia Community Organization," thus SEACOR.

region or some of its members, regardless of whether such problem is political, economic, or otherwise.[19]

Thailand conceded that the new group probably would devote most of its attention to economic problems and, on that premise, sought to make specific recommendations. Market arrangements and commodity pricing, it suggested, would be an excellent place for cooperation to begin, because the countries' economies were so dependent on their agricultural exports.

Although Manila and Kuala Lumpur had stressed already the scope for cultural cooperation, Bangkok concluded that—in a region in which each state tends to be heavily Buddhist, Christian, or Muslim—attempts at cultural cooperation might prove more divisive than cohesive. The Thai study recommended, therefore, that "cultural activities which have been suggested by some countries should be dropped and replaced by educational, artistic, and technical activities." [20] And these educational and technical activities were seen by Bangkok, not as ends in themselves, but as instruments designed to further the common economic interests of the area. Indeed, Bangkok officials pointed to the high cost of the most modern "technical and technological undertakings" and hoped that cooperation in those fields would yield large economic benefits.

Unlike many other suggestions for international cooperation, Thailand's proposals seemed consistently directed against dramatic public symbols of achievement. Instead of suggesting, for example, that a permanent headquarters be established, Bangkok emphasized that the administrative machinery of the organization should be "kept at a minimum," and stressed its desire for an "informal" and "practical" organization. Bangkok also suggested that the new association conduct its meetings in private, with press and public attendance permitted only at the formal opening sessions, and, specifically, that "there shall be no record kept of the prime-ministers' and foreign-ministers' meetings." [21]

[19] Ministry of Foreign Affairs, "Preliminary Working Paper on Cooperation in South-East Asia" (Bangkok: 1959), Mimeo. In author's possession.

[20] *Ibid.*

[21] How different this is from the strong sentiment of leaders in many other nations to conduct every negotiation in public. Compare, for an understanding of the gap between the "style" of the Thai government, and the American-influenced Philippines, a remark of then Philippines Foreign Minister S. P. Lopez. In January, 1964, when he was asked whether Macapagal would enter into any secret understandings with President Sukarno (on Malaysia), his reply was emphatically

These are precisely the lines along which ASA has developed. There has been a conscious effort to keep the group's internal workings quite private, and to avoid the kinds of public announcements that can lead to a hardening of positions. ASA's annual public announcements have been no more than a brief record of agreements, and the yearly foreign-ministers' report is merely a listing of topics discussed by delegates and on which more negotiation is necessary. Even ASA's "confidential" documents, normally restricted to officials of the member governments, are far from complete records of what actually transpired. There is, for example, no such thing as the classified "verbatim transcript," which has been a product of British Commonwealth prime-ministers' meetings. Consequently, ASA public records have very limited utility as historical documents, and even its confidential records will leave future historians with the feeling that something is missing.

This is all quite intentional, and reflects a sensitive and sophisticated approach to the problem of conducting international organizations. No ASA delegate need fear that his private negotiating position will soon become public knowledge, becoming thus a public commitment from which he can no longer gracefully retreat. Similarly, Thailand's early recommendation against a permanent headquarters—that modern symbol of world prestige—has proved a major asset to ASA: it has avoided any possibly irritating debate on location, and forced each of the three governments' relevant bureaucracies (because there is no "international secretariat") to become intimately involved with ASA proceedings and to assume responsibility for planning and implementing cooperative steps.

This organizational style, emphasizing privacy, the softening of conflict, and joint responsibility, appears to be quite consistent with Haas' findings in Europe. In a discussion of the "essential" requirements for community-formation, he writes:

> Leadership groups must continue to practice skill in *de-emphasizing divisive values* and in stressing common aspirations, and to facilitate easy interchange in group and personal roles in common tasks.[22]

Haas also regards this factor as a "background requirement," and notes that a "willingness to de-emphasize clashing aspirations" was found

---

negative. The principle that would govern the Macapagal-Sukarno talks, Lopez said, "will be the Wilsonian doctrine of open covenants openly arrived at." Lopez statement to the press at Manila International Airport, January 7, 1964.

[22] Haas, *op. cit.*, p. 226. Italics added.

(in Europe) only among a very small group of politicians and administrators. This is also the general pattern so far evident in the development of ASA. Perhaps Thailand, with its longer experience as an
independent state, was more aware of these organizational principles
than either the Philippines or Malaya; at any rate, it deserves much
credit for insisting on the qualities of informality, pragmatism, and
privacy, that characterize ASA.

Yet it was largely the continuing interest and enthusiasm of Kuala
Lumpur and Manila that insured the establishment of ASA. Bangkok, essentially conservative in its approach to regional cooperation, initially would have preferred no organization at all to one that
was not reasonably consistent with its views. Rahman and Garcia, on
the other hand, wanted to see a start made, and they cared less than
the Thais about each and every detail. This blend of enthusiasm and
caution may have been precisely what was needed.

THE MALAYAN CORRESPONDENCE

The Bangkok proposals were only the first of two unilateral steps,
n mid-1959, leading toward regional cooperation. The second was
Rahman's effort to contact the region's leaders. The environment in
vhich ASA was established is highlighted in those letters. All the notes
vere similar in substance, and their general nature is revealed in por-
ions of the Tunku's message to Sukarno, dated October 28, 1959:

> The objective of this association is to encourage closer relations among
> the countries of Southeast Asia by discussion, conferences, or consultation,
> and to achieve agreement freely. It is hoped by this method that countries
> will be able to understand each other more deeply. It is also the objective
> of this association to study ways and means of helping one another—
> particularly in economic, social, and cultural and scientific fields. . . .
> You will understand that because of historical circumstances, the economic
> growth of most of the countries in Southeast Asia in this century has been
> influenced by relations with countries outside the region. Because of this,
> the feeling of "one region" has been stunted, . . . and because of these
> historical circumstances, we have looked for help and examples from the
> outside and seldom look to ourselves. . . .
>
> Mr. President, you of course realize that this region is not rich only in
> natural resources but also in culture, history, population, and so on. I
> believe that, by getting together more closely, we will be able to make
> more advantageous use of all of these resources, for the benefit of all,
> and will be able to enrich our own countries by cooperation of all kinds.
>
> I also believe that, from the viewpoint of international relations, by

establishing this form of association we will be able to put forward our view more convincingly, especially in international economics, because we share many common interests. Even if we cannot achieve full agreement on a particular subject, we will be at least better able to understand, through this association, why we cannot achieve agreement.[23]

These letters, which provide some indication of the nature of Rahman's approach (and which shed some light on later Indonesian-Malaysian relations), accomplished little. Despite Rahman's stress on economic and technical cooperation, and his de-emphasis of "politics," the replies he received from Djakarta, Rangoon, and Phnom Penh were unfavorable. Djakarta was curt, even condescending; while Rangoon found it "inadvisable" to participate "at this stage." It was clear from these responses that cooperation in Southeast Asia would include, at least initially, only Thailand, Malaya, and the Philippines, and no effort made during the next two years succeeded in enticing a fourth member.[24] Indeed, had officials of the three states not been so concerned with finding a "neutral" fourth member for the proposed group, ASA would very likely have been established months sooner.

THE FINAL STAGES
AND ORGANIZATIONAL PATTERNS

Concrete planning for ASA seems to have begun in April 1960, when a Malayan official visited the foreign ministers of Thailand and the Philippines[25] to set guidelines for later meetings of substantive "experts." Progress was slowed during the rest of 1960, partly because threatening security developments in the area commanded the attention of senior officials. In February 1961, foreign ministers of Thailand and the Philippines met with the Tunku in Kuala Lumpur and the

[23] From a copy in the files of one of the governments concerned (translated for the author).

[24] Thai officials continued to hope almost right up to the actual forming of ASA (July 1961) that Burma might join. As for Indonesia, President Sukarno's reply to the Tunku, on December 31, 1959, negates the Indonesian claim that its leaders were not consulted about the establishment of ASA. Sukarno answered, for example, that although "it is good, in fact necessary," for Southeast Asian countries to establish close cooperation, "a new association . . . will only raise doubts and . . . become a stumbling block to our desire to cooperate." Sukarno suggested, therefore, that the countries of the region concentrate instead on bilateral arrangements. He added that if wider cooperation were desired, "I can foresee possibilities within the Afro-Asian context. . . " From Sukarno's letter to the Tunku (typescript).

[25] Inche Mohammed Sopiee was the Tunku's special representative.

three announced their intention to "proceed with the formation of the proposed organization for economic and cultural cooperation in Southeast Asia." [26]

Each government now established its own "working group," and (with trade and finance officials playing a major role) each drew up those proposals and projects which it wanted to emphasize as objects of cooperation. By late June, members of the three groups combined into the "Joint Working Party." Acting now as a single group, their task was to present first the nations' separate proposals and then select categories on which all felt cooperative efforts might be developed. Thus, when the three foreign ministers met in Bangkok, they had available as an agenda the recommendations of this Joint Working Party. Accordingly, on July 31, 1961, the formation of ASA was officially announced, amid widespread reports that many of its sponsors saw economic cooperation as its major objective.[27]

It cannot be too strongly emphasized that the initial concrete planning for ASA was the responsibility of officials already involved heavily in their own states' developmental efforts, not that of a "central" staff. This is particularly significant in light of Guetzkow's hypothesis, which emphasizes "indigenous techniques" and "internal procedures" as conditions conducive to collaboration. He adds, moreover, that Professor Percy Corbett, an early student of modern international organization, had implicitly used this hypothesis. In an analysis of international service agencies, Corbett wrote that international groups learned that "the best means of achieving the common object in each country is to stimulate the development of resourceful and devoted *native organs*." As Guetzkow writes, in words suggestive of Chester Barnard's perspectives on organization: "internal procedures are familiar procedures." [28]

This seems to have been the organizational model for the steps that led to the formation of ASA. Those procedures, rather than being far-off and unfamiliar, were internal and national—in Guetzkow's term, "proximate." The Joint Working Party, for example, met for just three days (June 19-21, 1961); thus it necessarily relied heavily on the results submitted by each of the three national working parties, which had deliberated separately for several months. Clearly, the effort that

[26] Ministry of External Affairs, Federation of Malaya, "The Story of ASA" (January 1963), 3. Mimeo.

[27] See M. P. Gopalan, "The Launching of ASA," *Far Eastern Economic Review*, (September 21, 1961).

[28] Guetzkow, *op. cit.*, p. 156. Italics added.

established ASA was not exerted by an ad hoc "international secretariat," but came from within each nation. This style, which emphasized intensive national participation by involving a relatively large segment of the bureaucracy, and which continued to characterize ASA, may help to explain the organization's relative survivability. As Guetzkow suggests, there is probably a built-in factor inhibiting international collaboration when (and because) its procedures are unfamiliar: "Citizens often can perceive more clearly the structure of the initiation, control, and results of intragroup means." The ASA experience would seem to support this analysis. For example, officials responsible for the development of ASA have consistently emphasized familiar methods: they have avoided establishing glamorous new agencies, and they have utilized the existing institutions and communications paths within each government.

At the same time, it is clear that if a new organization is to survive, and achieve some of its goals, new patterns of behavior and communication—in this case international communication—must be developed. Professor Haas found that (in Europe), "new modes of conduct and new channels of communication among elites did not develop until *after* the institutional constitutive act." [29] In Southeast Asia, the effects of formal establishment were even more apparent, probably because communication among Asian elites had been so weakly developed. But the greatest impact of ASA's formal establishment and the intensified communications it produced, has probably been in the new ways of thinking that were generated. One area in particular has been notably affected: economic cooperation.

ASA's Economic Environment and Its Early Expectations

Proposals for economic cooperation, especially in trade, have been a prominent feature of ASA's environment since its inception. Central banks and economics ministries were heavily represented in the first Joint Working Party; when that was divided into three major committees, the one dealing with "economics and related matters" was believed by many participants and observers to be the most significant.[30] In the Philippines, for example, Vice-President Pelaez (on his return from the April 1962 meetings of ASA) "presumed the future

[29] Haas, *op. cit.*, p. 231.
[30] The other two committees dealt with "cultural and social questions," and problems of "ASA procedures and organization." See Gopalan, *op. cit.*

of ASA will be a common-market scheme," [31] and months before ASA was established Under-Secretary for Commerce Laguio had suggested

> . . . lowering of intrabloc tariffs, industrial complementarity, joint bargaining over the marketing of raw materials, expansion of members' merchant marines for trading purposes, an organization to stabilize prices and supply of essential consumer goods and possibly operate a price stabilization fund, technical interchange based on liberalized immigration procedures, and a multilateral payments system to secure maximum trade reciprocity.[32]

Yet the same report noted that many of Laguio's colleagues in Manila felt that advocacy of these steps was at least "premature." Their doubts underscore a major element in the Asian environment which applies to ASA as well: the general skepticism about the practicality of a regional approach.[33] Any description of the economic environment of Asia must distinguish between fact and judgment. The facts (pointed to in Chapter V and relevant also for the ASA subregion) are fairly clear: they show a dismal pattern of economic interaction among the three ASA countries. Seen from the Philippines, for example, Malaya in recent years has occupied twelfth place in terms of import value, and twenty-first place in terms of export value;[34] Thailand ranked even lower—

---

[31] Mr. Pelaez was then foreign minister as well. If by *future* he meant a period fifteen to twenty years from now, there might be wide agreement, but regarding the near future, few economists in the three countries now feel that a common market is in the offing for ASA.

[32] Daniel Wolfstone (pseud.), "Manila's Image of ASA," *Far Eastern Economic Review* (September 15, 1960), 600.

[33] What often exists, sometimes even in the statements and thoughts of the same individual, is a striking ambivalence towards the whole subject. Thus in interviews, many leaders have spoken with considerable enthusiasm about their personal attraction to the goal of regional cooperation, and a moment later have ticked off the many obstacles in the path of achieving this goal. The ambivalence, no doubt, derives from their commitment to regionalism, which they tend to regard as a "good," and their simultaneously strong commitment to rapid national economic development, which is of course also seen as a "good." The inconsistent policy choices which tend to flow from an emphasis on one or the other are often very clearly recognized. What led to the establishment of ASA was the belief that the inconsistencies can be resolved.

[34] With the inclusion of Sabah (North Borneo) into Malaysia, a localized ASA trade must be taken into account: in 1961 North Borneo reported $4.1 million in imports from the Philippines, and $6.4 million in the other direction. Generally speaking, however, total Philippines exports to the other ASA countries do not exceed $1 million each year. Figures for imports to Malaya have included Singapore, although Singapore was not independent and not a part of Malaya when ASA was formed. Singapore's withdrawal from Malaysia in 1965 may not be significant in this context, for if ASA is revived, Singapore would benefit by joining.

twenty-third in terms of import value, and twenty-sixth in terms of export value.[35] Tables VI-1 and VI-2 provide recent intra-ASA trade figures.

TABLE VI-1. MALAYA AND SINGAPORE TRADE BY VALUE
(Millions of U.S. Dollars)

Country	Exports			Imports		
	1957	1959	1961	1957	1959	1961
Philippines	22.6	18.9	9.3	1.0	0.88	0.8
Thailand	37.4	40.7	35.0	115.4	114.7	110.8
ECAFE Region	491.1	480.0	472.0	860.3	967.8	859.8
World	1362.1	1510.2	1412.8	1440.3	1532.0	1496.2

TABLE VI-2. PHILIPPINES TRADE IN ASIA BY VALUE
(Millions of U.S. Dollars)

Country	Exports			Imports		
	1957	1959	1961	1957	1959	1961
Malaya and Singapore	0.5	0.5	0.8	16.4	5.8	7.3
Thailand	0.3	0.2	0.2	6.6	0.1	16.9
ECAFE Region	92.1	132.2	138.7	144.0	154.5	167.9
World	431.7	529.5	499.5	614.6	509.1	611.3

Source: The data necessary for compiling both tables is in ECAFE, "Intra-regional Trade Statistics" (November 5, 1962). Mimeo. In both, apparent discrepancies are attributable to smuggling and weak statistical reporting; so that Nation A will publish a larger import figure from B than B reported as exports to A.

Clearly, intra-ASA trade, running to no more than 7-8 per cent of each country's total trade value, is exceedingly small; and, despite certain specific sectors of variation, it is not increasing.[36] The reasons are

[35] See ASA, Second Meeting of the Joint Committee of Economic Experts, "Annual Report on the Economies of the ASA Countries, 1961-1962," Manila, November 21-24, 1962 (mimeo.).

[36] There is for example a relatively sizable value of Malaysian imports from Thailand, of which about 40 per cent has been in rice. But another 40 per cent represents tin and rubber destined for the outside world, and passing through Singapore in its entrepôt role. Similarly, the Philippines occasionally buys large quantities of Thai rice to compensate for bad years, but those are unpredictable purchases and intended to be stop-gap measures only. On the other hand, reflecting the growth of rubber products industries in Manila, the Philippines in recent years increased its rubber imports from Malaya and Singapore—though again much of the rubber represented re-exports from Indonesia.

as familiar as they are fundamental. First, there has been no pattern of trade—or any other form of interaction—among these countries. Second, the products of any one ASA country are able to find only small markets in the other two; in a word, the national economies have not been complementary. This low-level trade pattern, typical of Asia, has led some economists to conclude that efforts to increase trade are the necessary first step toward cooperation. As one specialist has put it: "It is natural that at this time the idea of a common market for Asia and other forms of regional trade cooperation should get serious consideration." [37]

Others, of course, have come to the conclusion that—"natural" or not—the emphasis on a common market, customs union, free-trade area, or any of the other measures designed primarily to remove obstacles to trade is misplaced. Indeed, this was the lesson learned by many of the participants in ASA. Professor Lim Tay Boh made this point with precision:

> The expansion of the intraregional market cannot, however, be fully achieved by the removal of trade obstacles alone. The removal of trade obstacles and the creation of a common market or free-trade area for the whole region will provide a larger market for the foodstuffs, raw materials and manufactured goods exported by the countries of the region. *But regional cooperation at the liberalization of trade alone will not be sufficient to exploit the potentialities of intraregional trade without a vigorous policy of regional cooperation in spreading industrial know-how and promoting investment in a wide range of diversified production.* For the relatively low per capita incomes of the countries of the region have been one of the main obstacles to the expansion of intraregional trade. What is needed in the region is not only more trade but more rapid industrial growth.[38]

THE DIRECTION ASA MAY TAKE

Professor Lim's conclusion, with its emphasis on industrial development, is consistent with the goal of enhanced regional cooperation. Because economic development is a widely accepted value among the elites of this region, perceiving development steps as supportive

---

[37] D. T. Lakdawala, "Trade Cooperation Within the ECAFE Region," *Pakistan Development Review* (Spring 1962), 506.

[38] Lim Tay Boh, "Regional Trade Cooperation Among Asian Countries." *Pakistan Development Review* (Spring 1962), 550. Italics added. Professor Lim, formerly chairman of the economics department, is now vice-chancellor of the University of Singapore.

of—or convergent with—extranational cooperation may add impetus
to the trend toward regionalism. Guetzkow suggests that the forces for
and against collaboration are additive, and offers illustrations of forces
working toward collaboration:

> The citizens of one nation might seek external relations because of a
> strong collaborative ideology . . . and, in addition, a widespread percep-
> tion of collaboration as an advantageous direct route to the solution of
> their problems. . . . Those of another nation might encourage their gov-
> ernment to be active internationally because of highly successful past ex-
> periences in this area . . . and because the very nature of their task seems
> to require it.[39]

Guetzkow's emphasis on "the nature of the task" seems particularly
applicable to the conditions for collaboration in Southeast Asia, especially in view of the thesis that trade cooperation is premature without
greater emphasis on cooperation in development. In the three ASA
countries, moreover, officials who have participated in ASA meetings
appear to be turning toward this view, probably for two reasons: because they have found the environment not yet conducive to cooperation in trade,[40] and because they perceive that such things as technical
cooperation may enable small states to undertake developmental steps
that would be impractical if attempted alone.

The thesis that ASA must first concentrate on cooperation in development has been argued eloquently by Dr. Puey, Governor of the Bank
of Thailand. His recommendations for ASA, as a small, subregional
group, parallel Kitamura's suggestions for the ECAFE area as a whole.
Drawing on his experience in both groups, Puey has argued that regional
"specialization of labor" is a realistic goal, and that it would reduce
the present diversion of capital to regionally redundant enterprises.
He remarked, for example, that—with few exceptions (tin-smelting
and sugar production)—his own country could readily accept agree-

---

[39] Guetzkow, *op. cit.*, p. 159.

[40] Haas pointed out that in the European instance new channels of communications among elites developed only after the establishment of formal organization.
ASA's experience would seem to show that these new channels of communication,
necessarily uncovering the "disheartening" economic data we have presented, have
led to a revision in goals. It can be said that in some cases ASA participants have
engaged in a process of "undoing" some of the goals first projected. Increased
trade remains as a purpose, but the learning that has resulted from the newly
established communications has led to a recognition of the many prior steps that
can be taken which will both facilitate and induce intensified trade.

ments for regional industrial specialization.[41] Another prominent and influential Thai, the banker and economist, P. Sithi-Amnuai, has made much the same case in advocating a regional bank.[42] Along with Puey's suggestion for a single "ASA investment prospectus" for industrial development, such steps would be designed to attract capital to coordinated projects, rather than encouraging Thais, Malaysians, and Filipinos to compete for the same investment resources.

Each of these suggestions reflects a basic change: officials in Southeast Asia approach the subject of cooperation with greater sophistication now than when ASA was forming. At first, ASA seemed to be an organization that was trying to accomplish everything at once. Even the basic organizational structure, seven or eight main committees, seemed to be trying to cover every foreseeable avenue of cooperation. And, as late as April 1962, the very meaning of *cooperation* had not lost very much of the vagueness it had in Rahman's early letters. There was, similarly, a good deal of talk of "exchanges": of "social workers," "women leaders," and so on. By November 1962, however, as a result of the second meeting of the Joint Working Party, both the organization and focus of ASA underwent significant development and alteration.

First Steps Toward Cooperation

First, the format of ASA was drastically revised and a structure was formed to rest on only three major committees: an economic committee, a social and cultural committee, and a technical-cooperation and research committee. The goals of ASA—or, rather, the priorities attached to them—were revised, for the first year's experience showed that certain goals, however desirable, were not likely to be achieved for some years. In essence, ASA participants had learned that regional cooperation requires far more than agreements among foreign ministers, that effective cooperation will develop only after frequent and intensive contacts among the involved institutions and groups in each nation.

For example, in support of its goal to encourage business, ASA arranged for regular meetings among leaders of each of the national chambers of commerce. ASA officials hope that these business leaders will discuss among themselves very specific aspects of interaction, in such areas as customs procedures, tax regulations, and other concrete details. This is a remarkably important development for, as a leading

[41] Interview with the author, Bangkok, July 24, 1963.
[42] P. Sithi-Amnuai, "A Regional Bank as a First Step Towards an Asian Common Market," *Bangkok Bank Monthly Review* (March 1963), 76.

business figure in Bangkok remarked, there has generally been total ignorance about opportunities for, say, Thai businessmen in the Manila market.[43] ASA meetings, he pointed out, have had the considerable virtue of developing an essential communications net. Thai businessmen interested in exporting to Manila now know specifically to whom they should write and are learning to expect concrete, useful, and businesslike answers. To an impatient observer, looking for quick developments in regional integration, this will seem a small advance, but it must be remembered that Southeast Asian businessmen have known much more about markets and procedures in San Francisco or London than about conditions in Bangkok or Singapore. Against that background, these "small" increments of knowledge about the region are of considerable significance, and support the thesis that a formal cooperative organization of states can be critical in opening up these communications.

ASA'S GOALS ARE NARROWED

Many of ASA's other activities also illustrate the point that a first task of regionalism may be to identify those things that cannot be done, as well as the small though practical things that can. For both purposes an institution may be crucial. For example, when ASA was formed, there was an implicit expectation that scholars, students, and universities in the member states generally, would be able to engage readily in a variety of cooperative and exchange ventures. This has not happened—not even when excellent physical arrangements have been offered (including reimbursement for tuition and travel costs) have students from ASA countries shown much interest in neighboring institutions.[44] The causes of this disappointing performance relate essentially to problems of language, schedules, and standards.

The language problem primarily concerns Thailand, for university students in Malaya and the Philippines generally use English.[45] In Thailand, although English is widely taught, most new university students have little facility in it. Consequently, ASA's educational committees, when considering Thai students for university admission, im-

---

[43] Interview with Mr. Banchert Cholavichan, Chairman of the Thai Chamber of Commerce, Bangkok, July 24, 1963.

[44] With the exception of a certain number of Thai students, for the past several years, studying in the Philippines (apparently in engineering and related fields).

[45] In Malaya, although there will be increasing recognition given to Malay as a teaching tongue, university authorities expect that students will continue to be conversant in English.

mediately faced this practical obstacle to easy exchanges. Another
problem, however, arising from differences in standards, proved to be
even more difficult. Because a Malayan student enters the university
with two years' more preparation than a Filipino, and a year more than
a Thai, it is widely assumed that his education can begin on a more
advanced level than the other two. Although ostensibly this is a matter
only of historically different systems, it presents the more difficult problem of accreditation and standards. "Malayan standards for the universities are too strict," [46] was the view of an informed Filipino, while
a Malayan official commented: "Our student is best prepared when he
enters the university because the standards are accepted throughout
the Commonwealth." [47] Because these differences proved to be the
major (but not the only) impediment to ASA arrangements for large-
scale educational exchanges,[48] participants sought to resolve the problem. Thai and Malayan representatives suggested that some outside
body, perhaps the Educational Testing Center at Princeton, should
evaluate Philippine standards (because those seemed to be the least
stringent). The Philippines did not oppose this idea, and this willingness
to accept an independent evaluation of domestic programs is a good
illustration of a clear tendency in ASA: the willingness to compromise,
even on some sensitive subjects, on behalf of cooperative goals.[49]

Malaya, for its part, showed the same willingness to compromise
when ASA asked that students from the other two countries be admitted
to the University of Malaya. That raised special problems in Kuala
Lumpur, where the already-intense pressure for admission to the university is increased by problems of ethnic "balance": because ethnic

[46] Mr. Ramon Hermano, formerly of the National Science Development Board,
Manila.
[47] Foo Yeow Hoke, Registrar, University of Malaya, and member of ASA committees. His reference is to the Cambridge certificate examinations, and undoubtedly Malayan officials are proud of the large number of their students
accepted in Australian, Canadian, and British universities.
[48] Observers generally feel that such exchanges might contribute handsomely to
building a sense of regional "identity," and ASA participants certainly accept this
as one of their goals.
[49] Before adopting this proposal, ASA officials hope to resolve the problem with
an internal evaluation; they have asked a vice-president of the University of the
Philippines (Dr. Virata) to begin a full-scale study of high school programs in
order to report to ASA. In the meantime, the three countries agreed that persons
who already hold a B.A. or equivalent would be admitted to graduate schools
in the other ASA countries on the same basis as local students (see ASA, "Report
of the 2nd Meeting of Foreign Ministers," 1963, p. 43).

Malays are given preference,[50] Malayan students of Chinese and Indian origin must meet particularly high entrance requirements. This problem has already received parliamentary attention, and in a political environment extremely sensitive to any question of ethnic "balance," a decision to admit Thais and Filipinos (who might take places away from local Chinese and Indian candidates) will hardly be popular. Nevertheless, University of Malaya authorities assured ASA that somehow "places would be found," and indicated other areas in which they were willing to change their procedures.[51] In sum, ASA's experiences in other educational "exchanges" constituted a descent from lofty heights, where everyone could agree on ideal goals, to the pragmatic task of putting those ideals into effect.

Roughly the same experience characterized the efforts to build an "ASA Airline," a notion inspired by the Scandinavian example in SAS.[52] It seemed a good idea, especially because the newest long-range jet aircraft were so expensive. Hardly had the first discussion of the problem begun, however, when it became clear that each of the ASA governments might not be the real masters of what they chose to call their "national" airlines.[53] Thai Airways is under a heavy financial and management obligation to Scandinavian Airways;[54] Philippines Airlines (PAL) has a special routing arrangement (which limits its freedom) with KLM; and Malayan Airlines (MAL) is almost completely (90-94 per cent) owned by British interests.[55] As these facts, amusing only to

[50] Scholarship awards favor Malay students by three or four to one. Nevertheless, the more education-oriented Chinese still dominate: in 1963 the student body was 1736, of which 1042 were Chinese and 358 Malay (see *Review of the Second Five Year Plan,* University of Malaya).

[51] Especially the anomaly by which Malaya refuses to recognize most foreign degrees. This is changing, and part of the incentive is said to derive from a genuine desire to cooperation with neighboring ASA states.

[52] See the first ASA foreign-ministers' report, which urged that a study be made of forming "a consortium similar in structure to the Scandinavian Airlines system. . . ."

[53] Daniel Wolfstone (pseud.), "Blueprints for ASA," *Far Eastern Economic Review* (November 30, 1961). The information provided there was later heavily amplified in a series of interviews during June and July 1963, in each of the capitals.

[54] The Thais owe SAS something in the range of $40 million, although the director-general of the economics division in the Thai foreign ministry maintains that 75 per cent of the airline's ownership is controlled by Thai nationals.

[55] This is in combination with Cathay Pacific, which is in turn owned largely by BOAC. According to Malayan officials, it will not be before 1970 that MAL will be sufficiently in local hands for Kuala Lumpur to exercise controlling interest.

outsiders, became clear to ASA, it seemed obvious that the goal of a regional ASA airline was years off. Nevertheless, the three countries, stressing the role of ASA, arrived at some mutual scheduling arrangements, and—despite some comments that these arrangements would have come anyway—most local officials maintain that ASA's existence facilitated the "pooling" of schedules. A senior Thai official commented: "ASA quickened the agreement that was arrived at." [56] Moreover, although the major goal of a regional airline has not been achieved, ASA participants know precisely where they stand, and this is an important contribution in itself.

It will be remembered, for example, that two years before ASA was established, when Rahman wrote to Sukarno and the other leaders, he concluded with the hope that "even if we cannot achieve full agreement on a particular subject, we will at least be better able to understand through this association why we cannot. . . ." The experience of ASA so far would indicate that this expectation certainly has been fulfilled. There have, of course, been a number of tangible accomplishments in cooperation, although none of them is of major proportions. Some, like the $3 million joint fund, seem especially promising.[57] But, just as important for a new and unprecedented effort, ASA has achieved

---

[56] Interview with the author, Bangkok, Office of the Foreign Minister, July 1963.

[57] See ASA, *Report of the Second Meeting of Foreign Ministers* (Kuala Lumpur: Federation of Malaya, 1963), pp. 1-7. Among the most interesting of the completed agreements is this fund for joint research, largely in technical cooperation and steps related to development. There are also a number of joint informational programs, including radio and television exchanges, and a series of agreements for much freer exchange of data on the production and marketing of primary commodities. These can be quite important, as one example may illustrate: For years, Thai officials have wanted from Malaya information and samples of high-yield rubber seed, but were met by a total lack of cooperation, including prohibitive prices or a flat refusal by the Malayans to export the seed which was giving them a market advantage. With the advent of ASA, according to Malayan and Thai officials, the situation underwent complete reversal: Thai specialists can now obtain the needed data, and the price of the seed is also reasonable. The terms in which this change was described, for example by a member of the Thai cabinet, and by a department head, were strongly evocative of Professor Guetzkow's "advantages hypothesis." Director-General of the Department of Economic Affairs, Chuanchuen Kambhu, remarked that without ASA Thailand would still be ignorant of a number of important Malayan achievements which are at the same time of great value to Thailand. He felt that ASA would contribute significantly to the well-being of each of the states, as such exchanges multiply. Guetzkow, similarly, has suggested that "if the advantages to be derived from collaboration are vivid and concretely tied to clearly formulated means, they are likely to be more adequately perceived." *Op. cit.,* p. 156.

two basic intangibles: it has survived; and it has opened up a remarkable number of formal and informal communications channels.

Conclusion: Achievement in International Organization

Like the venture into educational cooperation, and another effort to form an "ASA shipping line," the primary product of the "ASA airline" experience was its lesson value. In each of these and other instances, a grandiose set of objectives was forced to undergo very practical scrutiny. For the first time, the realities and difficulties of "cooperation" were laid out and examined in practical detail, and came to the attention of each country's senior policy-makers as well as its working-level officials. The results of this examination of the practical and complex details of cooperation have provided three benefits.

First, officials from the ASA countries found that there is probably a larger variety of workable and worthwhile subjects for joint ventures and cooperation than had been foreseen. This applies especially to research ventures affecting both agricultural and industrial development, from which there promise to be substantial potential benefits to each country.

Then, too, now that the really difficult issues have been exposed, these can, on the assumption that ASA will be revived, be subjected to the kind of study which must precede satisfactory international cooperation.[58] It will no longer be necessary for busy senior officials in each country to devote precious time in an attempt to salvage "face" from the necessarily ill-fated attempts to bring about some prestigious ASA project.

Finally, it became possible for officials to think in terms of priority planning, concentrating on those fields in which each country's leading experts and policy-makers believe achievements to be realizable. In mid-1962, for example, there was a widespread feeling that ASA needed to do something quick and dramatic in order to demonstrate that it would succeed and was of immediate import. A year later, however, officials had more frankly come to grips with the nature of ASA's development. As a result, a calm willingness developed, to expect only modest

---

[58] It should again be stressed that when ASA temporarily postponed its activities in the wake of the diplomatic upset between Manila and Kuala Lumpur concerning North Borneo, officials in both capitals were at great pains to stress that ASA would be resumed.

new advances on a year-to-year basis—although, of course, considerable satisfaction is drawn from the achievements already recorded. Indeed, even as ASA was being put into "cold storage" temporarily, efforts were devoted to planning for the next three to five years on the basis of the 1963 report, and also to bringing about those step-by-step cooperative agreements that were closest to fruition.[59]

As a result of this continuing experience, there is within the bureaucracies in Bangkok, Kuala Lumpur, and Manila a fairly widespread satisfaction with ASA that outsiders seldom share. Despite the very apparent lack of major tangible accomplishments, the level of achievement justifies this satisfaction. Among Southeast Asian leaders, this pattern of thought is not held to be inconsistent. In Bangkok, for example, both Foreign Minister Thanat Khoman and his principal assistant, Ambassador Konthi (later Secretary-General of SEATO) are clearly proud of their role in developing ASA—although perfectly forthright in remarking that ASA has not yet contributed anything of great material significance either to Thailand or to the region. Philippine Vice-President Pelaez was equally blunt when he discussed "ASA achievements." [60] Yet these men, and many others at lower levels (even in the face of the strained relations between Manila and Kuala Lumpur), are remarkably sanguine about ASA's future. In their assessment, not only the material accomplishments but the intangible experiences and achievements of regional cooperation as well, must be weighed in arriving at a judgment. And what must be emphasized is that local leaders stress steady, slow, and practical accomplishment for ASA. From this perspective—and it may be the only one that matters—the future for subregional cooperation symbolized so far by ASA, may be bright.

One strong element leading to this local confidence is the simple fact that ASA has not been scrapped. Although full diplomatic relations have not yet been resumed between Malaysia and the Philippines, the offices of the ASA national secretariat in Kuala Lumpur are still in exist-

---

[59] There were, moreover, continuing conversations directed toward the signing of an ASA trade treaty, though as our previous discussion should have made clear, not a great deal should be expected from that development for several years. The treaty probably will be signed shortly after ASA itself is reactivated, but it is likely to be an essentially "most-favored-nation" type. At the same time, the draft may contain provisions not commonly found in instruments of this sort, pertaining particularly to joint action on commodity disposals by the United States; joint participation in trade fairs, and so on. See ASA, "Report of the First Meeting of the Committee on Trade Policy and Promotion," Annexes.

[60] Interviews with the author, Manila and Bangkok, June and July 1962, 1963, October-November 1964.

ence, and its personnel have every expectation that their work will be resumed. Indeed, each of the three foreign ministers, in conversations at the end of 1964, made precisely this point. Foreign Minister Mendez in Manila said that the "ASA group" in Manila would soon be "reactivated," and Foreign Minister Thanat Khoman in Bangkok reported that he had extracted a promise from his prime minister that as soon as ASA is re-established, the million-dollar Thai contribution to the ASA fund would immediately be restored.[61] Yet, in view of Manila's claim to North Borneo, it could have been supposed that ASA would be allowed to die off altogether. That likelihood was of course increased, once Malaysia was established in 1963, by the break in relations between Kuala Lumpur and Manila, and the resulting Philippine overtures to Indonesia.

Manila and Kuala Lumpur continued "speaking" to one another, however, and by mid-1964 had resumed consular relations—largely through the efforts of Thailand's foreign minister, but also because leaders in both capitals were willing to have the effort made. This *rapprochement* is, in large part, a result of the intensive communications paths established in the wake of ASA, for ASA developed new contacts and understandings between the leaders of these governments. Indeed, when Philippine-Malayan relations were at a very low point, and Thailand's foreign minister was making strenuous efforts to prevent them from worsening, Philippines Vice-President Pelaez asked this author to convey his best wishes to Thanat: "President Macpagal, you know, has appointed him 'ASA Ambassador.' "[62]

Precisely what the Thai foreign minister said or did to keep the Malayans and Filipinos talking to one another is not known. It is understood, however, that the major point of his argument with both parties was that their dispute should not be allowed to get out of control, for they had something of mutual benefit between them—the organizational entity of ASA—which should be preserved.[63]

What seems clear is that both Kuala Lumpur and Manila attach

[61] Based on interviews in Manila, October 1964, and Bangkok, November 1964, with both foreign ministers and members of their staffs.

[62] Interview with the foreign minister and vice-president, Manila, June 26, 1963.

[63] Thanat would like to claim that he did only what any third party would when two of his mutual friends are arguing; but he too believes that political relations between Malaya and the Philippines probably would have deteriorated much further had it not been for the existence of an organizational tie (ASA) between them. Interview with Foreign Minister Thanat Khoman, Bangkok, July 24, 1963. In January 1963, before departing for Manila, Thanat is said to have told the American ambassador in Bangkok that "ASA must be saved if possible."

special significance to this first indigenous effort at regional cooperation. Officials in both capitals are aware that their leaders—Rahman and Garcia in their 1959 meeting—formed the first link in the chain of events that led to ASA. These officials recognize that it would be particularly galling if ASA fell apart as a result of Malayan-Philippine differences, especially on the unrelated and relatively noncritical North Borneo issue. Many of them want, instead, to preserve ASA, the existence of which has provided both a reason and a framework for reducing tension among its members. Indeed, the leaders of all three countries, seemingly aware of the growing pains suffered by any new organization, have acted in a manner calculated to maintain ASA's existence. They recognized, for example, that to hold the scheduled ASA foreign-ministers' meeting at the end of 1962, when Philippine-Malayan relations were strained, could have wrecked ASA by giving public vent to these irritations; therefore, they simply postponed the meeting. The decision suggests one of the "background conditions" for successful international organization proposed by Haas: the "willingness to de-emphasize clashing aspirations." This is precisely what Manila and Kuala Lumpur did within ASA, rather than face an uncomfortable, divisive, and possibly organizationally-fatal issue head on.

This indicates a recognition—of which ASA is itself a manifestation —that the shared attitudes and goals of the Philippines and Malaysia are greater than their differences. In this light, ASA generated not only a convenient rationale against hasty action, but also provided a neutral third party (Thailand) to act as informal mediator and communications link. No doubt this is not what observers generally look for when evaluating international organizations for regional cooperation, nor was this ASA's primary purpose. Yet, one of the functions of an organization is to provide—intentionally or not—a rubric for the settlement of disputes among its participants. Mediation need not be through a formal structure or device; the fact of the organization's very existence will, if each member concerned benefits from participation, provide a significant incentive for not permitting the association to end.[64]

In this case, it seems clear that one of the major reasons that Manila and Kuala Lumpur avoided a sharp and more bitter break in their relations, and have begun the groping steps back toward normalcy, lies in the existence of ASA. ASA can legitimately regard this avoidance of

[64] See generally, Chester Barnard, *The Functions of the Executive* (Cambridge, Mass.: Harvard University Press, 1938).

worse relations as one of its accomplishments—not in its role as a body for achieving specific measures of cooperation in Southeast Asia, but simply as a continuing organization of three states. In sum, ASA not only provided a set of goals and a framework for achieving them, but functioned as an instrument for absorbing some of the region's conflicts. Its revival would probably represent a step toward stability in the region, and if it were enlarged it might again perform as a modulator of conflict.

CHAPTER VII: PROSPECTS FOR STABILITY IN SOUTHEAST ASIA

The main purpose of this book has been to examine the conditions that affect stability in Southeast Asia's international relations. Some forces internal to the region, such as the interest in economic cooperation, do tend toward stability; others, indeed those that so far have dominated the region's international politics, clearly tend toward instability, and perhaps the most important of these is the nation of Indonesia. The sheer size of its population and territory, its undoubted resources, the dynamics and appeals of its leaders' ideologies, and the size and strength of its armed forces insure that Indonesia's impact on the international affairs of the region will be significant and could be decisive.[1]

Until recently, Indonesia has generally been a "loner" insofar as the specifically regional affairs and politics of the area are concerned. Indonesian leaders have preferred bilateral, rather than regional, arrangements; when they have thought in broader terms they have preferred the multi-regional Afro-Asian framework. Yet Indonesia did participate in Maphilindo, the loose "confederation" designed by Macapagal, although Sukarno and Subandrio viewed it not as a contribution to regional cohesion, but as a device for furthering their anti-Malaysia campaign.

Despite this background, three factors could give Maphilindo future importance: it was—like ASA—indigenous; it represented in some ways a departure from Indonesia's general disdain for region-wide efforts; and, most important, its offshoots could point the way toward the development of regional stability.

Maphilindo is without question an indigenous creation, for it grew almost entirely out of proposals made in the Philippines. The outlines for Maphilindo were sketched, by and large, in the study prepared at the University of the Philippines (see chapters II and IV), when President Macapagal enlarged his 1962 confederation ideas to include Indonesia. When compared with the university study, the text of the

---

[1] To a large extent this is independent of President Sukarno's future. Whether he is succeeded by a prominent nonparty leader, or some group of his immediate associates, or perhaps a coalition of the army and others, the role of Indonesia in the region's politics will become more, not less, important.

official Philippines proposal (the essence of which became Maphilindo) shows almost complete identity.[2]

The fact that Sukarno was even briefly willing to channel the Malaysia dispute through Maphilindo, despite his past disdain for regional diplomacy, may be important for its long-term effects. It sparked renewed Philippines interest in a close relationship with Indonesia. Second, in Malaysia it helped remind ethnic Malays who still continue to look to Djakarta with admiration that—if pressed too hard by their resident Chinese—an association with Indonesia would provide a final answer to the problem of ethnic balance. Indonesian leaders know all this, and the knowledge that they are *wanted* (for different reasons) by their neighbors could provide a powerful weapon should they decide to press their foreign policy goals within a regional framework like Maphilindo or an enlarged ASA.

Such a decision, which could be the third offshoot of the Maphilindo experience, deserves very special attention, for it can be argued that

[2] Space allows only two illustrations, one taken from the introductory paragraphs in both documents, the other taken from the sections in both documents dealing with the organizational framework for the proposed confederation. In the following illustration, the university study is in Column 1, the official Philippines document ("the Macapagal plan") in Column 2:

From the University Study, "General Principles"	From the official Manila document, "Aims of the Proposed Confederation"
(1)	(2)
"The proposed confederation shall aim to— (a) Restore and strengthen the historic unity and common heritage among the Malay peoples, and draw them to closer political, economic, and cultural relations."	"5. The proposed confederation shall aim to restore and strengthen the historic unity and common heritage of the Malay peoples and draw them into closer political economic, and cultural relations."

The second illustration deals with the organizational framework for Maphilindo recommended by Manila and initially proposed in the university study. The study, it should be said, considered three formats for the confederation, ranging from integrated military, economic and political ties, to one that had "loose political bonds but with an integrated economy;" and finally, the recommended version, which was known as Plan C. This was the loosest form. It was designed to be similar to the Arab League, and what follows is a comparison, under the heading of "General Organs," and "Political Organs," of the respective texts of the university study and the official Philippines proposal:

University Study	Official Proposal
A council of heads of state shall be constituted and shall meet once or twice a year. This body shall determine the broad principles of cooperation and harmonization of policies.	A supreme council composed of the heads of government shall be constituted and shall meet once or twice a year. This body shall determine the broad principles of cooperation and coordination of policies.

stability in the region probably would be enhanced if Indonesia became regularly associated with a continuing regional organization. Even without material benefits from such an association (and Indonesian participation, with that country's economic and administrative weaknesses, could mean some initial net loss to the other states), the political gains could be significant.

It is at least conceivable that an organizational affiliation might provide Indonesia's leaders (as ASA did for Malaya and the Philippines) with a reason and a rationale for smoothing the roughest edges of their regionally de-stabilizing foreign policies. Indeed, this is suggested by Sukarno's behavior since shortly after the Malaysia crisis developed, for he has appeared eager to invoke the authority of some prestigious, and potentially friendly, outside body as a justification for modifying his policy toward Malaysia. In the attempts to resolve the conflict, Sukarno's efforts were devoted to calling for, or accepting, a series of mediators: Thai Foreign Minister Thanat, Robert Kennedy, Maphilindo, and, finally, an Afro-Asian commission. These efforts indicate a belief that, from time to time, Indonesian leaders genuinely desired to settle the issue. Of course, it might also be argued that Indonesia intends to continue pressing Malaysia until that new nation breaks apart,[3] and that the invoking of Maphilindo, Kennedy, Thanat, and the Afro-Asian commission were nothing more than temporary posturings. Careful analysis, however, does not allow that view to be accepted. It is far more likely that Sukarno did indeed want, after mid-1963, to settle the Malaysia crisis, but only on terms that could not reasonably be seen as humiliating, or inconsistent with the view of Indonesia's "great destiny." [4]

Yet to say that Sukarno has wanted to end confrontation—given certain conditions—is not to say that Indonesian leaders have not had relatively clear goals regarding the territories that now comprise Ma-

[3] This would be a good interpretation of *Ganjang Malaysia*.

[4] There is evidence to suggest that one reason for Sukarno's constant exhortations to his people to be a "great people, a heroic people," is that he suspects lacksadaisical qualities in them, which he regularly condemns as the attributes of a "bean-curd folk": "Only yesterday, I said . . . that Indonesia at present is not like Indonesia of the past [when it] was a nation of toads, a bean-curd nation. . . . But the Indonesian nation today is not a bean-curd nation . . . but a heroic nation. . . ." (Sukarno's speech of May 3, 1964.) It is perhaps Indonesia's history of relative subservience to the Dutch which gives rise to this concern; a cabinet minister in Thailand, for example, remarked to the writer that "no people which tolerated three centuries of Dutch rule can really pose a threat to this region."

laysia. In essence, those goals have been to exercise major influence, and, if possible, to dominate, for it is clear that Indonesia's perception of its role requires that its voice be taken seriously.

There are several ways in which other nations can attempt to deal with this Indonesian role. In 1958-59, for example, Britain and the United States encouraged the dissolution of Indonesia, at least as presently constituted. It is unlikely that similar efforts will be undertaken soon again. Another way may be to recognize Indonesia as a "trouble-maker," and hope to build countervailing strength around it. But for a variety of reasons, among them the many weaknesses of Malaysia and the many potential strengths of Indonesia, that effort, too, appears doomed to failure.

Yet another approach is to *internalize* the role of Indonesia within the system of Southeast Asia's international politics. This approach would recognize that Indonesian aspirations and resources represent destabilizing forces, and would endeavor to channel and accommodate those forces. For example, a regional or subregional association that combined the dramatic nature of Maphilindo with the concreteness of ASA could bring major advantages—both for the stability of the region and for the internal well-being of Indonesia. Such a body (let us call it ASANEFOS to designate the "Association of Southeast Asian New Emerging Forces") would include Indonesia, the ASA members, and perhaps even Burma and Cambodia. To that extent it might help provide Indonesia with the framework for a grand foreign-policy role in Asia, and would thus help satisfy its need for a major voice in world affairs. But the main feature of the group would be to combine the membership of both ASA and Maphilindo, and could thereby integrate Indonesia with practical efforts at cooperation. Moreover, ASANEFOS would provide a rationale, for the first time, within which Sukarno could support the development efforts of the "administrators" and "economists" in Indonesian politics. No such rationale now exists, and a central malaise of Indonesian politics has been that the practical and moderate men, whose overriding concern is with economic development, have lacked a grand ideological design and symbol with which to attract support for their efforts. Clearly, their goal of development-for-its-own-sake has not been enough. As a result, the gap between nation-building (the task to which Sukarno has addressed his great talents) and economy-building, (the job on which such men as Hatta and the late Djuanda have hoped to concentrate) has not been bridged. The nation-builders have so far tended to dominate,[5] and under that leadership Indonesia's economy has suffered greatly, and its foreign policies have been frustrating both to itself and to its neighbors.

A multinational framework, however, perhaps along the lines of the new Maphilindo (or ASANEFOS, suggested here) could bridge this gap. This is its major attraction as a device for contributing to stability both in the region and in Indonesia. If such a new group carefully provided for Indonesia's style (as in its name and stated goals), it could satisfy certain of the foreign-policy aspirations of many leading Indonesians, and at the same time provide the incentive and rationale for domestic efforts aimed at the economic development of the country. This would be especially so if practical aspects of the new group were modeled after ASA—and one would expect that, if Thailand participated, the ASA model, with concrete projects in cooperation for development, would be important. Especially after its first year, one of the main features of ASA was its attachment to regional cooperation—not as an end in itself—but as a practical instrument within which to press ahead with the development of each participating state.

A regional effort along new lines, if it is to be established, and to attract the willing support of Indonesia, must meld two quite different perspectives: a hard-headed knowledge of the needs and requirements of economic and political development (and how regional cooperation can help achieve those goals), and a strident—sometimes flamboyant—Asian nationalism. Both are already to be found in every one of the Southeast Asian countries. A new effort at regional cooperation, if it is to succeed, will have to combine the energies of both. Clearly, it would contain more of the trappings of the new Asian nationalism than was displayed by ASA, which was dominated by three relatively conservative nations. At the same time, the new effort would have to be far more meaningful and concrete than the very vague Maphilindo.

---

[5] Partly this is because Sukarno believes that building a single Indonesian national consciousness is the priority task, and he is unable or unwilling to understand and grapple with the requirements of state and economy-building. It is also partly because the Indonesian Communist party (at least until September 1965) has been willing to go along with, and take its chances on, nation-building. For "nation-building" contributes little in the short run to a prosperous Indonesia, and is for that reason consistent with and in support of the PKI's own hopes to succeed to power in the state. Steps designed to develop the economy, on the other hand, such as the brief flirtation with "stabilization of the economy" of mid-1963, have always been opposed, if not openly and publicly, by the Indonesian Communist party.

Such an effort, by combining the two approaches in ways that Indonesian leaders could accept and justify at home (calling it ASANEFOS might help) and starting only when Indonesia's full participation were guaranteed, would give the concept of regional cooperation in Southeast Asia, for the first time, truly important meaning. Without Indonesia, any effort in the region can be nothing more than transitional; with Indonesian participation, a new effort at regional cooperation would represent a potential giant step toward stability—both in Southeast Asia and in Indonesia.

The formation of a group like the proposed ASANEFOS would represent one of the two essential elements for practical regionalism: the interest of the Southeast Asian states themselves. More specifically, it would mean that the interest in regionalism of the administratively and economically more efficient small states (the ASA group) would have been reinforced by the interests of the colorful but less prosperous states (like Indonesia).

The second essential element is now becoming apparent, and this is the interest in Asian regionalism on the part of the great powers. Their support—and their capital—are essential to make regional cooperation work. That support was signalled in April 1965 when President Johnson proposed a $1 billion American contribution toward cooperative developmental efforts in Southeast Asia. Later, when Japan and the United States subscribed $200 million each to an Asian Development Bank, this great-power support for regionalism was given concrete meaning.

As these two essential elements come together for the first time in history, they can provide the practical basis for making regionalism real in Southeast Asia. And that eventuality—regional cooperation well grounded in economic and political realities—could contribute mightily to the stability of international politics in Southeast Asia.

INDEX

Abdulgani, Ruslan, **99**
Adloff, Richard, 47, 49, 62, **65-66**
Afro-Asians, 164 (*see also* Indonesia)
Albert, Carlos, 27, 34-35
Anand, Panyarachun, 124
Anderson, Benedict R. O'G., **85**
ANZUS, 72
Armstrong, Hamilton Fish, 167
Arreglado, Juan M., 24, 26-28
ASA (Association of Southeast Asia):
 and Burma, 167, 171; and Cambodia,
 167, 171; and communications, 168,
 172-73, 177-79, 183; and cooperation, 183-84, 192; and education,
 179-81, 183; established, 165-71,
 173-74, 177-78, 186; and Indonesia,
 25, 167, 171, 190-91, 193; Joint
 Working Party, 178; and Malaya,
 40, 166-68; 170-72, 174, 178, 183-
 84, 186; and Manila meeting, 69-
 70, 165; organizational style, 169-
 70, 172-73, 178-79, 186; Pelaez on,
 19, 173-74, 185; and Philippines,
 25-26, 40, 167-68, 170-72, 174, 178,
 183-84, 186; and regional airline
 proposal, 181-82; and regionalism,
 162, 170-71, 179, 182, 184, 186-87,
 192; suspended, 9-10, 162, 183-84;
 and Thailand, 167-68, 170-72, 174,
 178, 184, 186; trade within, 175-78
ASANEFOS (Association of Southeast
 Asian New Emerging Forces), proposal for, 191-93
Asian Development Bank, 1, 146, 149,
 159, 193 (*see also* Johnson, Lyndon B.)
Asian Productivity Organization, **160**
Aung Gyi, 136
Aung San, 145
Australia, 1, 38-39, 72, 84, **151**
Azahari, and Brunei Rebellion, **36, 69,
 80, 86, 97-98, 117**

Balmaceda, Cornelio, 32
Bandung Conference, 104, **164**
Bangkok (as port), 49
Barnard, Chester, 172, **186**
Battambang, 45, 64

Battista, 40
Bigart, Homer, **51-52**
Borneo, 16, 79
 and Indonesia, 72-74, **71, 92, 94, 97,**
 99-100, 109-14, 118
Brackman, Arnold, 2
Britain:
 and Borneo, 72; and Cambodia, **45;**
 and Malaya, 89; and Malaysia, 3,
 20, 22, 24, 72, 78-79, 91; and Singa-
 pore base, 3, 73, 102
British North Borneo Company, **11, 13,**
 16
Brunei, 17, 97
 and Azahari revolt, 36, 69, 80, 86, **97-**
 98, 117; Sultan of, **13**
Buddhists, 168
Bunker, Ellsworth, **131**
Burma:
 and ASA, 167, 171; and Communist
 China, 59; Economic development
 and cooperation, 147, 151 (table),
 166; foreign policy, 3-4, 136; and
 Rahman, 171; Shan people, 8; and
 Thailand, 8, 136-37
Buttinger, Joseph, 41, **48**
Buttwell, Richard, 69

Cady, John F., 7
Ca Mau Peninsula (*see* Cambodia)
Cambodia (*see also* Sihanouk):
 and ASA, 167, 171; and Bangkok
 (port of), 49; and Battambang,
 45, 64; and Ca Mau Peninsula, 42,
 45 (maps, 44, 50); Chinese minority, 47; Cochin-China, 46, 48,
 51-53; and Communist China, 53-
 56, 58-60, 62-63; culture, 41; customs revenues, 65-66; economic
 development and cooperation, 143;
 table, 147; foreign policy, 3-5, 48,
 51, 53-54, 58, 60-64, 67, 121, 123;
 and France, 41, 45-46, 48-49, 51,
 53-54, 122; history, 42, 45-46, 63
 (maps, 44, 50); and Indochina,
 45, 65; Khmer empire, 42, 129
 (maps, 44, 50); and Laos, 49, 53,
 126; neutrality, 42, 55, 58, 62-64;

The Modern Nations in Historical Perspective Series

The American Assembly Series

The Classics in History Series